T0226671

Advances in
COMPUTERS
VOLUME 80

Advances in
COMPUTERS

EDITED BY

MARVIN V. ZELKOWITZ

Department of Computer Science
University of Maryland
College Park, Maryland
USA

VOLUME 80

AMSTERDAM • BOSTON • HEIDELBERG • LONDON • NEW YORK • OXFORD
PARIS • SAN DIEGO • SAN FRANCISCO • SINGAPORE • SYDNEY • TOKYO
Academic Press is an imprint of Elsevier

ELSEVIER

ACADEMIC
PRESS

Academic Press is an imprint of Elsevier

32 Jamestown Road, London, NW1 7BY, UK
Radarweg 29, PO Box 211, 1000 AE Amsterdam, The Netherlands
30 Corporate Drive, Suite 400, Burlington, MA 01803, USA
525 B Street, Suite 1900, San Diego, CA 92101-4495, USA

First edition 2010

Library of Congress Cataloging-in-Publication Data
A catalog record for this book is available from the Library of Congress

British Library Cataloguing-in-Publication Data
A catalogue record for this book is available from the British Library

ISBN: 978-0-12-381025-0

ISSN: 0065-2458

For information on all Academic Press publications
visit our web site at elsevierdirect.com

Working together to grow
libraries in developing countries
www.elsevier.com | www.bookaid.org | www.sabre.org

ELSEVIER   BOOK AID
International   Sabre Foundation

Contents

Agile Software Development Methodologies and Practices

Laurie Williams

A Picture from the Model-Based Testing Area: Concepts, Techniques, and Challenges

Arilo C. Dias-Neto and Guilherme H. Travassos

Advances in Automated Model-Based System Testing of Software Applications with a GUI Front-End

Atif M. Memon and Bao N. Nguyen

Empirical Knowledge Discovery by Triangulation in Computer Science

Ravi I. Singh and James Miller

StarLight: Next-Generation Communication Services, Exchanges, and Global Facilities

Joe Mambretti, Tom DeFanti, and Maxine D. Brown

Parameters Effecting 2D Barcode Scanning Reliability

Amit Grover, Paul Braeckel, Kevin Lindgren, Hal Berghel, and Dennis Cobb

Advances in Video-Based Human Activity Analysis: Challenges and Approaches

Pavan Turaga, Rama Chellappa, and Ashok Veeraraghavan

Contributors

Prof. Hal Berghel is currently Professor and Director of the School of Informatics and Associate Dean of the Howard R. Hughes College of Engineering, and Professor and past-Director of the School of Computer Science, all at the University of Nevada, Las Vegas. He is also founding Director of both the Center for Cybersecurity Research, and the Identity Theft and Financial Fraud Research and Operations Center. Berghel has held a variety of research and administrative positions in industry and academia during his 30-year career in computing. His current research focuses on computing and network security, digital forensics, and digital crime. Berghel is a Fellow of both the Institute for Electrical and Electronics Engineers and the Association for Computing Machinery, and serves both societies as ACM Distinguished Lecturer and an IEEE Distinguished Visitor. He holds a Ph.D. from the University of Nebraska–Lincoln.

Paul Braeckel has more than 10 years of experience in software development, using a wide variety of languages, platforms, and technologies, and currently leads the development of Ephemeral Credentialing Products as Project Manager at the Identity Theft and Financial Fraud Research and Operations Center in Las Vegas, Nevada. He specializes in Object Oriented development of cybersecurity applications using .NET languages and his software development experience is broad, ranging from desktop business applications to complex web applications. Paul holds a M.S. in Computer Science from the UNLV and a B.S. in Mechanical Engineering from Washington University in St. Louis, and is working on his Ph.D. in Informatics at the UNLV.

Maxine D. Brown is an Associate Director of the Electronic Visualization Laboratory at University of Illinois at Chicago (UIC) and coprincipal investigator of the NSF International Research Network Connections program's TransLight/StarLight award. She serves on the External Advisory Committee of Argonne National Laboratory's Leadership Computing Facility and is the UIC representative and President Elect of the Board of Directors of the Great Lakes Consortium for Petascale Computing. Brown was recipient of the 1998 ACM SIGGRAPH Outstanding Service

Award. In 2009, Chicago's TV/radio series "Chicago Matters: Beyond Burnham" designated her 1 of 15 Global Visionaries for her role in codeveloping StarLight. Her email address is maxine@uic.edu.

Prof. Rama Chellappa is a Minta Martin Professor of Engineering, Professor of Electrical and Computer Engineering, and a Permanent member of the University of Maryland Institute for Advanced Computer Studies (UMIACS) at University of Maryland, College Park. He also directs the Center for Automation Research. Prof. Chellappa has published numerous book chapters, peer-reviewed journal and conference papers in image and video processing, analysis, and recognition. He has received several research, teaching, and service awards. He is a Fellow of IEEE, IAPR, and OSA. He is serving as the President of IEEE Biometrics Council. His research interests are image processing, image understanding, and pattern recognition. His email address is rama@umiacs.umd.edu.

Dennis Cobb is retired from the Las Vegas Metropolitan Police Department Deputy Chief and now president of DCC Group, Inc. assisting public and private organizations with critical communications technology, processes, and capabilities. Dennis is a founding participant in the UNLV/LVMPD Identity Theft and Financial Fraud Research and Operations Center. Dennis served as Nevada's Interoperable Communications Coordinator and chaired Nevada's Communications Steering Committee, and as a member of US DHS SAFECOM Emergency Response Council. He assisted in developing the US National Emergency Communications Plan and assists with radio interoperability issues in National Institute of Justice Technology Working Groups. Dennis Cobb holds a B.A. in Political Science and M.S. in Crisis and Emergency Management from the University of Nevada, Las Vegas. He is a graduate of the FBI National Academy, a 1992 Fulbright Fellow, and 1994 White House Fellow.

Dr. Tom DeFanti is a research scientist at the California Institute for Telecommunications and Information Technology at the University of California, San Diego and a distinguished professor emeritus of Computer Science at the University of Illinois at Chicago, where he cofounded the Electronic Visualization Laboratory. He is principal investigator of the NSF International Research Network Connections Program TransLight/StarLight Project. DeFanti was recipient of the 1988 ACM Outstanding Contribution Award and was appointed an ACM Fellow in 1994. He also shares recognition along with EVL director Daniel J. Sandin for conceiving the CAVE virtual reality theater in 1991.

Amit Grover has over 14 years of experience in Information Technology and has played an instrumental role in the development, implementation, and commissioning of a wide variety of Defense-related IT applications. He has had the opportunity of designing and implementing INFOSEC policies in Military units and has worked on interfacing Information Systems on board warships, submarines, and UAVs (Unmanned Aerial Vehicles). Amit holds a Master of Science degree in Computer and Information Science from East Tennessee State University and a Bachelor's Degree in Mechanical Engineering. Currently, he is affiliated to the Identity Theft and Financial Fraud Research and Operations Center at Las Vegas, where he is contributing on various aspects of a comprehensive secure credentialing system.

Kevin Lindgren is an undergraduate student in the UNLV School of Informatics concentrating in cybersecurity and an undergraduate research associate in the Identity Theft and Financial Fraud Research and Operations Center. Kevin returned to higher education after devoting 5 years of service to the US Army, performing a tour of duty in Iraq.

Dr. Joe Mambretti is Director of the International Center for Advanced Internet Research at Northwestern University, which is focused on developing digital communications for the twenty-first Century (iCAIR, www.icair.org). The Center designs and implements large scale infrastructure and applications. He is also Director of the Metropolitan Research and Education Network (MREN, http://www.mren.org), an advanced high-performance network interlinking organizations in seven upper-midwest states, and he is co-Director of the StarLight communications exchange. His publications include two books published by Wiley, "Next Generation Internet" and "Grid Networks: Enabling Grids with Advanced Communication Technology." His email address is j-mambretti@northwestern.edu.

Prof. Atif M. Memon is an Associate Professor in the Department of Computer Science, University of Maryland. His research interests include program testing, software engineering, artificial intelligence, plan generation, reverse engineering, and program structures. He is the inventor of the GUITAR system for automated model-based GUI testing. He is the founder of the International Workshop on TESTing Techniques & Experimentation Benchmarks for Event-Driven Software (TESTBEDS). He serves on various editorial boards, including that of the *Journal of Software Testing, Verification, and Reliability.* He has served on numerous National Science Foundation panels and international program committees. He is currently serving on a National Academy of Sciences panel as an expert in the area of Computer Science and Information Technology, for the Pakistan–US Science and Technology Cooperative Program, sponsored by United States Agency for International Development (USAID). In addition to his research and academic interests, he handcrafts fine wood furniture. He can be reached at atif@cs.umd.edu.

Prof. James Miller received his B.Sc. and Ph.D. degrees in Computer Science from the University of Strathclyde, Scotland. In 2000, he joined the Department of Electrical and Computer Engineering at the University of Alberta as a full professor. He has published over 100 refereed journal and conference papers on Software and Systems Engineering, currently serves on the program committee for the IEEE International Symposium on Empirical Software Engineering and Measurement, and sits on the editorial board of the *Journal of Empirical Software Engineering*. He can be reached at jm@ece.ualberta.ca.

Dr. Arilo Dias-Neto is a software engineer with a D.Sc. degree obtained in 2009 from COPPE/Federal University of Rio de Janeiro (Experimental Software Engineering Group), Brazil. He is an Adjunct Professor of Computer Science at Computer Science Department/Federal University of Amazonas, Brazil. He has conducted research regarding model-based testing, software testing, and experimental software engineering. Contact him at ariloclaudio@gmail.com.

Bao N. Nguyen is a Ph.D. student in the Department of Computer Science, University of Maryland. He received his B.S. degree in Computer Science with first class honors from Vietnam National University, Hanoi, in 2005. Before that, he was awarded the "The Bridge over Asian Countries" scholarship to study in Japan for 1 year. He received the Vietnam Education Foundation fellowship for his Ph.D. research. His research interests include software engineering, software testing, and reverse engineering. His email address is baonn@cs.umd.edu.

Ravi I. Singh received his B.Sc. in Computer Science from the University of Alberta, Canada. He began his M.Sc. in 2008 at the University of Alberta. He is also a member of IEEE. His major areas of research interest include triangulation, persuasion and machines, and electronic government. He also has a background in linguistics and speaks eight languages.

Prof. Guilherme H. Travassos is a Professor of Software Engineering in the Systems Engineering and Computer Science Program at COPPE/Federal University of Rio de Janeiro, Brazil. He is also a 1D CNPq, Brazilian Research Council and FAPERJ researcher. He received his doctorate degree from COPPE/UFRJ in 1994 and spent 2 years in the Experimental Software Engineering Group at the University of Maryland, College Park for a postdoctoral position from 1998 to 2000. He leads the Experimental Software Engineering Group at COPPE/UFRJ. His current research interests include experimental software engineering, e-science and nonconventional web applications, software quality, VV&T concerned with object-oriented software. He is a member of ISERN, ACM, and SBC (Brazilian Computer Society). Contact him at ght@cos.ufrj.br.

Dr. Pavan Turaga received his B.Tech. in Electronics and Communication Engineering from the Indian Institute of Technology, Guwahati in 2004, and M.S. and Ph.D. degrees in Electrical and Computer Engineering from the University of Maryland, College Park in 2007 and 2009, respectively. He is a research associate in the Center for Automation Research, at the University of Maryland Institute for Advanced Computer Studies (UMIACS). His research interests are in computer vision, pattern recognition, machine learning, and their applications. He can be reached at pturaga@umiacs.umd.edu.

Dr. Ashok Veeraraghavan received his B.Tech. in Electrical Engineering from the Indian Institute of Technology, Madras in 2002 and M.S and PhD from the Department of Electrical and Computer Engineering at the University of Maryland, College Park in 2004 and 2008, respectively. He is currently a Research Scientist at Mitsubishi Electric Research Labs in Cambridge, MA. His research interests are in computational imaging, computer vision, and signal processing. His email address is veerarag@merl.com.

Prof. Laurie Williams is an Associate Professor at North Carolina State University. She received her undergraduate degree in Industrial Engineering from Lehigh University. She also received an MBA from Duke University and a Ph.D. in Computer Science from the University of Utah. Prior to returning to academia to obtain her Ph.D., she worked in industry, for IBM, for 9 years. Dr. Williams is the lead author of *Pair Programming Illuminated* and a coeditor of *Extreme Programming Perspectives*. Dr. Williams has done several empirical studies of agile methodologies and practices, pair programming, and test-driven development. You can contact Dr. Williams at williams@csc.ncsu.edu.

Preface

This is volume 80 of the *Advances in Computers*. Annually, three volumes are produced describing the latest developments in the realm of computer technology. Each volume contains five to seven chapters, each exploring some new facet of this ever-changing field. The *Advances* have been published since 1960 and represent the longest continuously published series concerning information technology. In this volume, seven chapters explore two main themes: (1) Current advances in software development processes are discussed in Chapters 1 through 5 and (2) Computer understanding of visual information is covered in Chapters 6 and 7.

For the past 10 years, several approaches aimed at increasing the productivity and reliability of software development have been proposed. Under the general name of "agile development," these methods all aim at changing the software development cycle into short manageable pieces. While many organizations claim to be using agile practices, there is no clear consensus of what that really means. In Chapter 1, "Agile Software Development Methodologies and Practices," Dr. Laurie Williams discusses the evolution of agile software development and gives a rundown of the various practices that go under the general name "agile."

Testing of software during development is well recognized as the most expensive phase of software development and approaches toward improving testing are active research areas. Both in Chapter 2 and in Chapter 3, ways to automate the testing process are discussed. "A Picture from the Model-Based Testing Area: Concepts, Techniques and Challenges" by Dr. Arilo C. Dias-Neto and Dr. Guilherme H. Travassos is the content of Chapter 2. By describing software by some formal model, it is often possible to automatically generate test conditions based on the model. This greatly shortens the time and effort to generate and run such tests. While an active research area, model-based testing (MBT) is not a readily used practice in industry. In Chapter 2, the authors look at the literature and discuss how much impact the MBT approaches have actually had on industrial practices. They discuss the various risk factors that MBT must address in order to become more widely accepted.

In Chapter 3, Dr. Atif M. Memon and Bao N. Nguyen, in "Advances in Automated Model-Based System Testing of Software Applications with a GUI Front-End," continue the discussion of MBT, discussed earlier in Chapter 2. In their case, they focus on graphical user interface (GUI) testing. With much of software development now focused on interactive software controlled via a user interface running either on a local machine or via a web browser over the Internet, the testing of such interfaces becomes crucial. They provide a catalog of various testing strategies useful for building such MBTs for evaluating such user interfaces.

While the previous three chapters are concerned with new approaches toward solving software development problems, ultimately the evolution of any science depends upon experimentation and validation of those theories. In computer science, especially in software engineering, such experimentation often means studying several software developments to understand how the new techniques work in practice. Such experiments are necessarily costly and time consuming. Since they also involve the efforts of the individual developers with varying talents, the results of such experiments are often imprecise. In Chapter 4, "Empirical Knowledge Discovery by Triangulation in Computer Science," the authors, Ravi I. Singh and Dr. James Miller, propose methods of triangulation in order to obtain additional knowledge from each such experiment. By triangulation they mean a multiple method approach toward understanding a phenomenon more precisely. It is expected that this multidimensional approach should allow quicker convergence on the actual effects of each such method.

"StarLight: Next Generation Communication Services, Exchanges, and Global Facilities" by Dr. Joe Mambretti, Dr. Tom DeFanti, and Maxine Brown, in Chapter 5, looks at the software infrastructure that manages Internet traffic. They are developing a service-oriented architecture for providing communication services on a network. Because of the 40-year legacy of the Internet from its ARPANET beginnings in the early 1970s, there are many inherent designs and implementations limiting its future growth. They are proposing a design to support an almost unlimited range of services and capabilities.

The last two chapters in this volume look at various applications of video processing technologies. In Chapter 6, "Parameters Effecting 2-D Barcode Scanning Reliability" by Amit Grover, Paul Braeckel, Kevin Lindgren, Dr. Hal Berghel, and Dennis Cobb, the authors look at the various technologies used in barcode scanning. They look at various forms of barcode systems, from the ubiquitous barcodes on almost every consumer product today which can hold up to 11 data digits, to two-dimensional codes that are able to encode several thousand characters of data. The main focus of this chapter is to evaluate the reliabillity of scanning such codes.

In the last chapter, "Advances in Video-based Human Activity Analysis: Challenges and Approaches" by Dr. Pavan Turaga, Dr. Rama Chellappa, and Dr. Ashok Veeraraghavan, the authors explore the current status of computer technology for creating and interpreting videos, especially those involving human activities. Applications of such technologies include security by interpreting actions of those photographed, neuroscience in developing new prosthetics, video game designs, animation, search strategies based on video content, among many others. This chapter provides an overview of these applications, and more, as well as a brief overview of the underlying technology that currently exists for processing video data.

I hope that the reader finds these seven chapters interesting. I am always looking for new topics to explore. If you have an idea for a theme that has not appeared here recently, or feel qualified to write such a chapter yourself, please contact me at mvz@cs.umd.edu. I am always open to new ideas for these volumes.

Marvin Zelkowitz
College Park, Maryland

Agile Software Development Methodologies and Practices

LAURIE WILLIAMS

Department of Computer Science, North Carolina State University, Raleigh, North Carolina, USA

Abstract

Beginning in the mid-1990s, a number of consultants independently created and evolved what later came to be known as agile software development methodologies. Agile methodologies and practices emerged as an attempt to more formally and explicitly embrace higher rates of change in software requirements and customer expectations. Some prominent agile methodologies are Adaptive Software Development, Crystal, Dynamic Systems Development Method, Extreme Programming (XP), Feature-Driven Development (FDD), Pragmatic Programming, and Scrum. This chapter presents the principles that underlie and unite the agile methodologies. Then, 32 practices used in agile methodologies are presented. Finally, three agile methodologies (XP, FDD, and Scrum) are explained. Most often, software development teams select a subset of the agile practices and create their own hybrid software development methodology rather than strictly adhere to all the practices of a predefined agile methodology. Teams that use primarily agile practices are most often small- to medium-sized, colocated teams working on less complex projects.

ADVANCES IN COMPUTERS, VOL. 80
ISSN: 0065-2458/DOI: 10.1016/S0065-2458(10)80001-4

1

Beginning in the mid-1990s, a number of consultants independently created and evolved what later came to be known as *agile software development methodologies* after unsuccessful attempts to aid clients with currently available "plan-driven" [1] development methodologies. Agile methodologies and practices emerged as an attempt to more formally and explicitly embrace higher rates of change in software requirements and customer expectations.

Agile methods [2–4] are a subset of iterative and evolutionary methods [5,6] and are based on iterative enhancement [7] and opportunistic development processes [8]. Each iteration of an agile methodology is a self-contained, mini-project, with activities that span requirements analysis, design, implementation, test, and customer acceptance [5]. Each iteration leads to an *iteration release* (which may be only an internal release) that integrates all software across the team and is a growing and evolving subset of the final system. Agile methods recommend/require short development iterations because the feedback obtained before and after iterations N, and any other new information, can lead to refinement and requirements adaptation for iteration $N+1$ and beyond. The customer adaptively specifies his or her requirements for the next release based on observation of the evolving product, rather than speculation before the project has begun [9]. Frequent deadlines reduce the variance of a software process and, thus, may increase its predictability and efficiency [10].

The predetermined iteration length serves as a timebox[1] for the team. Scope is chosen for each iteration to fill the iteration length. Rather than increase the iteration length to fit the chosen scope, the scope is reduced to fit the iteration length. A key difference between agile methods and earlier iterative methods is the prescribed length of each iteration. In previous iterative methods, iterations might have been 3 or 6 months long. With agile methods, iteration lengths vary between 1 and 4 weeks, and intentionally do not exceed 30 days. Research has shown that shorter iterations have lower complexity and risk, better feedback, and higher productivity and success rates [5].

This chapter provides background information on the origins and principles underlying agile software development. Agile software development practices are then discussed in Section 3. Teams of all sizes producing large and small systems of varying criticality may selectively integrate a smaller subset of these agile practices

---

[1] A timebox is an inflexible period of time in which to accomplish a task. The start date and end date is set in stone and may not be changed.

in which it can still be considered a primarily plan-driven [1] methodology. Teams that choose a larger subset of these practices would use what could be considered an agile methodology, such as those agile methodologies presented in Section 4. Boehm and Turner [1] consider smaller, higher skilled teams that are amenable to change working on noncritical projects with a significant amount of requirements churn to be best suited for an agile methodology.

1. Agile Origins and Manifesto

In February 2001, 17 software engineering consultants had independently created change-tolerant methodologies retreated to Snowbird, Utah, to discuss commonalities between their respective methodologies. They classified their methodologies as *agile*, a term with a decade of use in flexible manufacturing practices [11,12]. The term promoted the professed ability for rapid and flexible response to change of the methodologies. The consultants also formed the Agile Alliance and wrote "The Manifesto for Agile Software Development" and the "Principles Behind the Agile Manifesto" [13,14]. The methodologies originally embraced by the Agile Alliance were Adaptive Software Development (ASD) [15], Crystal [3,16], Dynamic Systems Development Method (DSDM) [17], Extreme Programming (XP) [18], Feature-Driven Development (FDD) [19,20], Pragmatic Programming [21], and Scrum [22,23].

The Agile Alliance documented its value statement in the succinct Manifesto [13]:

We are uncovering better ways of developing software by doing it and helping others to do it. Through this work we have come to value:

Individuals and interactions	*over*	*processes and tools*
Working software	*over*	*comprehensive documentation*
Customer collaboration	*over*	*contract negotiation*
Responding to change	*over*	*following a plan*

That is, while there is value in the items on the right, we value the items on the left more.

Each of the tenets of the Manifesto will now be discussed as they formulate the basis of agile methodologies.

- *Individuals and interactions over process and tools*: The implication is that formalization of the software process and inflexibility hinder the human and practical component of software development, and thus reduce the chance for success. An area of commonality among all agile methodologies is the importance of the people performing the roles and the recognition that, more so than any process or tool, these people are the most influential factor in any project. Brooks acknowledges the same in *The Mythical Man Month* [24], which he authored decades ago: "The quality of the people on a project and their organization and management, are more important factors in success than are the tools they use or the technical approaches they take."

- *Working software over comprehensive documentation*: In agile methods, the progress of the team is measured in working software. Gone are the days of developers reporting they are "80% complete" with the code that only exists on their personal workstation or spending 6 months to produce paper documents, such as a 200-page requirements document and 800-page design specification of no practical value to a customer[2] or user. Instead, the team quickly produces a partial system that the customer can try and provide feedback on before the team launches into the next evolution of the working software. Minimal documentation is produced with agile processes, "just enough" to support the development of working software and to satisfy the customers' explicit needs for documentation.

- *Customer collaboration over contract negotiation*: When requirements are specified in a contract at the start of a project, assumptions are made such that (1) the development team can implement those requirements without much further clarification; and (2) the customer knows enough at the start of the project to specify the desired product. Conversely agile teams work with a "give and take" as the customer discovers their real requirements as working software is gradually evolved through the software development lifecycle (SDLC).

- *Responding to change over following a plan*: Rather than attempting to produce a plan for the entire SDLC, agile methods tend to have a high-level release plan followed by short-term iteration plans created at the start of every iteration. The iteration plan can reflect any changes that have occurred and new discoveries and priorities since the last iteration. Customers have a tendency to change what they want once they see the software "in action" [25].

- *...while there is value in the items on the right, we value the items on the left more*: The authors of the Manifesto recognize that the items on the right of each bullet (processes and tools, comprehensive documentation, contract negotiation, and following a plan) have value. The Manifesto states a priority is given toward the items on the left when resources and time force a choice to be made.

---

[2] The customer can be the organization paying for the software, as with customer software. Alternatively, the role of customer can be "played" by a product owner or business analyst in the software development organization.

2. Agile and Lean Principles

After completing the "Manifesto for Agile Software Development," the original group of 17 created the "Principles Behind the Agile Manifesto" [13]. Subsequently, Lean Software Development Principles [26] were authored by Mary and Tom Poppendieck. Principles are basic generalizations that are accepted as true and that can be used as a basis for reasoning or conduct. Alternatively, principles can be defined as underlying truths that do not change over time or space [25]. In this section, both agile and lean principles will be described and compared. These principles are used as the basis for agile software development practices, as will be discussed in Section 3.

2.1 The Agile Principles

The Agile Alliance documented the 12 principles they follow that underlie the Manifesto [13]. As such the agile methods are principle-based [5]. The whole team is guided by these principles:

1. *Our highest priority is to satisfy the customer through early and continuous delivery of valuable software.* Early and continuous delivery of software allows the software development team to get feedback on the evolving product. Customers also feel more confident in a software development team when they can "touch and feel" the evolving product. Additionally, the most valuable features are delivered to the customer. Therefore, customers are given the flexibility to change lower priority requirements over time and the team can deliver a partial, fully functioning, valuable product if time constraints prevent all requirements from being implemented prior to release.

2. *Welcome changing requirements, even late in development. Agile processes harness change for the customer's competitive advantage.* Agile methods allow a team to accommodate change throughout the process because the project is replanned for every iteration. When a change had a large impact upon the design/architecture of the working software, the implications and associated risks and the need for refactoring[3] are discussed during the iteration plan.

3. *Deliver working software frequently, from a couple of weeks to a couple of months, with a preference to the shorter time scale.* This principle puts some bounds around the "early and often delivery" first principle.

---

[3] Refactoring is the process of changing a software system in such a way that it does not alter the external behavior of the code yet it improves its internal structure [27].

4. *Business people and developers must work together daily through the project.* Project managers/business analysts are available to provide feedback and to answer the questions of the development team. Whenever a software developer or tester makes an assumption of what the customer desires, the project is at risk for straying from the desired functionality.

5. *Build projects around motivated individuals. Give them the environment and support they need, and trust them to get the job done.* Agile methods emphasize empowering the individuals on the team to make decisions and trusting that the individuals will do their job for the benefit of the team as a whole.

6. *The most efficient and effective method of conveying information to and within a development team is face-to-face conversation.* This principle emphasizes synchronous human communication rather than "talking" through documents. Best case, the communication occurs face-to-face but phone calls or instant messaging can also be used when face-to-face is impractical or impossible.

7. *Working software is the primary measure of progress.* As stated by Cockburn [3], "Rely on the honesty that comes with running code rather than on promissory notes in the form of plans and documents." Initially, the team may feel that a project cannot be broken down into smaller pieces for which working code can be produced. However, through group ingenuity, the team can accomplish the breakdown and achieve the benefits of early and often software delivery.

8. *Agile processes promote sustainable development. The sponsors, developers, and users should be able to maintain a constant pace indefinitely.* Sustainable development means that the team is working at a pace that can be sustained indefinitely as opposed to teams working excessive overtime. Errors can be introduced into the product and ingenuity and creativity decline when the team is too weary. Additionally, if a team member's personal life is impacted by his or her profession for too long, the team member may quit leaving a hole in the team that can be costly to the project.

9. *Continuous attention to technical excellence and good design enhances agility.* To remain agile, designers must produce good designs and be ready to dedicate time to refactor code when the design has diverged from tidy, well-encapsulated design principles.

10. *Simplicity—the art of maximizing the amount of work not done—is essential.* The emphasis is on producing a product that is simple enough to handle change while fulfilling customer requirements.

11. *The best architectures, requirements, and designs emerge from self-organizing teams.* These artifacts emerge because of the knowledge and discovery that occur throughout a project.

12. *At regular intervals, the team reflects on how to become more effective, then tunes and adjusts its behavior accordingly.* With each iteration, the team reflects upon what worked and what did not work about their recent work. The team makes plans to continue the practices that served the team well and to alter their practices that were troublesome.

2.2   The Lean Principles

Several years after the Agile Alliance, Manifesto, and Principles were formulated, Mary and Tom Poppendieck melded the concepts of lean manufacturing with agile software development through their seven Principles of Lean Software Development [25,26]. The use of the word *lean* was popularized in the early 1990s to refer to the Japanese approach to automobile manufacturing, particularly Toyota and Honda [28]. The seven lean principles are summarized:

1. *Eliminate waste.* "Waste is anything that interferes with giving customers what they value at the time and place where it will provide the most value" [25]. The focus of this principle is on eliminating waste from the time the team begins to address a customer's need and the time when software has been implemented to address that need. In manufacturing, the inventory of component parts is waste. In software development, partially done code implementation or work-in-process (such as untested code or a partial implementation of a customer requirement) is waste. Consider a software developer who is given three large requirements to complete in the next 6 months without the need to demonstrate any working code in the interim. This developer accumulates a large inventory of unfinished code for the 6 month period, during which time the customer is not able to provide intermediate feedback and testing cannot commence.

   Another large source of waste in software development is extra features. When product managers[4] and/or customers[5] feel their only time to provide their requirements is 6 months to 2 years prior to a release, they are likely to add any requirement to the list that could possibly be conceived of. Otherwise,

---

[4] In this chapter, the term *product manager* refers to the individual within an organization responsible for the day-to-day management and welfare of a product or family of products at all stages of the product lifecycle. A primary responsibility of a product manager is to elicit requirements from external customers and, based upon these requirements, to provide a development organization with information about the desired functionality of a new product or the next release of a product. In many teams that do not produce customer software, the product manager acts as a proxy for the customer set.

[5] Primarily in custom software development, the real customer will work with the team to specify the system requirements.

they could face criticism, contract renegotiation, and an arduous change control process for adding or changing requirements. As a result, typical software products can be created with 64% of the features and functions rarely or never used by a customer [29] at significant expenses. Often the Pareto Principle [30] will apply and 20% of the requirements will provide 80% of the value to the customer. The remaining 80% of the code which will provide only 20% of the value should be carefully chosen each iteration to reduce waste.

2. *Build quality in.* When many defects are found in late-cycle testing, the software development process is faulty and should be fixed. A defect found in late-cycle testing is orders of magnitude more expensive to fix than one found right after the defect is injected [31], or better yet, than the defects that can be prevented from being injected. The incremental creation of automated unit tests (the practice referred to as test-driven development [32]), automated acceptance test, pair programming [33], and continuous integration including integration tests can be used by organizations to enable efficient defect removal and defect prevention. Additionally, the defect tracking system is considered a queue of work-in-process because code with one or more defects cannot be considered completed code.

3. *Create knowledge.* As a team progresses through a project, they learn more and more about what is really desired by the customer and what the system architecture can support. Teams that try to anticipate all requirements and create a detailed design for those requirements inevitably face requirements changes and make many design changes in the actual implementation that do not correspond to the initial architecture and design. Additionally, a large upfront requirements and design effort may cause a team to feel inertia due to their early effort which may cause them to not be as flexible as they could be. Agile processes anticipate the evolution of design and requirements, and therefore do not waste time locking either down prematurely. Additionally, agile teams gain knowledge by reflecting upon the success (or lack thereof) of their interim progress and adapt their software development process accordingly. Finally, knowledge gained through the iterations can be used to make more accurate estimates of future work. Estimates based upon desires far in advance of a product release, conversely, are speculations that can be quite inaccurate.

4. *Defer commitment.* Planning a project is an important learning exercise, but sticking to a detailed long-term plan is generally not healthy. Planning does not need to be considered making a commitment. To prepare for inevitable change, defer critical design decisions until the last responsible moment, particularly focusing on maintaining options at the points where change is likely. The Poppendiecks advise "...plan thoughtfully and commit sparingly" [25].

5. *Deliver fast.* Companies that compete with others on speed generally have a cost advantage over their competitors. If a company strives for repeatable and predictable delivery speed, they must also focus on quality and customer understanding. Otherwise, their progress could come to a halt with rework and customer problems. As a result, speed requires the team members to be empowered to find the best way to do their jobs and to adjust the software development process.

6. *Respect people.* Teams should be given general plans and reasonable goals. The members of the team should then be empowered to self-direct themselves, to "use their heads" to determine the best way to meet the goals.

7. *Optimize the whole.* The whole multidisciplinary team responsible for delivering a product needs to have one common, ultimate goal, such as maximizing Return on Investment (ROI), which optimizes the overall results. Conversely, teams might decompose their overall goal into subgoals with different groups responsible for each. These subgoals might conflict with each other or cause an overall ROI suboptimization, compromising on the team's ability to achieve its ultimate goal. For example, if the developers are measured on productivity, they might be inclined to send as much code as possible to the testers as rapidly as possible without concern for the quality of the code. The testers would need to worry about quality. As a result, the overall quality of the code could decrease. The Poppendiecks, instead, encourage teams to focusing on their ultimate team goal, enabling prudent trade-offs between organizations.

2.3 Comparison of Agile and Lean Principles

Table I provides a comparison of agile and lean software development principles. The Poppendiecks [25,26] have stated that the lean principles can be used to explain why the agile principles seem to work. An X in the cell between an agile and lean principle indicate that the two principles support each other.

3. Agile Practices

As stated earlier, principles are underlying truths that do not change over time. Conversely, practices are the applications of principles to a particular situation. Practices change as one moves from one environment and situation to another [25]. As a result, software development teams who wish to be agile must first determine whether they agree with the agile principles. Subsequently, the team can choose

TABLE I
A COMPARISON OF AGILE AND LEAN PRINCIPLES

Agile principles	Lean principles						
	Eliminate waste	Build quality in	Create knowledge	Defer commitment	Deliver fast	Respect people	Optimize the whole
Early and continuous delivery	X		X		X		
Welcome changing requirements			X	X			X
Short iterations/releases	X		X		X		
Business/developers work together daily			X	X	X		X
Motivated individuals					X	X	
Face-to-face communication			X			X	
Working software as measure of progress	X		X				
Sustainable development						X	
Technical excellence/good design			X	X			X
Simplicity		X		X			
Self-organizing teams					X	X	X
Reflections			X		X	X	X

among software development practices that support these principles based upon the team's preferences, project, and team composition.

In this section, an overview of software development practices that are used by agile teams is presented. Some of these practices are prevalent only in agile methodologies, others are used in both agile and plan-driven methodologies. The practices are presented in alphabetical order. Some practices refer to other practices, so in this section, a forward reference to another practice may occasionally be required to understand a practice. At the end of the section, the practices are mapped to the agile principles supported by the practices. Section 4 of this chapter provides an overview of agile methodologies, such as Extreme Programming and Scrum. In Section 4, a mapping of the practices to the two methodologies that utilize the practices is presented.

3.1   Acceptance Test-Driven Development

Acceptance testing is a formal process that is conducted to determine whether or not a system satisfies a set of criteria (i.e., "acceptance criteria") that are predetermined by the customer to enable the customer to determine whether or not to accept the system [34]. Acceptance test-driven development is a practice whereby acceptance tests are written as a collaborative effort between the product manager/customer, software tester, software developer, and user interface designer early in the iteration such that development can proceed with more knowledge of the desired functionality [35,36]. The product manager describes his or her desired functionality and answers questions of the tester, developer, and user interface designer. The tester translates the product manager's desires into discrete steps by creating test cases documenting the product manager's desires. The developer provides information on the technical feasibility of the desired new functionality. The user interface designer makes development more concrete by specifying the user interface with which the system user will interact. The developer provides information about the technical feasibility of the feature and obtains significant information about the expectation of the customer. The net result of this collaborative activity is a set of test cases for each feature that provide examples of the expected behavior of the new functionality of the system in a variety of scenarios, removing ambiguity from the feature prior to any significant code development or test case planning.

The set of acceptance test cases that is collaboratively developed by the product manager, tester, and developer is not all the test cases planned for and run by the software tester [37]. Software testers plan and execute additional functional, integration, and system test cases to examine the behavior of the new functionality in a wider set of possible scenarios. As necessary, the tester contacts the product manager to obtain additional information about the desired behavior in these additional scenarios.

Most preferably tests written by the tester are automated, particularly the acceptance tests. These tests become part of the executable documentation of the system and can be run periodically (at least daily as part of the nightly build, if not more often) as regression tests to check whether new functionality has broken previously working functionality.

The development of acceptance tests and ongoing clarification of these tests drive collaboration and communication between the product manager, developer, tester, and user interface designer. The tester who had traditionally been involved toward the end of the process is now the hub of requirements clarification via acceptance test creation at the start of the iteration.

Related practices:

- Stories/features: Acceptance tests aid turning a story/feature into a specification to which the developer can write code and the testers can write tests.

3.2 Automation-Driven Root Cause Analysis of Failures

In the general sense, the aim of root cause analysis is to identify the underlying reason(s) for an adverse event has occurred. The premise of root cause analysis is that problems are best solved by attempting to correct or eliminate root causes, as opposed to merely addressing the immediately obvious symptoms. By directing corrective measures at root causes, the aim is that the likelihood of problem recurrence will be minimized.

Automation-driven root cause analysis of failures focuses on finding the underlying reason a failure has been found by a tester or has been experienced by a user. This practice proceeds as follows when a failure has been found:

1. One or more automated functional-level tests are written which will expose the failure and test the desired behavior.
2. One or more automated unit-level tests are written which will expose the failure.
3. The code is fixed such that the desired behavior is demonstrated through the passing of the test cases in Steps 1 and 2.

Through automation-driven root cause analysis of failures, the team can examine both (1) how has a fault been injected into the code or why a requirement been missed; and (2) what kinds of tests were not written such that testing not discover the fault or missing requirement. Additionally, the new automated tests are additions to the executable documentation of the system and the automated regression tests.

3.3   Code Ownership

The code ownership practice specifies that code is owned by a particular developer, often based upon a developer's area of expertise (such as database coding or user interface development). Teams that use an object-oriented language often assign ownership of classes to a particular developer. Team members who need to have a change made to code they do not own must go to the code owner to have the change made. Developers have specific responsibility for the quality, improvement, and appearance of a software system or subsystem and for problems, flaws, and routine maintenance [38].

Advantages of code ownership include ease in establishing a clear and single-minded vision; opportunity for specialization; pride in the work product; a focus on the technical excellence of the code; and increased ability to create a simple solution due to in-depth knowledge of code. Disadvantages include the team having a lower "truck number[6]"; and latency when the person who needs to make a change is unavailable.

The converse of this practice, collective code ownership, is described below. Agile teams select their code ownership strategy.

3.4   Code and Tests

The code and tests (or executable documentation) practice advocates that the primary permanent artifacts that should be invested in for a software system are the code and automated tests. Other artifacts, such as requirements or design documents, only become obsolete with time and are not valued by customers. Code and tests cannot become obsolete due to the need for them to be compiled. New developers to a project or to a certain area of the system can read automated acceptance tests to see what scenarios can be handled. Changes made to the code can be checked for regression and interaction problems by running the automated tests. This practice also relies on social mechanisms, such as face-to-face communication, to keep alive the history of the project.

Synonym: Executable documentation.

---

[6] The truck number is the count of the people who possess expertise in a particular area of the system. If any one of these people were hit by a truck, the organization will have lost a critical resource. With code ownership, the truck number can be one [39]

3.5   Collective Code Ownership

With collective code ownership, all code is collectively owned. Every team member can contribute to every subsystem and is free to work across all subsystems [38].

Advantages of collective code ownership include distribution of system knowledge; greater team interaction; and increased speed in handling change when key team members are not available; and ability to respond rapidly and effectively to changing requirements. Some problems that have been found with collective code ownership practice include: poor or missing documentation; source code being unreadable due to a variety of styles; unity of purpose may be difficult to achieve; and long debugging cycles [38] (presumably because ownership is unclear).

Synonym: Shared code

Related practices. The practices below can provide a "check-and-balance" for the collective code ownership practice.

- *Continuous integration.* The continuous integration practice would increase the likelihood that integration problems due to the code change will surface earlier in the software development process.
- *Automated tests run often/nightly.* After a change is made to code, all automated tests should be run to detect whether the change has caused a regression problem.
- *Use of a coding style guideline.* Developers can more easily acclimate to the code of their teammates if all use a common coding style.
- *Pair programming.* Two people making a change are less likely to inject a new fault.

3.6   Continuous Integration

Continuous integration is a software development practice where members of a team integrate their work frequently. Usually each developer integrates at least daily. Each integration is verified by an automated build involving the running of all automated tests that should detect integration errors as quickly as possible. Martin Fowler defines practices for continuous integration[7]:

1. Maintain a single source repository. The source repository should include code and tests.
2. Automate the build. The system should be able to be built by checking the source out of the repository and issuing a single command.
3. Make your build self-testing. Include automated tests as part of the build process.

---

[7]   http://www.martinfowler.com/articles/continuousIntegration.html

4. Everyone commits to the mainline every day. Developers should not "secretly" develop their code in a sandbox which enables them to keep their latest code out of the build, possibly creating more and more integration problems over time.
5. Every commit should build the mainline on an integration machine. If the mainline build fails, the problem should be fixed right away rather than waiting for the nightly build.
6. Keep the build fast. If the build is not fast, developers will commit less often and will be provided feedback on problems less often.
7. Test in a clone of the production environment. Testing in a different environment introduces risk when the system is deployed in production.

The main benefit of continuous integration is reduced risk of integration problems. Additionally, regression and integration bugs can be found and fixed more rapidly. Related practices.

- Unit test-driven development. All automated unit tests should be run as part of the continuous integration practice.
- Acceptance test-driven development. All automated acceptance tests should be run as part of the continuous integration practice.

3.7 Done Criteria

With agile methodologies, working code is the primary measure of progress works. However, teams cannot be satisfied with code that "works" for the acceptance tests only. In theory, agile teams strive to have code being in a condition to release to a customer at the end of every iteration (also known as "potentially shippable"). As a result, code cannot be considered "working code" and "done" until it passes the set of done criteria established by a team at the start of the release. Once established, the done criteria apply to all features. Some examples of done criteria include the following:

- Passing all acceptance tests
- 80% unit test coverage
- Testers have run all planned test cases
- No high severity defects are open for the feature
- Help screens for the feature have been developed

During the iteration review meeting, without compromise all done criteria features must be demonstrated to be considered done; otherwise, the feature must be moved into the next iteration during which time the done criteria can be completed.

3.8   Energized Work

The energized work practice states that individuals and teams should not work excessive overtime for long periods of time. The motivation behind this practice is to keep the code of high quality (tired programmers inject more defects) and all team members happy (to reduce employee turnover). Tom DeMarco contends that, "Extended overtime is a productivity-reducing technique" [40]. The longer people stay at work, the less work they do. Kent Beck adds that "Software development is a game of insight, and insight comes to a prepared, rested, relaxed mind" [35].

Synonym: Sustainable pace

3.9   Executable Documentation

Synonym: Code and tests (defined in Section 3.4)

3.10   Features

Features are short statements of the functionality desired by a system user or customer. Features are pieces of customer-visible, customer-valued functionality that can be completed in a single iteration. Some agile methodologies state features in a specific format. Two of these are now provided.

As a <user role>, I want to <desired functionality> so that I can <goal>.

Example: As a coffee machine owner, I want to provide the recipes for three coffee types so I can offer a variety of coffee to my customer.

<action> <results> <object>

Example: Input the recipe for a coffee type

The statement of what is desired for the feature is intentionally short. A feature statement is a "token for further conversation" between the product manager and customer during which the real desires for the functionality are discussed in greater detail. Traditionally, requirements have been stated such that a developer can read the statement and feel he or she knows the expectation of what is to be implemented. Under this scenario, a requirements statement must be very thorough. Conversely, the details of the desired behavior for a new feature are intentionally left up to conversation so that (1) more details than the product owner alone could have thought to document can be brought out during the conversation; and (2) no time is spent documenting the details for requirements that may never be chosen for an iteration due to changing requirements, competition, and changing environments. As such, the details for a feature are discussed on a "just-in-time" basis.

When a feature is too large to be completed in a single iteration, it can be called an "epic." A requirement can be stated as an epic until the functionality is to be developed in the next iteration. At that time a piece of functionality that can be completed within a single iteration is extracted from the epic and stated as a feature. The rest of the functionality of the epic remains in the backlog.

As stated, a feature must be completed in a single iteration. By breaking down desired functionality into iteration-sized "chunks," the development team can get feedback on their progress. This feedback is used to guide future functionality. Developers can demonstrate their new functionality with pride at the iteration review meeting. Additionally, work-in-process is eliminated each iteration.

Synonym: Story.

3.11   Incremental Design

Rather than develop an anticipatory detailed design prior to implementation, invest in the design of the system every day in light of the experience of the past and the current needs. The viability and prudence of large investments in anticipatory design have changed dramatically in our volatile business environment [4]. Teams often develop a "good enough" view of the architecture and design of a system during what is referred to as "Iteration 0." The length of Iteration 0 is as long as the other iterations. Teams then relook at the impacts to the architecture and design of the system each iteration based upon the features that have been chosen for that iteration. Rework may be required for the new features. However, teams have avoided large investments in anticipatory design. Instead, the time for design (and possibly rework) is shifted to each iteration.

Related practices.

- Refactoring. Refactoring [27] to improve the design of previously written code is essential when the incremental design practice is used.
- Unit test-driven development. Teams with automated unit tests with relatively high coverage can safely experiment with refactoring because a safety net is in place whereby regression faults due to the refactoring can be detected.

3.12   Inspections

Software inspections involve members of the software development team. Inspections are a static analysis technique that relies on visual examination of development artifacts to detect errors, violations of development standards, and other problems [34]. Artifacts that are commonly inspected include requirements documents, design, code, and test plans. Many organizations utilize Fagan-style [41] inspection. With a Fagan-style inspection, artifacts that will be inspected are distributed to participants prior to the meeting. A Fagan-style inspection requires several participants to be present, each with a required role to play (for smaller reviews participants may take on more than one role). The roles are defined below:

- *Author:* The author is the person who wrote the document being inspected. He or she is present at the inspection to answer questions to help others understand the work, but not to ''defend'' his or her work.
- *Moderator:* The moderator runs the inspection and enforces the protocols of the meeting. The moderator's job is mainly one of controlling interactions and keeping the group focused on the purpose of the meeting—to discover (but not fix) deficiencies. The moderator also ensures that the group does not go off on tangents and sticks to a schedule.
- *Reader:* The reader calls attention to each part of the document in turn, and thus paces the inspection.
- *Recorder:* Whenever any problem is uncovered in the document being inspected, the recorder describes the defect in writing. After the inspection, the recorder and moderators prepare the inspection report.
- *Inspectors:* Inspectors raise questions, suggest problems, and criticize the document. Inspectors are not supposed to ''attack'' the author or the document but should be objective and constructive. Everyone except the author can act as an inspector.

Organizations that have embraced inspections have often found that they have far fewer defects discovered in test or by customers once the product is released [42,43]. Inspections have also been shown to reduce SDLC defect detection costs [44].

3.13 Informative Workspace

A team member should be able to walk into the team space or common hallway and quickly get a general idea of how the project is going [35]. This information can be provided by ''big, visible charts'' [35] (or ''information radiators'' [3]) that provide updated status information such that it is worth the team member's time to look at the display. Two common forms of status information among agile teams are the burn down chart and the iteration status board. A burn down chart is a graphical representation of work left to do versus time, as is shown in Fig. 1A. The outstanding work (or backlog) is often on the vertical axis and time along the horizontal axis. The iteration status board provides information on features that are to be completed in an iteration, as is shown in Fig. 1B. Features are written on ''sticky notes.'' Features that have not been started yet are in the ''To Do'' column. When a feature is started, the sticky note is moved to the ''In Process'' column. Often the person who now

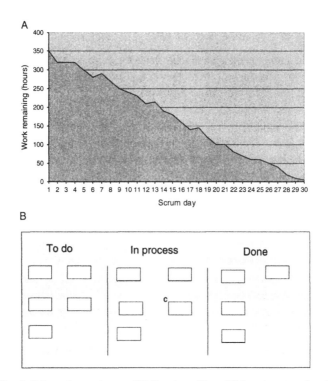

FIG. 1. Informative workspace. (A) Burndown Chart. (B) Iteration status board.

owns the implementation of the feature will write their name on the note. When a feature is completed, it is moved to the "Done" column.

Teams also can provide intranet- or Internet-based informative workspaces, such as team-based task tracking software, which are particularly beneficial for distributed teams.

3.14   Iteration Demonstration

At the end of each iteration, the development team demonstrates the acceptance test for the functionality completed during the iteration to the development team, the customer (or customer proxy, such as the product manager), and other interested parties. The demonstration serves several purposes. First, the development team obtains feedback on their latest work from the customer. The customer is more likely to be able to think of feedback because a tangible software product is shown. This feedback can be incorporated into the work of the next iteration. At times, the feedback may lead to the creation of a new feature for reworking some of the demonstrated functionality. A second purpose is for team motivation, as the team can proudly display their completed, working code. Finally, the demonstration is a means of raising awareness of the evolving product among support groups such as field service, security engineering, or performance engineering.

3.15 Negotiated Scope

Agile iterations and releases are "timeboxed" such that the end date is known and is not changed. As a result, time and resources (i.e., the number of people assigned to a project) are fixed. Additionally, the desired quality level should be known prior to project inception via the "done criteria" (see Section 3.7). The negotiated scope practice acknowledges that, time, resources, and quality are fixed and calls for an ongoing, iteration-based negotiation on the precise scope of the project based upon the customer's view of working software and current desires for the project. Formal contracts can be written as a "time and materials" contract whereby the customer pays for a certain number of developers for a certain number of iterations. In each iteration, the customer decides what the team should do. Negotiated scope is a means for structuring the implementation based upon current desires, reality, and knowledge rather than what was defined in a contract before the project began [35].

3.16 Nightly Build

In the best case, teams that are using the continuous integration practice (see Section 3.6) render a nightly build unnecessary. However, many teams use a nightly build system with which the product is built and all automated tests are run overnight. Upon returning to work in the morning, the development team obtains feedback on whether anyone has broken the build or has tests that are not passing. A good build is often considered as having the following characteristics: all files, libraries, and other components compile successfully; all files, libraries, and other components link successfully; the program can be launched; and all automated test cases pass.

The nightly build has been considered a software engineering best practice for more than a decade [45,46]. Benefits of having a nightly build are stability, minimization of integration risk, reduction of the risk of a low quality product, early and continuous quality feedback, early fault detection, and improvement of morale [45,47].

3.17   Pair Programming

Pair programming is a style of programming in which two programmers work side-by-side at one computer, continuously collaborating on the same design, algorithm, code, or test [33]. Pair programming has been practiced sporadically for decades [33]; however, the emergence of agile methodologies and Extreme Programming (XP) [35] has recently popularized the pair programming practice. With pair programing, one of the pair, called the *driver*, types at the computer or writes down a design. The other partner, called the *navigator*, has many jobs. One of these is to observe the work of the driver—looking for tactical and strategic defects in the driver's work. Some tactical defects might be syntax errors, typos, and calling the wrong method. Strategic defects occur when the driver's implementation or design will fail to ultimately accomplish its goals. The navigator is the longer range thinker of the programming pair. Because the navigator is not as deeply involved with the design, algorithm, code, or test, he or she can have a more objective point of view and can better think strategically about the direction of the work. Both in the pair are constant brainstorming partners.

An effective pair will be constantly discussing alternative approaches and solutions to the problem [33,48]. A sign of a dysfunctional pair is a quiet navigator. Periodically, the driver and the navigator should switch roles. On a software development team, team members should pair program with a variety of other team members to leverage a variety of expertise.

Among practitioners, the practice of pair programming has been shown to improve product quality, improve team spirit, aid in knowledge management, and reduce product risk [33].

3.18   Planning Poker

Planning Poker is "played" by the team as a part of the iteration planning meeting for the purpose of estimating resources required to implement a feature. For each feature, the customer or marketing representative begins by explaining each requirement to the extended development team. We use the term *extended development team* (often called the "whole team" [35] by agile software developers) to refer to all those involved in the development of a product, including product managers, project managers, software developers, testers, usability engineers, security engineers, and others. In turn, the team discusses the work involved in fully implementing and testing a requirement until they believe that they have enough information to estimate the effort. Each team member then privately and independently estimates the effort in units of "story points" (discussed in more detail below). The team members reveal their estimates simultaneously. Next, the team members with the lowest and highest estimate explain their estimates to the group. Discussion ensues until the group is ready to revote on their estimates. More estimation rounds take place until the team can come to a consensus on a quantity of story points for the requirement. Most often, only one or two voting rounds are necessary on a particular requirement before consensus is reached.

In Planning Poker, estimation is based upon the notion of story points [49]. Story points are unit-less measures of effort relative to previously completed requirements. The unit-less story points do not directly correspond to traditional effort estimates such as person-hours or person-days. As a result, estimation is generally done more quickly because participants focus on relative size and not on thinking about how long the work will take. The latter might depend upon which engineer is assigned the task and what their work schedule might be. The team can focus on the estimation with discussions like the following:

- "<requirement> is similar to <other requirement> which was a 5, so we'll give this a 5"; or
- "<requirement> is likely to take twice as long as <other requirement>"; or
- "<requirement> will take the entire iteration, let's give it an 8"

Team members are constrained to estimating from a set of possible story point values on an exponential scale (most commonly 1, 2, 3, 5, 8, 13, 20, 40, and 100) [49] that are the relative amount of effort necessary for the correct implementation, including software development, usability engineering, testing, and document authoring/updating. There are two reasons behind the use of a limited set of possible values. First, humans are more accurate at estimating small things, hence there are more possible small values than large values [49]. Second, estimation can be done more quickly with a limited set of possible values. For example, why argue over whether the estimate should be 40 or 46 when our ability to estimate such large requirements is most likely inaccurate?

The values are often calibrated such that a very small task is given the value of 1, and a value of 8 indicates that the requirement will take the entire iteration. The values of 2, 3, and 5 are given relative to these endpoints. A requirement which is given an estimate of more than 8 is referred to as an *epic* [49] and can remain an epic for a future iteration. Once an epic is to be implemented in the next iteration, the epic must be broken down into small independent stories with estimates of 1, 2, 3, 5, or 8. A team computes its velocity [35,49]; *velocity* is a historical number of how many story points the team is able to implement in an iteration. In an iteration planning meeting, the team determines which requirements to implement in the next iteration by choosing the higher priority requirements whose story points fit within the capacity determined by the velocity estimate.

Practicing Planning Poker has three major benefits:

1. *Effort Estimate*. The team obtains effort estimates via the expert opinion of all the members of the extended development team. The incorporation of all expert opinions leads to improved estimation accuracy [50,51], particularly over time as the team becomes experienced with Planning Poker.
2. *Estimate Ownership*. The estimate is developed collaboratively by the extended development team. Therefore, the members will feel the estimate is realistic and will feel more accountable since they own the estimate.
3. *Communication*. The conversations that take place during the process are useful for sharing knowledge and for structuring conversation between those on the extended team with a diversity of perspectives. When one or more team members have a low estimate and others have a high estimate, team members have a very different perception of what is involved in the implementation and verification and/or have a range of technical knowledge or experience. As such, Planning Poker provides a structured means for:
   • obtaining a shared understanding;
   • exposing hidden assumptions of the technical aspects of implementation and verification;
   • discussing the implications throughout the system for implementing a requirement;
   • surfacing and resolving ambiguities realized via divergent perspectives on the requirement; and
   • exposing easy and hard alternatives for achieving desired goals.

Planning Poker is a Wideband Delphi-based practice (see Section 3.32).

3.19   Release and Iteration Backlog

The release backlog [23] is an evolving, prioritized queue of business and technical requirements that needs to be developed into a system during the release. For each requirement, the release backlog contains a unique identifier for the requirement, the category (feature, enhancement, defect), the status, the priority, and the effort estimate (such as a story point estimate, see Section 3.18) for the feature. The general scope of the release backlog is formulated prior to a release beginning, and the features are given an initial prioritization. In each subsequent iteration, the features can be added or deleted from the release backlog, and the current feature list is reprioritized.

The iteration backlog [23] is a list of all business and technology features, enhancements, and defects that have been scheduled for the current iteration.

The iteration backlog is updated each day by team members who implement and test the features. The features are taken off the backlog when they are accepted by a customer or product manager and can pass the done criteria (see Section 3.7).

3.20   Retrospective

At the end of each iteration, teams gather for retrospective meetings [52]. In this meeting, data is presented on how the iteration went, such as how much working software was produced, if iteration goals were met, and how many defects are in the defect backlog. Additionally, the team discusses what went well for them during the iteration and what they should do differently for the next iteration [3]. Specific action items are taken out of the retrospective and made as stories for the next iteration so that the team allocates necessary resources toward process improvement.

3.21   Scrum Meeting

Short meetings, called Scrum meetings (or stand-up meetings, see Section 3.26), are daily meetings that last no more than 10–15 min [39]. While managers and the product manager may attend the meeting, only the developers, testers, and others directly contributing to working code speak at the meeting. Each team member answers the following questions:

- What did you do yesterday?
- What will you do today?
- What is getting in the way of you doing your work?

The purpose of these meetings is for critical information exchange between the team members, with minimal overhead. The focus is on technical progress and the work plan for an empowered team to make daily decisions that will lead to the team being as successful as possible during the iteration. An additional purpose of the meeting is for the team members to publicly commit to their work plans. Such public commitment increases the likelihood the work will be completed that day, supporting the energized work (see Section 3.8) practice because work is more likely to be done at a consistent pace rather than clustering at deadlines.

3.22   Sit Together

Teams that utilize the sit together [35] practice sit together in one open space, as in a "warroom" set up. The purpose of sitting together is to enable communication between team members. Communication drops off if a team member has to walk more than 10 m to see colleague [53]. Warrooms have been shown to double the productivity of a software team [54].

The need for periodic privacy of team members can be achieved by having a "caves and commons" [3] set up whereby there is a "common" area for team members to work to maximize communication and information transfer. A "caves" area gives people a place to make phone calls, check e-mails, or to work quietly.

3.23   Short Iterations

Each iteration is a self-contained mini-project composed of activities such as requirements, design, programming, and test [5]. Agile teams generally have time-boxed iterations that last between 1 and 4 weeks. When an iteration is timeboxed, the iteration length is fixed and is not allowed to be moved out, even if the team knows that they have not met their iteration objectives. Rather than move out the schedule, the scope of the iteration is reduced. At the end of the iteration, the team delivers working code that passes the done criteria (see Section 3.7) and is considered to be potentially shippable. The team then obtains feedback on this working code from their customer, product manager, and other team members.

3.24   Short Releases

The teams deliver code to customers in the form of supported releases more often, preferably as often as every 3 months [35]. The purpose of having such short releases is to get the product out to customers as quickly as possible for the customer's competitive advantage and so that feedback on the product can be obtained and fed back into the development process. The short release practice necessitates the team considering what coherent groupings of functionality can be delivered to the field in a short period of time.

3.25   Sprint

Synonym: Short iteration (defined in Section 3.23).

3.26   Stand-Up Meeting

Synonym: Scrum meeting (defined in Section 3.21)

The name "stand up meeting" is based upon teams conducting meeting in spaces without chairs. When the team has to stand for the meeting, the meeting is less likely to exceed the 15 min maximum time allowance.

3.27   Stories

Synonym: Features (defined in Section 3.10).

3.28   Sustainable Pace

Synonym: Energized work (defined in Section 3.8).

3.29   Ten-Minute Build

Teams that use the 10-min build practice [35] structure the project and its associated tests such that the whole system can be built and all the automated tests can be run in 10 min and thus the process can be done often. The purpose of being able to build and run so rapidly is to enable developers to get feedback on recent changes. If the build is so quick, the developers are more likely to run the tests and integrate new code more often and to be able to see the impact of the new code.

3.30   Unit Test-Driven Development

Unit test-driven development [32] is a practice that has been used sporadically for decades [1,32]. With this practice, a software engineer cycles on a minute-by-minute basis between writing failing automated unit tests and writing implementation code to pass those tests.

Case studies [55–58] were conducted with four development teams at Microsoft (Windows, MSN, Visual Studio, and one unnamed application) developed in C++ and C# and one IBM device driver team that developed in Java. All had transitioned from an *ad hoc* unit testing practice to the team-wide use of automated unit testing using the NUnit[8] or JUnit[9] frameworks. Table II shows a comparison of the results of these teams relative to a comparable team in the same organization that did not use TDD. Except for the Microsoft application, the TDD teams realized a significant decrease in defects, from 39% to 91%. The main difference between the Windows, MSN, Visual Studio, and IBM teams versus the Microsoft application team was that the first four developed automated unit tests incrementally on a minute-by-minute basis. The Microsoft application team developed their test cases every few days. These results indicate that writing unit tests more often leads to greater defect reduction. Developers took from 15% to 35% longer to achieve this quality gain.

---

[8] http://www.nunit.org/index.php
[9] http://junit.org/

TABLE II
MICROSOFT AND IBM UNIT TEST-DRIVEN DEVELOPMENT CASE STUDIES

	MS Windows	MS MSN	MS Visual Studio	MS App	IBM Drivers
Pre-TDD defects/LOC	A	C	C	D	E
Decrease in defects/LOC	0.38A	0.24B	0.09C	0.80D	0.61 W
Increase in development time	25–35%	15%	25–30%	30%	15–20%

However, the quality improvement due to reduced defects, leading to less debug and field support time, more than makes up for this increase in development time.

3.31   Whole Team

Agile teams that utilize the whole team practice [35] which consider the cross-functional team of all those necessary for the product to succeed as one team. The whole team consists of developers, testers, product managers, project managers, user interface designers, documentation specialists and anyone else involved in the production of working code. When operating as a whole team, the "we-them" mentality goes away in favor of the team striving for joint objectives.

3.32   Wideband Delphi Estimation

Wideband Delphi is based upon the Delphi practice [59], developed at The Rand Corporation in the late 1940s for the purpose of making forecasts rather than estimates. With the Delphi practice, participants are asked to make their forecast individually and anonymously in a preliminary round. The first round results are collected, tabulated, and returned to each participant for a second round, during which the participants are again asked to make a new forecast regarding the same issue. This time each participant has knowledge of what the other participants forecasted in the first round but not any explanation by the participants of the rationale behind their forecast. The second round typically results in a narrowing of the range in forecasts by the group, pointing to some reasonable middle ground regarding the issue of concern. The original Delphi technique avoided group discussion [60].

Boehm created a variant of this technique called the Wideband Delphi technique [31]. Group discussion occurs between rounds in Wideband Delphi; participants explain why they have chosen their value. Wideband Delphi is a useful technique for coming to some conclusion regarding an issue when the only information available is based more on experience than hard empirical data [60].

Planning Poker (see Section 3.18) is a Wideband Delphi technique.

3.33   Practices Versus Agile Principles

Table III below maps the agile practices discussed in this chapter to the agile principles supported by the practices.

4.   Examples of Agile Software Development Methodologies

This section provides a brief introduction to three agile methodologies: XP, FDD, and Scrum. The three were chosen to demonstrate the range of applicability and specification of the agile methodologies. For each methodology we provide an overview, discuss documents and artifacts produced by the development team, the roles the members of the development team assume, the process, and a discussion. The methodology descriptions in this section refer to the agile practices defined in Section 3.

Often industrial teams create their own hybrid software development process by picking and choosing among the practices discussed in Section 3, rather than strictly adhering to the complete set of practices laid out in one of these three methodologies.

4.1   Extreme Programming (XP)

The Extreme Programming (XP) [18,35] originators aimed at developing a methodology suitable for "object-oriented projects using teams of a dozen or fewer programmers in one location." [36]

4.1.1   Documents and Artifacts

In general, XP relies on "documentation" via oral communication, the code itself, and tacit knowledge transfer rather than written documents and artifacts. The following relatively informal artifacts are produced:

- *Story cards*, paper index cards that contain brief requirement descriptions. The user story cards are intentionally not a full requirement statement but are, instead, a commitment for further conversation between the developer and

TABLE III

AGILE SOFTWARE DEVELOPMENT PRACTICES AND THE AGILE PRINCIPLES THEY SUPPORT

Agile practices	Agile principles										
	Early delivery	Change req'mnt	Short iteration	Business & development	Motivate individual	Face–Face	Work software	Sustain dev	Technical excellence	Simplicity	Reflection
Acc Test				X		X			X		X
Root cause									X		
Code ownership		X	X		X					X	
Code and tests									X		
Collect code own					X		X				
Cont integ			X				X		X		
Done criteria			X				X				
Energized	X							X			
Features		X	X				X				
Incremental Design		X	X		X		X		X	X	
Inspections											
Inform workspace	X	X	X	X	X	X	X				
Iteration demo	X	X	X	X		X	X				
Negotiate scope			X	X							
Nightly build			X						X		
Pair Program							X		X	X	
Planning Poker	X	X	X	X	X	X	X				
Rel & Iter Backlog	X	X	X	X		X	X				
Retrospective								X			X
Scrum meeting	X		X	X	X	X					
Sit together				X	X	X					
Short iterations	X	X	X	X			X				
Short releases	X	X	X				X				
Ten-minute build	X						X				
Unit TDD		X	X	X	X				X		
Whole team				X	X	X	X				

the customer. During this conversation, the two parties will come to an oral understanding of what is needed for the requirement to be fulfilled. Customer priority and developer resource estimate are added to the card. The resource estimate for a user story must not exceed the iteration duration.

- *Task list*, a listing of the tasks (typically 1.5–3 days in duration) for the user stories that are to be completed for an iteration.

- *CRC cards* [61] *(optional)*, paper index card on which one records the responsibilities and collaborators of classes which can serve as a basis for software design. The classes, responsibilities, and collaborators are identified during a design brainstorming/role-playing session involving multiple developers. CRC stands for *Class-Responsibility-Collaboration*.

- *Customer acceptance tests*, textual descriptions and automated test cases which are developed by the customer. The development team demonstrates the completion of a user story and the validation of customer requirements by passing these test cases.

- *Visible wall graphs*, to foster communication and accountability, progress graphs are usually posted in team work area. These progress graphs often involve how many stories are completed and/or how many acceptance test cases are passing.

4.1.2 Roles

- *Manager*, owns the team and its problems. He or she forms the team, obtain resources, manages people and problems, and interfaces with external groups.

- *Coach*, teaches team members about the XP process as necessary, intervenes in case of issues; monitors whether the XP process is being followed. The coach is typically a programmer and not a manager.

- *Tracker*, regularly collects user story and acceptance test case progress from the developers to create the visible wall graphs. The tracker is a programmer, not a manager or customer.

- *Programmer*, writes tests, design, and code; refactors; identifies and estimates tasks and stories (this person may also be a tester).

- *Tester*, helps customers write and develop tests (this person may also be a programmer).

- *Customer*, writes stories and acceptance tests; picks stories for a release and for an iteration. A common misconception is that the role of the customer must be played by one individual from the customer organization. Conversely, a group of customers can be involved or a customer proxy, such as the product manager, can play this role.

4.1.3 Process

The initial version of the XP software methodology [18] published in 2000 had 12 programmer-centric, technical practices. These practices interact, counterbalance, and reinforce each other [4,18]. However, in a survey [62] of project managers, chief executive officers, developers, and vice-presidents of engineering for 21 software projects, none of the companies adopted XP in a "pure" form wherein all 12 practices were used without adaptation. In 2005, XP was changed to include 13 primary practices and 11 corollary practices [35]. The primary practices are intended to be useful independent of each other and the other practices used [35], though the interactions between the practices may amplify their effect. The corollary practices are likely to be difficult without first mastering a core set of the primary practices.

The 13 primary technical practices, most described in Section 3, are sit together, whole team, informative workspace, energized work, pair programming, stories, short iteration, quarterly release, slack, ten-minute build, continuous integration, acceptance- and unit test-driven development, and incremental design. The slack practice, not defined above, guides teams toward including some lower priority tasks in each iteration. These lower priority tasks would be the last to be completed in the iteration in case time runs out. In this way, the customer should be able to see their higher priority stories completed by the end of each iteration.

XP also has 11 corollary technical practices. Four of these are defined in Section 3 due to their commonality with other agile processes: root cause analysis, collective code ownership, code and tests, and negotiated scope contract. The other seven are now briefly described:

- *Real customer involvement*, the customer is available to clarify requirements questions, is a subject matter expert, and is empowered to make decisions about the requirements and their priority. Additionally, the customer writes the acceptance tests.
- *Incremental deployment*, gradually deploy functionality in a live environment to reduce the risk of a big deployment.
- *Team continuity*, keep effective teams together.
- *Shrinking team*, as a team grows in capacity (due to experience), keep their workload constant but gradually reduce the size of the team.
- *Daily deployment*, put new code into production every night.
- *Single code base*, the team works with only one code stream.
- *Pay-per-use*, charge the user every time the system is used to obtain their feedback by their usage patterns.

4.1.4 Discussion

The main advantages of XP relative to small, colocated teams have been demonstrated by several industrial case studies, including [63–67]:

- Improved quality
- Improved productivity (though the measures were relatively inexact)
- Improved team morale
- Anecdotally, improved customer satisfaction

The possible drawbacks of XP are as follows:

- May not be applicable for other than small, colocated teams developing non-critical software, though XP has been successfully used with mission-critical projects [68], distributed teams [69], and for scientific research [70].
- XP deemphasizes documentation and relies upon social mechanisms to keep alive the important history of the project. Due to his de-emphasis on documentation, XP must be adapted for projects that require traceability and audit-ability.
- Some developers may not transition to pair programming easily; transitioning to the test-driven development practice may require technical training for some developers.
- The real customer involvement practice has shown to be very effective for communicating and clarifying requirements, but is a pressured, stressful, and time-consuming role [71].

4.2 Feature-Driven Development (FDD)

FDD [19,20] authors Peter Coad and Jeff de Luca characterizes the methodology as having "just enough process to ensure scalability and repeatability and encourage creativity and innovation all along the way" [4]. Throughout, FDD emphasizes the importance of having good people and strong domain experts. FDD is build around eight best practices: domain object modeling, developing by feature, individual class ownership, feature teams, inspections, regular builds, configuration management, and reporting/visibility of results. UML models [72,73] are used extensively in FDD.

4.2.1 Documents and Artifacts

- *Feature lists*, consisting of a set of features whereby features are small, useful in the eyes of the client, results; and a client-valued function that can be implemented in 2 weeks or less. If a feature would take more than 2 weeks to implement, it must be further decomposed.

- *Design packages* consist of sequence diagrams and class diagrams and method design information.
- *Track by Feature*, a chart which enumerates the features that are to be built and the dates when each milestone has been completed.
- *"Burn Up" Chart*, a chart that has dates (time) on the *x*-axis. On the *y*-axis is an increasing number of features that have been completed. As features are completed this chart indicates a positive slope over time.

4.2.2 Roles

- *Project manager*, is the administrative lead of the project responsible for reporting progress, managing budgets, and fighting for and managing resources including people, equipment, and space.
- *Chief architect*, is responsible for the overall design of the system including running workshop design sessions with the team.
- *Development manager*, is responsible for leading the day-to-day development activities including the resolution of resource conflicts.
- *Chief programmer*, as outlined by Brooks' ideas on surgical teams [24], is an experienced developer who acts as a team lead, mentor, and developer for a team of 3–6 developers. The chief programmer provides the breadth of knowledge about the skeletal model to a feature team, participates in high-level requirements analysis and design, and aids the team in low-level analysis, design, and development of new features.
- *Class owner*, is responsible for designing, coding, testing, and documenting new features in the classes that he or she owns.
- *Domain experts*, users, clients, sponsors, business analysts, etc. who have deep knowledge of the business for which the product is being developed.
- *Feature teams* are temporary groups of developers formed around the classes with which the features will be implemented. A feature team dynamically forms to implement a feature and disbands when the feature has been implemented (2 weeks or less).

4.2.3 Process

The FDD process has five incremental, iterative processes. Guidelines are given for the amount of time that should be spent in each of these steps, constraining the amount of time spent in overall planning and architecture and emphasizing the amount of time designing and building features. Processes 1–3 are done at the start of a project and then updated throughout the development cycle. Processes 4 and 5 are done incrementally on 2-week cycles. Each of these processes has specific entry and exit criteria, whereby the entry criterion of Process N is the exit criteria of Process $N-1$.

- *Process 1: Develop an overall model* (time: 1% initially, 4% ongoing)

Domain and development team members work together to understand the scope of the system and its context. High-level object models/class diagrams are developed for each area of the problem domain. Model notes record information about the model's shape and why some alternatives were selected and others rejected.

- *Process 2: Build a features list* (time: 4% initially, 1% ongoing)

Complete list of all the features in the project; functional decomposition which breaks down a "business activity" requested by the customer to the features that need to be implemented in the software.

- *Process 3: Plan by feature* (time: 2% initially, 2% ongoing)

A planning team consisting of the project manager, development manager, and chief programmer plan the order in which features will be developed. Planning is based on dependencies, risk, complexity, workload balancing, client-required milestones, and checkpoints. Business activities are assigned month/year completion dates. Every class is assigned to a specific developer. Features are bundled according to technical reasons rather than business reasons.

- *Process 4: Design by feature* (time: 34% ongoing in 2-week iterations)

The chief programmer leads the development of design packages and refines object models with attributes. The sequence diagrams are often done as a group activity. The class diagrams and object models are done by the class owners. Domain experts interact with the team to refine the feature requirements. Designs are inspected.

- *Process 5: Build by feature* (time: 43% ongoing in 2-week iterations)

The feature team implements the classes and methods outlined by the design. This code is inspected and unit tested. The code is promoted to the build.

Progress is tracked and made visible during the Design by feature/Build by feature phases. Each feature has six milestones, three from the Design by feature phase (domain walkthrough, design, and design inspection) and three from the Build by feature phase (code, code inspection, promote to build). When these milestones are complete, the date is placed on the Track by Feature chart which is prominently displayed for the team. When a feature has completed all six milestones, this completion is reflected on the "Burn Up" chart. All features are scoped to be completed within a maximum of 2 weeks, including all six milestones.

4.2.4 Discussion

The main advantages of FDD are as follows:

- Teams who value and are accustomed to object-oriented analysis and design and associated documentation and inspections will transition to FDD more easily than some of the other agile methods.
- The documentation produced could lead to higher quality projects and enable traceability and audit-ability.
- Project in which emergent properties, such as security, are important may be well suited for FDD due to its initial upfront planning. A web development team found that FDD was capable of dealing with the key challenges of their development: decreasing life-cycle times, frequently changing requirements, and risk analysis that can integrate security design throughout the development process [74].

Possible drawbacks of FDD are as follows:

- The upfront design may not make FDD as agile as other methodologies.
- Teams must purchase and use UML design tools.

4.3 Scrum

4.3.1 Overview

The Scrum process [4,23] puts a project management "wrapper" around a software development methodology. The methodology is flexible on how much/ how little ceremony but the Scrum philosophy would guide a team toward as little ceremony as possible. Often Scrum teams are colocated. However, with increasing frequency Scrum teams are working in a geographically distributed manner (e.g., Refs. [75,76]) whereby team members participate in the Scrum meeting via speakerphone. Scrum teams are self-directed and self-organizing teams. The team commits to a defined goal for an iteration and is given the authority, autonomy, and responsibility to decide how best to meet it.

Scrum uses the term "Sprint" to refer to the current iteration. Historically, Sprints have been 30 days. More recently, Scrum teams are using shorter Sprints, often 2-week sprints.

4.3.2 Documents and Artifacts

There are three main artifacts produced by Scrum teams, the Product Backlog, the Sprint Backlog, and the Sprint burn down chart as defined in Section 3.

4.3.3 Roles

- *Product Owner*, the person who is responsible for creating and prioritizing the Product Backlog, choosing what will be included in the next Sprint, and reviewing the system at the end of the Sprint.
- *Scrum Master*, knows and reinforces the Scrum practices, conducts the Scrum Meeting and the iteration demonstration (the Sprint Review), listens to progress, removes impediments (blocks), and provides resources.
- *Developer*, member of the Scrum team. The Scrum Team is committed to achieving the Sprint goals and has full authority to do whatever it takes to achieve the goal.

4.3.4 Process

In release planning, Scrum teams develop high-level stories for the release. Subsequently, the team estimates the size of these epics and stories for release via Planning Poker. Based upon the team's estimated velocity, a feasible release plan is developed by choosing the most important stories that can be completed during the release timeframe. Prior to launching into product implementation based upon this release plan, teams generally have what is referred to as Iteration 0. In Iteration 0, the team prepares for the ensuing product development. Also, teams estimate the story points for the first Sprint; and establish their work environment (i.e., build machine, test machine, continuous integration system) [77]. Additionally, they will establish a vision for the product architecture and the "look-and-feel" of the system. Teams also learn about any new technology that will be incorporated into the new release. Iteration 0 is timeboxed and is the same amount of time as all the other iterations. Teams may feel the need to make Iteration 0 longer than the Sprints, but keeping Iteration 0 no longer than the Sprints prevents the team from putting too much work and design into requirements that are likely to change as the release progresses.

After Iteration 0 has been completed, the Scrum process is composed of the following steps each Sprint cycle:

- A Sprint Planning meeting is held with the development team, management, and the Product Owner. The Product Owner is a representative of the customer or a contingent of customers. The Product Owner creates and prioritizes the

Product Backlog. In the planning meeting, the Product Owner chooses which features are included in the next Sprint usually driven by highest business value and risk. The development team estimates the resource required for each desired feature via Planning Poker. Jointly, they determine a reasonable number of features to be included in the next Sprint based upon the team velocity. Once this set of features has been identified, no reprioritization takes place during the ensuing Sprint.

- In the days following the Sprint Planning meeting, the development team and Product Owner collaborate on the development of acceptance tests for each Sprint feature. Additionally, the development team breaks the work required for each feature down into tasks and estimates the effort required to complete each task.
- During a Sprint, features are designed, implemented, tested integrated, and regression tested daily.
- The Scrum Meeting is an essential component of the methodology. Social promises are made in the meeting which seems to increase responsibility and follow-through and to keep the project on course. However, these meetings can become unmanageable if they are run with too many people. It is recommended that each team has a maximum of seven members. For use with larger teams, the team subdivides into smaller groups, each having its own Scrum meeting. One representative from each of the smaller groups attends a "Scrum of Scrums" meeting. This representative answers the Scrum questions, highlighting the activities of his or her own subteam. In this way, essential information is passed between subteams.
- At the end of a Sprint, a Sprint Review takes place to review progress; demonstrate features to the customer, management, users, and the Product Owner; and review the project from a technical perspective. The meeting is conducted by the Scrum Master. The latest version of the product is demonstrated in which the functions, design, strength, weaknesses, and trouble spots are shared with the Product Owner.
- The team conducts a retrospective on the activities of the Sprint.

4.3.5 Discussion

The main advantages of Scrum are as follows:

- Teams can adopt Scrum practices, such as the use of a Daily Scrum meeting, without much disruption to the development team.
- Scrum helps team manage change and eliminate work-in-process. Once the features have been chosen for a Sprint, no new features can be added to the Sprint, enabling the team to complete new functionality without direction change.

Possible drawbacks of Scrum are as follows:

- May not provide enough prescriptive guidance on engineering practices. For example, Scrum does not prescribe any testing practice.

4.4 Comparison of Practices of Three Methodologies

Table IV below provides a summary of the practices of the three explained agile software development methodologies. In the table, a practice is annotated as "no mention" if the methodologies neither include nor preclude the practice such that some teams may use the practice without "violating" the methodology. A practice is annotated as "no" when the methodology precludes the use of that practice.

5. Summary

Agile methodologies began to emerge in the mid-1990s in response to increased requirements and environmental change that was not able to be handled via existing plan-driven methodologies. In 2001, the agile methodology authors convened at Snowbird, Utah, USA, to discuss the similarities among their methodologies. They embodied these similarities in a statement of agile values called the "Agile Manifesto" [13]. The Snowbird participants then further defined their similarities by stating the "Principles Behind the Agile Manifesto" [13]. Subsequently, Mary and Tom Poppendieck provided a different perspective on agile software development by stating the Lean Software Development Principles [26]. The Lean Software Development Principles drew a parallel between agile software development and lean manufacturing such as was adhered to by automobile manufacturers such as Toyota.

Overviews of three representative agile methodologies, XP, Crystal, and FDD, were presented. These and other agile software development methodologies are all guided by the agile and lean principles. A summary of the distinguishing factors of these three methodologies is provided in Table V.

Other agile software development methodologies include ASD [15], Agile Modeling [78], and DSDM [17], and Crystal Software Development [3,16]. Additionally, teams can configure an agile Rational Unified Process (RUP) methodology [79]. Most teams in industry create their own hybrid agile methodology by choosing a selection of the agile practices presented in this paper rather than strictly adhering to any of the named agile methodologies.

TABLE IV

MAPPING OF AGILE PRACTICE TO METHODOLOGY

Agile practice	Extreme programming (XP)	Scrum	Feature-driven development
Acceptance test-driven development	Yes; primary practice	Not specified; often done by Scrum teams	No mention
Automation-centric root cause analysis	Yes; corollary practice	No mention	No mention
Code ownership	No	No mention	Yes
Code and tests	Yes; corollary practice	No mention	No
Collective code ownership	Yes; corollary practice	No mention	No
Continuous integration	Yes; primary practice	Not specified; often done by Scrum teams	No mention
Done criteria	Yes	Yes	Yes
Energized work	Yes	No mention	No mention
Features	Yes; called stories	Yes	Yes
Incremental design	Yes	Yes	Yes, but less so than XP or Scrum
Inspections	No; sometimes done	No; sometimes done	Yes; design and code
Informative workspace	Yes; primary practice	Yes; burndown charts	No mention
Iteration demo	Yes	Yes	No mention
Negotiated scope	Yes	Yes	Yes
Nightly build	No due to continuous integration; but common	No mention; but common	"regular build" from continuous to weekly; nightly build common
Pair programming	Yes	No mention	No mention
Planning Poker	No mention; done frequently	No mention; done frequently	No mention
Release and Iteration Backlog	Yes	Yes	Yes
Retrospectives	No mention; done frequently	Yes	No mention
Scrum meeting	Yes	Yes	No mention
Sit together	Yes	No mention	No mention
Short iterations	Yes	Yes	Yes
Short releases	Yes	Yes	Yes
Ten-minute build	Yes	No mention	No mention
Unit test-driven develop	Yes	No mention	No mention
Whole team	Yes	Yes	No mention

TABLE V

COMPARISON OF AGILE METHODOLOGIES

Agile methodology	Distinguishing factor
Extreme programming	• Intended for 10–12 colocated, object-oriented programmers
	• Disciplined, programmer-centric engineering practices that focus on building quality into the product as it is developed
	• Minimal archival documentation
	• Rapid customer and developer feedback loops
Feature-driven development	• Scalable to larger teams
	• Highly specified development practices
	• Five subprocesses, each defined with entry and exit criteria
	• Developments are architectural shape, object models, and sequence diagrams (UML models used throughout)
	• 2-week feature implementation cycles
Scrum	• A project management wrapper
	• Accommodating to the engineering practices of choice by the software development team

ACKNOWLEDGMENTS

Partial funding for the writing of this chapter was provided by the ScrumAlliance.

REFERENCES

[1] B. Boehm, R. Turner, Balancing Agility and Discipline: A Guide for the Perplexed, Addison Wesley, Boston, MA, 2003.

[2] P. Abrahamsson, J. Warsta, M.T. Siponen, J. Ronkainen, New directions in Agile methods: a comparative analysis, in: International Conference on Software Engineering (ICSE 2003), Portland, OR, 2003, pp. 244–254.

[3] A. Cockburn, Agile Software Development, Addison Wesley Longman, Reading, MA, 2002.

[4] J. Highsmith, Agile Software Development Ecosystems, Addison-Wesley, Boston, MA, 2002.

[5] C. Larman, Agile and Iterative Development: A Manager's Guide, Addison Wesley, Boston, 2004.

[6] C. Larman, V. Basili, A history of iterative and incremental development, IEEE Comput. 36 (June 2003) 47–56.

[7] V.R. Basili, A.J. Turner, Iterative enhancement: a practical technique for software development, IEEE Trans. Softw. Eng. 1 (December 1975) 266–270.

[8] B. Curtis, Three problems overcome with behavioral models of the software development process (Panel), in: International Conference on Software Engineering, Pittsburgh, PA, 1989, pp. 398–399.

[9] B. Boehm, A spiral model for software development and enhancement, Computer 21 (May 1988) 61–72.

[10] T. Potok, M. Vouk, The effects of the business model on the object-oriented software development productivity, IBM Syst. J. 36 (1997) 140–161.

[11] R. Dove, Response Ability: The Language, Structure and Culture of the Agile Enterprise, Wiley, New York, NY, 2001.

[12] Lehigh University, Agile competition is spreading to the world. http://www.ie.lehigh.edu/, 1991.

[13] K. Beck, M. Beedle, A. van Bennekum, A. Cockburn, W. Cunningham, M. Fowler, et al., The Agile Manifesto, http://www.agileAlliance.org, 2001.

[14] M. Fowler, J. Highsmith, The Agile Manifesto, in: Software Development, August 2001, pp. 28–32.

[15] J. Highsmith, Adaptive Software Development, Dorset House, New York, NY, 1999.

[16] A. Cockburn, Crystal "Clear": A Human-Powered Software Development Methodology for Small Teams, Addison Wesley, Boston, MA, 2005.

[17] J. Stapleton, DSDM: The Method in Practice, second ed., Addison Wesley Longman, Reading, MA, 2003.

[18] K. Beck, Extreme Programming Explained: Embrace Change, Addison-Wesley, Reading, MA, 2000.

[19] P. Coad, E. LeFebvre, J. DeLuca, Java Modeling in Color with UML, Prentice Hall, Englewood Cliffs, NJ, 1999.

[20] S.R. Palmer, J.M. Felsing, A Practical Guide to Feature-Driven Development, Prentice Hall PTR, Upper Saddle River, NJ, 2002.

[21] A. Hunt, D. Thomas, The Pragmatic Programmer: From Journeyman to Master, Addison Wesley, Reading, MA, 1999.

[22] K. Schwaber, Agile Project Management with SCRUM, Microsoft Press, Redmond, WA, 2004.

[23] K. Schwaber, M. Beedle, Agile Software Development with SCRUM, Prentice-Hall, Upper Saddle River, NJ, 2002.

[24] F.P. Brooks, The Mythical Man-Month, Anniversary Edition, Addison-Wesley, Boston, MA, 1995.

[25] M. Poppendieck, T. Poppendieck, Implementing Lean Software Development: From Concept to Cash, Addison-Wesley, Upper Saddle River, NJ, 2007.

[26] M. Poppendieck, T. Poppendieck, Lean Software Development, Addison Wesley, Boston, 2003.

[27] M. Fowler, K. Beck, J. Brant, W. Opdyke, D. Roberts, Refactoring: Improving the Design of Existing Code, Addison Wesley, Reading, MA, 1999.

[28] J. Womack, D. Jones, D. Roose, The Machine that Changed the World: The Story of Lean Production, Harper Perennial, New York, 1992.

[29] J. Johnson, Standish Group CHAOS Report, 2002, www.projectsmart.co.uk/docs/chaos-report.pdf.

[30] J.M. Juran, F.M. Gryna, Juran's Quality Control Handbook, fourth ed., McGraw-Hill, New York, NY, 1988.

[31] B.W. Boehm, Software Engineering Economics, Prentice-Hall, Englewood Cliffs, NJ, 1981.

[32] K. Beck, Test Driven Development—By Example, Addison Wesley, Boston, 2003.

[33] L. Williams, R. Kessler, Pair Programming Illuminated, Addison Wesley, Reading, MA, 2003.

[34] IEEE, IEEE Standard 610.12-1990, IEEE Standard Glossary of Software Engineering Terminology, 1990, http://standards.ieee.org/reading/ieee/std_public/description/se/610.12-1990_desc.html.

[35] K. Beck, Extreme Programming Explained: Embrace Change, second ed., Addison-Wesley, Reading, MA, 2005.

[36] R. Jeffries, A. Anderson, C. Hendrickson, Extreme Programming Installed, Addison Wesley, Upper Saddle River, NJ, 2001.

[37] L. Crispin, J. Gregory, Agile Testing: A Practical Guide for Testers and Agile Teams, Addison-Wesley, Upper Saddle River, NJ, 2009.

[38] M.E. Nordberg III, Managing code ownership, IEEE Softw. 20 (March–April 2003) 26–33.

[39] J.O. Coplien, N.B. Harrison, Organizational Patterns of Agile Software Development, Pearson Prentice Hall, Upper Saddle River, NJ, 2005.

[40] T. DeMarco, Slack: Getting Past Burnout, Busywork, and the Myth of Total Efficiency, Broadway, New York, NY, 2002.

[41] M.E. Fagan, Advances in software inspections to reduce errors in program development, IBM Syst. J. 15 (1976) 182–211.

[42] D. Hamlet, J. Maybee, The Engineering of Software, Addison Wesley, Boston, 2001.

[43] W.S. Humphrey, Introduction to the Personal Software Process, Addison-Wesley, Reading, MA, 1997.

[44] C. Wohlin, A. Aurum, H. Petersson, F. Shull, M. Ciolkowski, Software inspection benchmarking—a qualitative and quantitative comparative opportunity, in: IEEE Symposium on Software Metrics, Ronneby, Sweden, 2002, pp. 118–127.

[45] S. McConnell, Daily build and smoke test, IEEE Softw. 13 (1996) 144.

[46] S. McConnell, Rapid Development: Taming Wild Software Schedules, Microsoft Press, Redmond, WA, 1996.

[47] E. Karlsson, L. Andersson, P. Leion, Daily build and feature development in large distributed projects, in: International Conference on Software Engineering, Limerick, Ireland, 2000, pp. 649–658.

[48] J. Vanhanen, H. Korpi, Experiences of using pair programming in an Agile project, in: 40th Annual Hawaii International Conference on System Sciences (HICSS) 2007 Hawaii, 2007, p. 274b.

[49] M. Cohn, Agile Estimating and Planning, Prentice Hall, Upper Saddle River, NJ, 2006.

[50] N.C. Haugen, An empirical study of using Planning Poker for user story estimation, in: Agile 2006, Minneapolis, MN, 2006, 9pp (electronic proceedings).

[51] K. Moløkken-Østvold, N.C. Haugen, Combining estimates with Planning Poker—an empirical study, in: Australian Software Engineering Conference (ASWEC'07), Melbourne, Australia, 2007, pp. 349–358.

[52] E. Derby, D. Larsen, Agile Retrospectives: Making Good Teams Great, Pragmatic Programmers, Raleigh, NC, 2006.

[53] T. Allen, Managing the Flow of Technology, MIT Press, Boston, 1984.

[54] G.M. Olson, J.S. Olson, Distance matters, Hum. Comput. Interact. 15 (2001) 139–179.

[55] T. Bhat, N. Nagappan, Evaluating the efficacy of test-driven development: Industrial case studies, in: ACM/IEEE International Symposium on Empirical Software Engineering, Rio de Janeiro, Brazil, 2006, pp. 356–363.

[56] N. Nagappan, E.M. Maximilien, T. Bhat, L. Williams, Realizing quality improvement through test driven development: results and experiences of four industrial teams, Empirical Softw. Eng. 13 (June 2008) 289–302.

[57] J. Sanchez, L. Williams, M. Maximilien, A longitudinal study of the test-driven development practice in industry, in: Agile 2007, Washington, DC, 2007, pp. 5–14.

[58] L. Williams, G. Kudrjavets, N. Nagappan, On the effectiveness of unit test automation at Microsoft, in: International Symposium on Software Reliability Engineering, Mysuru, India, 2009, pp. 81–89.

[59] U.G. Gupta, R.E. Clarke, Theory and applications of the Delphi technique: a bibliography (1975–1994), Technol. Forecast. Soc. Change 53 (1996) 185–211.

[60] B. Boehm, C. Abts, S. Chulani, Software development cost estimation approaches—a survey, Ann. Softw. Eng. 10 (November 2000) 177–205.

[61] D. Bellin, S.S. Simone, The CRC Card Book, Addison-Wesley, Reading, MA, 1997.

[62] K. El Emam, Finding Success in Small Software Projects, Agile Project Management 4, 2003, http://www.cutter.com/project/fulltext/reports/2003/11/index.html.

[63] P. Abrahamsson, Extreme programming: first results from a controlled case study, in: 29th EURO-MICRO Conference, Belek, Turkey, 2003.

[64] J. Grenning, Launching extreme programming at a process-intensive company, IEEE Softw. 18 (November/December 2001) 27–33.

[65] L. Layman, L. Williams, L. Cunningham, Exploring extreme programming in context: an industrial case study, in: Agile Development Conference, Salt Lake City, UT, 2004, pp. 32–41.

[66] L. Layman, L. Williams, L. Cunningham, Motivations and measurements in an Agile case study, J. Syst. Archit. 52 (11) (2006) 654–667.

[67] L. Williams, W. Krebs, L. Layman, A. Antón, P. Abrahamsson, Toward a framework for evaluating extreme programming, in: Empirical Assessment in Software Engineering (EASE) 2004, Edinburgh, Scotland, 2004, pp. 11–20.

[68] J. Drobka, D. Noftz, R. Raghu, Piloting XP on four mission-critical projects, IEEE Softw. 21 (2004) 70–75.

[69] L. Layman, L. Williams, D. Damian, H. Buresc, Essential communication practices for extreme programming in a global software development team, Info. Softw. Technol. (TBD) 48 (9) (2006) 781–794.

[70] W. Wood, W. Kleb, Exploring XP for scientific research, IEEE Softw. 20 (2003) 30–36.

[71] A. Martin, R. Biddle, J. Noble, The XP customer role in practice: three studies, in: Agile Development Conference, Salt Lake City, UT, 2004.

[72] M. Fowler, UML Distilled, third ed., Addison Wesley, Reading, MA, 2004.

[73] J. Rumbaugh, I. Jacobson, G. Booch, The Unified Modeling Language Reference Manual, Addison Wesley, Reading, MA, 1999.

[74] X. Ge, R.F. Paige, F.A.C. Polack, H. Chivers, P.J. Brooke, Agile development of secure web applications, in: 6th International Conference on Web Engineering, Palo Alto, California, 2006, pp. 305–312.

[75] J. Sutherland, G. Schoonheim, N. Kumar, V. Pandey, S. Vishal, Fully distributed Scrum: linear scalability of production between San Francisco and India, in: Agile 2009, Chicago, IL, 2009, pp. 277–282.

[76] E. Uy, N. Ioannou, Growing and sustaining an offshore Scrum engagement, in: Agile 2008, Toronto, Canada, 2008, pp. 345–350.

[77] A. Shalloway, J.R. Trott, Lean–Agile Pocket Guide for Scrum Teams, Net Objectives, Bellevue, WA, 2009.

[78] S.W. Ambler, Agile Modeling, Wiley, New York, NY, 2002.

[79] P. Kroll, P. Kruchten, The Rational Unified Process Made Easy: A Practitioner's Guide to the RUP, Addison Wesley, Boston, 2003.

A Picture from the Model-Based Testing Area: Concepts, Techniques, and Challenges

ARILO C. DIAS-NETO

Computer Science Department, Federal University of Amazonas, Brazil

GUILHERME H. TRAVASSOS

Experimental Software Engineering Group, PESC/COPPE, Federal University of Rio de Janeiro, Brazil

Abstract

Model-Based Testing (MBT) represents a feasible and interesting testing strategy where test cases are generated from formal models describing the software behavior/structure. The MBT field is continuously evolving, as it could be observed in the increasing number of MBT techniques published at the technical literature. However, there is still a gap between researches regarding MBT and its application in the software industry, mainly occasioned by the lack of information regarding the concepts, available techniques, and challenges in using this testing strategy in real software projects. This chapter presents information intended to support researchers and practitioners reducing this gap, consequently contributing to the transfer of this technology from the academia to the industry. It includes information regarding the concepts of MBT, characterization of 219 MBT available techniques, approaches supporting the selection of MBT techniques for software projects, risk factors that may influence the use of these techniques in the industry together with some mechanisms to mitigate their impact, and future perspectives regarding the MBT field.

ADVANCES IN COMPUTERS, VOL. 80
ISSN: 0065-2458/DOI: 10.1016/S0065-2458(10)80002-6

45

1. Introduction

Software testing consists in an experimental investigation conducted to provide information for users and stakeholders about the quality of the software under test in the context where it will be deployed. It includes the process to run a software system aiming at to reveal failures [1]. According to Juristo et al. [2], software testing can be considered one of the most expensive activities in the software development process.

Considering all issues concerned with testing planning and design [3], it would be interesting to think about how to simplify or automate the execution and regression (reexecution after changes in the software or its specification) of tests, because the test cases generation activity would be the one that impacts more the testing coverage. According to Myers [4], one of the main factors influencing the software testing costs would be the number of identified test cases due to its relation to the resources that must be allocated for the generation and execution of each one of them.

There are several testing strategies that may be applied to generate test cases for a software project, such as code-based (test cases generation from software source code), specification-based (test cases generation from software specification), or model-based (test cases generation from software models) testing strategies, each one with its specific characteristics, challenges, advantages, and disadvantages. All of these characteristics should be considered while selecting and applying one of these strategies in a software project. Despite the importance of all these testing strategies for the success of a software project, this chapter is focused exclusively on Model-Based Testing (MBT).

According to Dalal et al. [5], MBT consists in a feasible strategy to control the software quality by reducing the testing process costs, because test cases can be generated from the artifacts (models) produced throughout the software development process. The MBT application makes possible to software engineers to apply an additional verification to the models developed throughout the software development before they can be delivered to the next process stages. By using these models for test cases generation they must be correct to assure the success of testing. Therefore, MBT can contribute for the software quality not just by running the test cases after software coding but also by allowing the model verification while generating the test cases set.

The intention of this chapter is to provide information regarding MBT that could allow software engineers to decide on the use of such testing strategy for their software projects. This text represents a summary of a comprehensive investigation regarding the selection of MBT techniques best suited for software projects [6]. On the basis of the results of a secondary study (systematic review) [7], 219 MBT techniques are highlighted. So far, this set can represent a picture of the state-of-the-art of such testing until 8/2009. Besides, some indications about risks on using MBT in software projects and suggestions of approaches that could support the decision about which MBT techniques could be used for a software project are also presented. This chapter is organized as follows: Section 2 presents the concepts concerned with MBT, the benefits introduced by this testing strategy, and the main difficulties reported at the technical literature regarding the MBT strategy in software projects. Section 3 describes the planning and results analysis of a systematic review that made possible the identification and characterization of 219 MBT techniques published at the technical literature from years 1990 until 8/2009. Besides, this section also includes the description of three approaches to support the selection of MBT techniques for software projects. Section 4 suggests some risks to be mitigated by researchers and software engineers aiming at to take advantage of the main benefits provided by the MBT strategy adoption of MBT in a software project. Finally, Section 5 presents the final considerations, conclusions, and further perspectives in the MBT field.

2. Model-Based Testing

2.1 Concepts and Background Regarding MBT

The use of models to represent a software system for tests generation and execution has been an area of study since at least 1976, when Ramamoorthy et al. [8] published a scientific paper describing the seminal technique for test-data generation.

In this approach, given a program graph for a FORTRAN program, a set of paths can be identified satisfying some given testing criteria. In 1978, Chow published a scientific paper describing a MBT technique adopting the control-flow criterion to evaluate software correctness from its representation by a finite state machine [9].

Since then, a number of different definitions regarding MBT have been presented. According to Utting and Legeard [10], MBT consists in a testing strategy where test cases are derived totally or partially from a model describing some aspects (e.g., functionality, security, performance, etc.) of a software system. In order to make feasible its use, it is necessary to have software behavioral or structural explicitly described by models designed with well-defined rules, such as formal models, finite state machines, UML diagrams, among others.

According to Dalal et al. [5], MBT depends on three key elements: the *model* used for the software behavior/structure description, the *test-generation algorithm* (criteria), and the *tools* that provide supporting infrastructure for the tests (including expected outputs). However, the MBT strategy usually still includes support to different testing levels (e.g., unit, integration, or system testing), the relationship between models and source code, and a discussion regarding what can be automated during the testing [11].

Despite some contexts confounds *MBT* with *Test Case Generation*, it is important to make clear the difference between these definitions to improve the MBT understanding. *MBT* uses models developed throughout the software development process that are adapted by the testing team for automatic test cases set generation. On the other hand, *Test Case Generation* is just one possible task composing the testing process, and it may or may not be performed using formal software models.

2.2   MBT Process and Overview of MBT Technique

A MBT technique represents an instance of the MBT strategy described in Fig. 1. It includes the definitions of some important characteristics concerned with MBT techniques, such as the type of model (notation) that must be used to represent the software behavior/structure, the test-generation criteria available in the technique, and the outputs generated by the technique. The specific activities associated to MBT are described below:

1. Build the software model (one of the main differences when compared to the other testing strategies).
2. Generate test cases.
   a. Generate inputs.
   b. Generate expected results or behaviors.

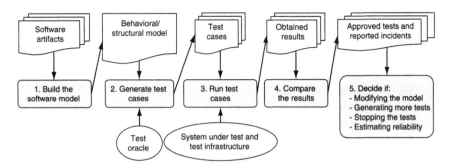

FIG. 1. MBT activities (adapted from Ref. [12]).

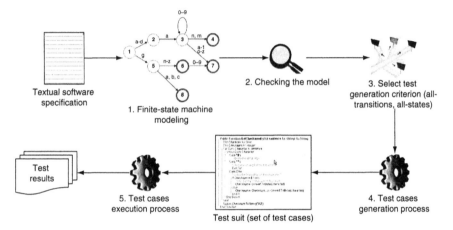

FIG. 2. Example of MBT technique. (See color insert at the back of the book.)

3. Run tests.
4. Compare obtained and expected results.
5. Decide further actions (modifying the model, generating more tests, stopping tests, or estimating software reliability/quality).

Figure 2 presents one example of a hypothetical MBT technique that allows deriving finite state machine models from the requirements specification. In this MBT technique, the input artifact is represented by the software specification written in a textual format. From this input, it is necessary to follow some steps:

1. Modeling a finite state machine. It is the model/notation used to represent the software behavior.

2. Checking the model, by executing an algorithm implemented in the MBT technique to evaluate if the constructed finite state machine model in step 1 is in accordance with the rules defined to generate test cases, for instance, analyzing if all states are connected or if there is at least one final state. If the model's validation rules are not attended, the MBT technique cannot follow to the next steps.

3. If the constructed model is correct, the MBT technique provides two test-generation criteria to be chosen by the testing team: (1) *all-transitions* that will generate test cases evaluating all transitions included in the finite state machine at least once or (2) *all-states* that will evaluate all states composing the model at least once.

4. Continuing, the MBT technique executes an algorithm to generate test cases according to the criterion selected in the step number 3, creating a test suit.

5. After the software coding, the test suit is executed to evaluate the developed software, generating a report with the test verdicts separating the approved and failed test cases and describing the revealed failures.

The results obtained by a secondary study [13] indicate a continuous evolution of MBT strategies and techniques along the years. This study was able to characterize 71 MBT techniques from the years 1990–1998/2006. As observed, these techniques use different models to represent the software, and these models usually describe different software characteristics. This scenario makes the identification, selection, and using of MBT techniques in software projects a hard decision-making task. An updated perspective based on the re-execution of Dias-Neto et al. [13] will be discussed in Section 3.

2.3   Benefits in Using MBT

The use of the MBT strategy may introduce several benefits for the testing process in a software organization, such as:

- Lower cost and effort for testing planning/execution and shorter testing schedule, because software engineers may reuse artifacts already built throughout the software development process that need to be just extended to provide the automatic test case generation;

- Improvement of the final product quality, because we are using models representing the software behavior/structure as an oracle for testing. Besides, software engineers can have the testing process almost fully automated;

- Facilities in the communication between the development and testing teams, because software engineers can use the same representation format (model) in the same abstraction level to exchange information about the software project;

- Support the exposition of ambiguities in the software specification and design, because software engineers can make an anticipated checking in the artifacts used as input for the test cases generation before defects can propagate in the next software development activities;
- Capacity of automatically generating and running a lot of useful and nonrepetitive (nonredundant) tests, because the generation is always based on predefined test-generation criteria and it is performed without any intervention;
- Facilities for updating the test cases set after the software artifacts used to build the software model changes, because when a new software model version is developed, the generation of new test cases can be automatically accomplished, and;
- Capacity of evaluating regression testing scenarios, because the execution of test cases may happen automatically in any time with low effort.

2.4 Lack of Transferring MBT Technologies into the Software Industry

Looking specifically at the MBT field, at the same time we can observe research producing interesting results regarding the development of new techniques and infrastructures to support MBT, there is a lack of scientific knowledge regarding these techniques, making hard their transferring to the software industry. According to Dias-Neto et al. [13], some factors observed in the technical literature seem to contribute for this scenario:

- *High number of MBT techniques available at the technical literature; however, poor scientific knowledge (evidence) published regarding these techniques*

In the survey published by Dias-Neto et al. [13] more than 200 scientific papers were identified describing MBT techniques published at the technical literature. In this survey, they observed each MBT technique has different characteristics when compared to other identified MBT techniques. On the other hand, they observed the most of MBT techniques has not been experimentally evaluated. Similar behavior has been observed by Juristo et al. [2] and Vegas and Basili [14] in the context of general testing techniques. This scenario highlights the need of obtaining scientific knowledge regarding the performance, scalability, effectiveness, and complexity of such techniques to support the technology transfer regarding the application of MBT from the academic to the industrial environment, motivating its use in software projects.

- *Inexistence of an updated body of knowledge regarding MBT techniques into the context of a software organization*

It would be interesting to provide a body of knowledge containing information regarding performance, scalability, effectiveness, complexity, and others characteristics of MBT techniques contextualized for a software organization scenario. However, one challenge would be to keep the information regarding the MBT techniques always updated and correct, allowing the decision-making regarding the selection and application of MBT techniques for a software project more reliable.

- *Existence of external factors influencing the application of MBT techniques in software projects*

The evaluation of MBT techniques presented in their original papers is usually performed using small examples and contextualized to a specific scenario defined by their researchers usually not integrated into a real software development process. However, in real software projects, testing is one activity that must be integrated into the software development process. Moreover, testing must be in accordance with a set of factors imposed by the software project planning, like schedule, budget, and team.

From these factors, we could observe at the technical literature the existence of a set of risk factors that may influence on the selection and application of MBT techniques in software projects. These factors indicate scenarios included in the testing process that are not included in the scope of a MBT technique. However, they need to be managed and considered in the moment of selecting and using a MBT technique because they can make unfeasible the test cases generated for a software project. These factors will be presented in the Section 4.1 of this chapter.

- *Each software project is unique and has specific characteristics*

Another aspect that makes difficult the application of MBT techniques in software projects is associated to the fact of each software project usually has specific characteristics, what makes it different from any other software project already developed by the software organization. Moreover, we can observe that usually MBT techniques are constructed to attend the specific context idealized by their developers, requiring the conduction of experimental studies aiming at to observe the behavior of these techniques in different contexts and under different conditions.

However, in order to know how to deal with these different aspects during the application of MBT techniques, we need to know which MBT techniques are available to be applied to software projects. Therefore, the next section updates the results of a systematic review conducted with the purpose of identifying and characterizing MBT techniques published at the technical literature from years 1990 to 2009.

3. MBT Techniques: A Systematic Review

It was planned and executed a systematic review with the purpose of identifying and characterizing MBT techniques published at the technical literature. A protocol was defined to support the primary studies' search and analysis. This protocol was executed in two different moments: August/2006 (first execution) and August/2009 (MBT techniques set updating).

The systematic review protocol was developed following the guidelines published by Biolchini et al. [7]. In this section, it will be presented details regarding the planning, execution, and results analysis of this systematic review, and the complete list of identified MBT techniques.

The identified and selected MBT techniques were quantitatively and qualitatively analyzed. It is important to highlight that the goal of this systematic review was not to compare the quality of the different techniques, but just to extract information from the scientific papers according to the text published by their authors and classify the MBT techniques accordingly. Because it represents a characterization study, without exploring comparison neither meta-analysis, we could refer to it as *quasi*-systematic review [15].

3.1   Systematic Review Planning and Execution

The steps followed to plan this systematic review were the definition of goal and research questions, selection of sources, definition of search strings and papers inclusion/exclusion criteria, and definition of the strategy to classify and extract information from the selected papers, summarized below:

- *Goal*: characterizing MBT techniques published at the technical literature.
- *Research Question*: which are the MBT techniques available at the technical literature and what are their main characteristics?
- *Sources*: six digital libraries—ACM Digital Library, Compendex IE, IEEEX-plorer, INSPEC, SCOPUS, and Web of Science. It is important to highlight that some books are very relevant in the MBT field (such as Refs. [10, 16, 17] were not included as sources, because the purpose of this systematic review would be to make possible the results repetition among the different executions, and we cannot assure every software engineers would have access to the cited books.
- *Search String*: (approach or method or methodology or technique) and (("model based test") or ("model based testing") or ("model driven test") or ("model driven testing") or ("specification based test") or ("specification based testing") or ("specification driven test") or ("specification driven testing") or ("use case

based test") or ("use case based testing") or ("use case driven test") or ("use case driven testing") or ("uml based test") or ("uml based testing") or ("uml driven test") or ("uml driven testing") or ("requirement based test") or ("requirement based testing") or ("requirement driven test") or ("requirement driven testing") or ("finite state machine based test") or ("finite state machine based testing") or ("finite state machine driven test") or ("finite state machine driven testing")) and (software).

In order to classify the identified scientific papers, five categories were adopted to separate papers describing MBT techniques using UML diagrams from those papers describing MBT techniques not using UML. Moreover, the categories separate papers describing MBT techniques applied for functional testing from those applied for structural testing (Fig. 3).

A. Model representing information from software requirements (functional testing), described by UML diagrams.
B. Model representing information from software requirements, described using any non-UML notation.
C. Model representing information from software internal structure (architecture, components, interfaces, units; structural testing), described by UML diagrams.
D. Model representing information from software internal structure, described using any non-UML notation.
E. Papers collected during the search, however unrelated to MBT. This category was included because eventually the digital engines used for searching may return papers containing the search strings, but for different contexts when compared with the goal of this systematic review. Therefore, these papers must be excluded.

Considering the two executions of this protocol, at total we identified 599 publications (Table I). However, 328 papers were excluded because their scopes were not related to this study, they were duplicated, or they were not electronically available.

The inclusion criteria used to identify the papers were

• The paper must be available in the Web (digital libraries or technical databases), because we need to access the original file to extract information regarding the MBT techniques;

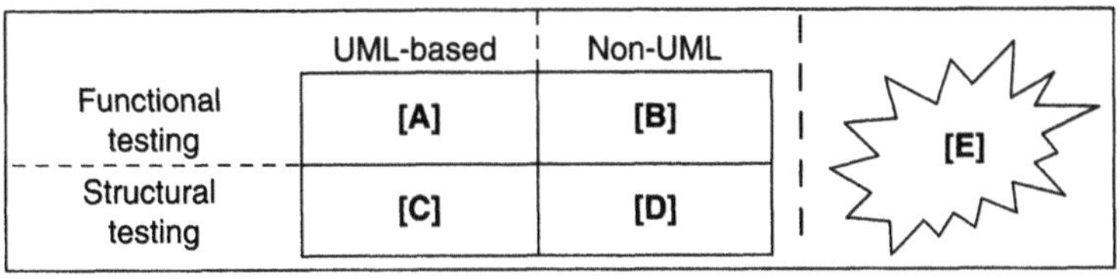

	UML-based	Non-UML	
Functional testing	[A]	[B]	[E]
Structural testing	[C]	[D]	

FIG. 3. Scientific papers categorization [18].

TABLE I
CLASSIFICATION OF THE IDENTIFIED PAPERS

Papers categories	Number of papers	Percent of papers
Category "A"	42	7.01
Category "B"	116	19.36
Category "C"	37	6.17
Category "D"	76	12.68
Category "E" or Not classified	328	54.75
Total	599	100

- The paper must be written in English;
- The paper must describe model-based software testing techniques, which is the focus of this systematic review;
- The paper must have been published from 1990. This year has been identified because it landmarks the publication of UML. Thus, we can classify MBT techniques as UML or non-UML considering the same period.

Not considering the papers in Category "E" because they do not relate with the description of MBT techniques, we totalized 271 remained papers. In Appendix A, it is described the list of 271 selected papers and their references. Among these papers, all of them were analyzed and they described 219 different MBT techniques, 76 UML-based MBT techniques, and 143 non-UML MBT techniques. The distribution of the selected papers (Categories "A"–"D") by publication per year is presented in Fig. 4, where it is possible to observe the increasing number of papers describing MBT techniques in the last years.

After the identification, selection, and classification, the next performed step was to extract the information regarding the MBT techniques from the selected paper. The list containing the 29 attributes used to extract information from each paper is described in Table II.

After the extraction of information from each MBT technique, they were analyzed considering different perspectives.

3.2 MBT Techniques Analysis

Firstly, we performed a statistical analysis regarding several aspects, such as type of experimental evidence obtained from each MBT technique, testing levels they are able to evaluate, the use of support tools, nonfunctional requirements (NFR) categories evaluated by MBT techniques, type of models used by MBT techniques, and the software execution platform.

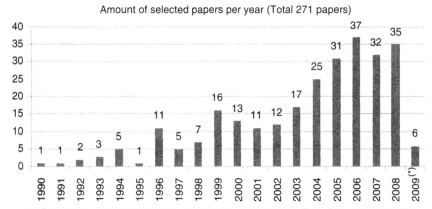

(*) This systematic review was re-executed in August/2009. Therefore, only scientific papers published and available until this month could be identified.

FIG. 4. Distribution of papers by publication year.

- *Analysis per Type of Experimental Evidence*

To determine how much evidence has been published regarding the usefulness of these MBT techniques, we categorized the papers according to the level of evidence they presented. In this analysis, we used the same five type of evidence's levels defined by Ref. [13] to make explicit that lessons learned and experiences from the field—not just academic studies—provide useful evidence. The categories are

- *Speculation*: These papers describe MBT techniques without presenting any study or example that would indicate their feasibility in software projects.
- *Example*: These papers describe MBT techniques and examples of their use. However, they provide no evaluation criteria against which to compare the described approach's performance.
- *Proof of concept*: These papers describe the use of a MBT technique for a "toy" system or a project without commercial pressure. Some measures might be collected that show that the approach can be successfully applied, but not necessarily its effectiveness.
- *Experience/industrial reports*: These papers describe real team developing software in industry using the MBT technique, and include some measures or subjective opinions to understand its utility.
- *Experimentation*: These papers evaluate the MBT technique in some detail through an experimental study (such as a case study, rigorous observation of

TABLE II

INFORMATION EXTRACTED FROM PAPERS DESCRIBING MBT TECHNIQUES

List of collected fields regarding MBT Techniques (alphabetical order)

Abstract
Approach description
Authors
Behavioral/structural model used for test generation
Category (A, B, C, D, or E)
Complexity level of each nonautomated steps
Existence of a model checker
Existence of a traceability mechanism
Inputs required to be used
Limitation/restriction to be used
List of automated and nonautomated steps
Needs of external tools
Programming Language of systems that can be evaluated (e.g., Java, C++, Ruby, .Net)
Results generated by the technique
Skills required to be used
Software development paradigm
Software execution platform (e.g., web application, embedded system)
Software Quality Characteristics the technique is able to evaluate (e.g., functionality, performance, security)
Source (e.g., Conference, Journal, University)
Supporting tool (name, cost, and platform)
Test cases generation criteria
Testing level (e.g., System, Integration, Unit, Regression)
Tests coverage criteria
Test modeling technology (e.g., UML, Z Language, ADA Language)
Title of paper
Type of failures that can be revealed
Type of experimental evaluation (speculation, example, proof of concept, experience/industrial reports, experimentation)
Type of testing technique (e.g., functional, structural, error-based)
Use of intermediate model

developers, or evaluations against a control approach). They include measures and analyses regarding the results in a specific environment.

Table III shows our results from the literature review, divided according to the type of evidence obtained from the MBT techniques.

Looking at Table III, we can see that most MBT techniques evidences fall into the proof of concept or example categories ($\sim$70%), and a small number of MBT techniques have been evaluated by experimental studies or industrial experience

TABLE III
TYPES OF EVIDENCES CONCERNED WITH MBT TECHNIQUES

Type of evidence	Number of MBT techniques	Percent of MBT techniques
Speculation	42	19.17
Example	63	28.76
Proof of concept	90	41.09
Experience/industrial reports	5	2.28
Experimentation	19	8.67
Total	219	100

TABLE IV
ANALYSIS OF MBT TECHNIQUES PER TESTING LEVEL

Testing levels	# MBT techniques
System	155 (71%)
Integration	34 (15%)
Unit	35 (16%)
Regression	7 (3%)

reports ($\sim$11%). These results suggest we have poor evidence regarding the use of MBT techniques *in loco*, and most of the evaluations are performed by who developed the approaches in small and specific scenarios, where the powerful of the obtained evidence is lower.

- *Analysis per Testing Level*

MBT techniques were characterized based on the testing level they can be applied. This information is very important to visualize the scope where researches on MBT have been developed.

Tests can be applied to small software units (*Unit Testing*), unit's collection (Integration Testing), or the entire system (*System Testing*). MBT may support the testing activities for all levels and in different ways. Moreover, *Regression Testing* may be performed with more simplicity, because in the case of changes in the model (or specification), new test cases may be generated from the automatic generation process. Table IV describes the results of the MBT techniques analysis per testing level.

MBT was originally designed for *System Testing*, justifying the high number of MBT techniques applied to this testing level (71%[1]). Continuing, MBT techniques

---

[1] The sum of MBT techniques in Table IV is a number greater than 219, because there are techniques that may be applied to more than one testing level.

are more applied to other testing levels, like *Unit* (16%), *Integration* (15%), and *Regression* (3%) testings. *Unit Testing* is not a popular abstraction level in MBT yet, because the purpose of this testing level is to test small modules, functions, or classes after their coding. Moreover, there are a lot of sounded techniques supporting structural testing from source code.

Regression Testing would not be, at first, considered a testing level because it represents a strategy to re-execute test cases that can be applied in all testing levels. However, some MBT techniques were specifically designed to support regression testing without indicating for which testing levels it could be applied. This is the reason regression testing has been classified as a different category to be able to include these specific MBT techniques.

- *Analysis per the Use of Supporting Tool*

The MBT techniques were also characterized according to the existence or not of a CASE tool supporting the test cases generation process. CASE tools may reduce the cost and effort for the application of MBT techniques, because some steps can be automated, simplifying the technique use. Table V presents the analysis results per supporting tool, where we can observe about 70% of the identified MBT techniques indicate the existence of a supporting tool. For the other techniques it was not possible to identify the existence of tools, because it was not identified any record in the selected papers.

However, besides the high number of MBT techniques using supporting tools, a more detailed analysis identified most of these tools are prototypes, possibly not representing products ready to be used in industrial software projects.

- *Analysis per Nonfunctional Requirements (NFR)*

Software requirements can be *functional* or *nonfunctional* [19]. Functional requirements define scenarios and functionalities to be provided by the software during its execution. On the other hand, NFR are essentials to define architectural aspects and restrictions during the software development. Both need to be tested, however, the test cases generation from NFR is sometimes not performed. Table VI presents an analysis of MBT techniques considering their evaluation of different NFR categories.

The NFR categories considered in this analysis were defined using the ISO-9126 (2001) standard that defines software quality attributes classified in six groups

TABLE V
ANALYSIS OF MBT TECHNIQUES PER SUPPORTING TOOLS

Use supporting tool	Not cited
153 (69.86%)	66 (30.14%)

TABLE VI

ANALYSIS OF MBT TECHNIQUES THAT EVALUATE NFR CATEGORIES

Nonfunctional requirements categories (according to ISO-9126)	Total
Efficiency	27
Usability	6
Reliability	2
Maintainability	0
Portability	0
Security	16

(*Functionality*, *Reliability*, *Usability*, *Maintainability*, *Portability*, and *Efficiency*). However, the group *Functionality* is composed of others subcategories, including NFR (e.g., security). Therefore, only the Functionality's subcategory *Security* was used to classify NFR in this work. Thus, the categories adopted in this work are efficiency, reliability, usability, maintainability, portability, and security.

From Table VI, we can observe most of MBT techniques able to evaluate NFR are applied to support *efficiency* requirements evaluation. At total, 27 MBT techniques use description of efficiency in the software models to provide test cases generation. Most of these MBT techniques are used to evaluate software response-time (performance). Moreover, 16 MBT techniques use *security* requirements during test cases generation, 6 MBT techniques are applied to *usability* evaluation, and two techniques evaluate *reliability*.

- *Analysis per model used to represent software behavior/structure*

The model used to represent the software behavior or structure is an important element in the study of MBT. The model defines the limitation of each technique based on the type of information it is able to represent about the software under test. Sometimes the model used for a software domain is not adequate to another domain. Table VII counts the type of models used by MBT techniques, classifying them as UML models or non-UML models.

Among the UML diagrams, the most adopted by the MBT techniques, in this order, are Statecharts, Classes, and Sequence Diagrams, followed by the other UML diagrams. Among the non-UML models, the most adopted are Finite State Machines, Z Language Specifications, Graphs, Markov Chains, and XML Files.

- *Analysis per Software Execution Platform*

According to the literature, certain specialized software categories use MBT. In Table VIII, we analyze the categories of software where MBT techniques can

TABLE VII
ANALYSIS OF MBT TECHNIQUES PER TYPE OF MODELS

UML models	Non-UML models
76 (34.70%)	143 (65.30%)

TABLE VIII
ANALYSIS OF MBT TECHNIQUES PER SOFTWARE CATEGORIES

Software Categories (*)	Number of MBT techniques		
	UML-based	Non-UML	Total
Not defined	42	65	107
Embedded system	5	18	23
Real-Time system	1	15	16
Reactive system	1	14	15
Safety-critical software	4	9	13
Distributed system	5	6	11
Web application	5	5	10
Web service	3	5	8
Concurrent system	2	5	7
COTS	5	1	6
Software product line	2	3	5
SIM smart card	1	3	4
Information system	2	1	3
Aircraft control system	0	2	2
Operating system	0	2	2
Telecommunication system	0	2	2
Medical system	1	0	1
Nondeterministic system	0	1	1
Synchronous software	0	1	1

*These categories are not orthogonal; some MBT techniques
fall under multiple ones.*

be applied. A high number of MBT techniques (49%) do not indicate a software
system category to which developers could apply them.

Table VIII shows that domains in which we find most of the examples of
non-UML techniques demand high reliability or require the system to react
within certain constraints, such as embedded systems, real-time, or safety-critical
systems. Looking at UML-based techniques, we can observe they are applied for

wider ranging software categories, including more recent software development categories, such as web applications, web services, and COTS.

3.3 Characterization of the Selected MBT Techniques

This section describes the selected MBT techniques characterization, presenting their category (A–D), testing level that they are applied to, software category, models used for test cases generation, indication of supporting tool, the categories of NFR evaluated by each MBT technique, and the complexity level of nonautomated steps composing the MBT techniques tests generation process. All MBT techniques have at least one nonautomated step, however, this(these) step(s) may require different complexity levels to be executed. Therefore, the column "complexity level" is represented using icons meaning *Low*, *Medium*, or *High*, according to the next explanation:

- *Low* (✓): composed basically of automated steps or manual steps where the testing team task is just to select small options (e.g., selecting test cases generation criterion or which test cases should be executed) available by the MBT technique.
- *Medium* (⚠): composed basically of manual steps requiring more effort to be executed, like intermediate model construction/generation or test-data definition. Several MBT techniques use intermediate models throughout the test cases generation process, but in most cases they are automatically generated (low complexity). When this generation is manually done, the step effort complexity would be medium;
- *High* (✗): composed basically of manual steps requiring high complexity, like manual transformations between models, because this task consists in the application of transformation rules and restrictions to derive a model, making the test cases generation process a very hard task in the software project.

Table IX presents a summary of the characterization of 219 MBT techniques identified by this systematic review. The list of references for these MBT techniques is presented in Appendix A.

3.4 Selecting MBT Techniques for Software Projects

Besides the large number of available MBT techniques, an additional difficulty when selecting MBT techniques to be used in a software project would be to identify which characteristics of MBT techniques should be considered to support the decision-making. In a survey conducted in 2006, 144 researchers and practitioners who have published at the technical literature for the development or use of MBT

TABLE IX
CHARACTERIZATION OF IDENTIFIED MBT TECHNIQUES

Authors	Cat	Testing level	Software category	Behavioral and structural models	Tools	Steps complexity	NFR[a] testing
Abdurazik and Offutt (2000)	C	System	OO	UML collaboration diagram	ND	✓	No
Aichernig and Delgado (2006)	B	Unit	Concurrent system	Specifications in input–output labeled transaction system	Yes	✗	No
Al-Amayreh and Zin (1999)	B	System	Not defined	Specifications in Z and PROLOG	Yes	✗	No
Alagar et al. (2000)	B	Unit	Reactive and real-time system	Specifications of system configuration and grid automaton	Yes	✗	Efficiency
Alava et al. (2006)	D	Integration	Web application	Design view (DView) and XML file	Yes	✗	No
Ali et al. (2005)	C	Integration	OO	UML statechart and collaboration diagrams and SCOTEM (State COllaboration TEst Model)	Yes	✓	No
Ambrosio et al. (2007)	D	System	Embedded system	State-based model	Yes	▲	Efficiency
Amla and Ammann (1992)	B	Unit	Not defined	Z specifications	ND	▲	No
Ammann and Offutt (1994)	B	System	Not defined	Z specifications	ND	✓	No
Andrews et al. (2005)	B	System	Web application	Finite state machine	Yes	✗	No
Auguston et al. (2005)	B	System	Reactive and real-time system	AEG (Attributed Event Grammar) models	Yes	✗	No

(continued)

TABLE IX   (*Continued*)

Authors	Cat	Testing level	Software category	Behavioral and structural models	Tools	Steps complexity	NFR[a] testing
Avritzer and Weyuker (1994)	B	System	Telecommunication system	Markov chain	Yes	X	Efficiency
Baharom and Shukur (2008)	D	Unit	Not defined	Interface specification and model intern design document	Yes	X	No
Bai et al. (2008)	A	System	Web service	TOL (Test Ontology Language)	Yes	◮	No
Barbey et al. (1996)	B	Unit	OO	CO-OPN/2	Yes	✓	No
Basanieri and Bertolino (2000)	C	Integration	OO	UML use case, classes, and sequence diagrams	ND	X	No
Bellettini et al. (2005)	C	System	Web application	UML statechart and extended classes diagrams	Yes	✓	No
Belli and Guldali (2005)	B	System	Not defined	Finite state machine, linear temporal logic	Yes	X	No
Benz (2007)	B	Integration	Distributed system	Task models	Yes	X	No
Bernard et al. (2006)	A	System	Not defined	UML classes, object, statechart diagrams, and objects constraint language (OCL)	Yes	✓	No
Bertolino et al. (2000)	D	Integration	Not defined	LTS dynamic models	Yes	X	No
Bertolino and Gnesi (2003)	B	System	Product line	Use cases	Yes	X	No
Bertolino et al. (2003)	C	Integration	Component-based system	UML use cases, sequence, and classes diagrams	Yes	✓	No
Bertolino et al. (2005)	C	Integration	OO	UML sequence and statechart diagrams, rational complete model	Yes	X	No

				DORIS/ADL models			
Biberstein and Fitzgerald (1999)	B	System	Real-time system		Yes	X	Efficiency
Bigot et al. (2006)	C	System	SIM smart card	UML statechart diagram	Yes	◢	No
Blackburn and Busser (1996)	B	System	Critical system	Specification model T-VEC	Yes	◢	No
Boden and Busser (2004)	D	System, Unit and Integration	Embedded system	Simulink models	Yes	X	No
Bogdanov and Holcombe (2001)	D	System	Embedded system, avionic control system	Statechart diagrams	Yes	X	No
Bonifacio et al. (2008)	D	Unit	Not defined	Finite state machine	ND	X	No
Botaschanjan et al. (2004)	A	System	OO	UML object and sequence diagrams and OCL	ND	◁	No
Botaschanjan et al. (2008)	D	System	Automotive system and safety-critical	AutoFOCUS task models	Yes	X	Efficiency
Bouquet et al. (2005)	B	System	Smart card SIM and real-life software	Abstract machine in B language	Yes	◁	No
Bouquet et al. (2006)	B	Unit	OO	Specification in JML	Yes	✓	No
Bouquet et al. (2007)	A	System	OO	UML classes, object, statechart diagrams, OCL expressions	Yes	✓	No
du Bousquet et al. (1999)	D	System	Reactive system	Environment description	Yes	✓	Security
Boyd and Ural (1991)	B	System	Not defined	Finite state machine	ND	✓	No
Briand and Labiche (2002)	A	System	OO	UML use cases + activity, sequence, collaboration, classes diagrams, and data dictionary (OCL)	Yes	✓	No

(continued)

TABLE IX (*Continued*)

Authors	Cat	Testing level	Software category	Behavioral and structural models	Tools	Steps complexity	NFR[a] testing
Briand et al. (2002)	A	Regression	OO	UML classes, use cases, and sequence diagrams	Yes	✓	No
Briand et al. (2002)	C	Integration	OO	UML classes diagram and graph	ND	✓	No
Briand et al. (2004)	C	System	OO	UML statechart, classes diagrams, OCL, and transaction test sequences	Yes	✓	No
Briand et al. (2004)	C	System	OO	UML statechart diagram + OCL, event/action flow graph	ND	✗	No
Briand et al. (2006)	C	Unit	COTS	UML classes and sequence diagrams + OCL, CSPE (constraints on succeeding and preceding events) restrictions and graph	Yes	⚠	No
Brinksma (2004)	B	System	Reactive and real-time system	VIZ	Yes	✗	Efficiency
Brito et al. (2009)	C	Integration and Unit	Embedded system	UML collaboration and sequence diagrams	Yes	✓	Efficiency
Buchs et al. (2006)	A	System	OO concurrent system	Environment, conceptual, protocol, operational CO-OPN (concurrent object-oriented Petri nets) models	Yes	✗	No
Calame et al. (2007)	A	System	OO	UML 2.0 diagrams	ND	✓	No
Carpenter (1999)	A	System	Safety-critical system	UML use cases and sequence diagrams	ND	✗	No

Reference		Test level	Paradigm	Model / notation	Automation	Support	Other
Cavarra et al. (2003)	A	System	OO	UML classes, statechart, object diagrams, intermediate format (ASM—Abstract state machine)	Yes	✓	No
Chang et al. (1990)	D	System	Distributed system	Petri nets	Yes	✗	Efficiency
Chang and Richardson (1999)	D	Unit	Not defined	ADL specifications and test-data description (TDD)	Yes	◁	No
Chang et al. (1996)	D	Unit	Not defined	ADL specifications	Yes	◁	No
Chen et al. (2005)	A	System	OO	UML activity diagram	Yes	✓	No
Chen and Liu (2004)	D	System	Not defined	Specification in SOFL	ND	✗	No
Chen et al. (2002)	A	Regression	OO	UML activity diagram	ND	✓	No
Chen et al. (2005)	D	Integration	Not defined	Conditions data flow diagram in SOFL (structured object-oriented formal language)	ND	◁	No
Chetali and Nguyen (2009)	D	Unit	Smart card	SyncCharts, Finite state machine	Yes	✗	No
Chevalley and Fosse (2001)	A	System	Critical system	UML statechart diagram	Yes	✓	No
Choi (2001)	B	System	OO	Extended use cases	Yes	◁	No
Chung et al. (1999)	B	System	Concurrent system	System specification in MSC	Yes	✗	No
Chung et al. (1996)	D	Unit	Not defined	Basic state machine, Compost state machine	ND	✓	No
Conrad and Krupp (2006)	B	System	Embedded system	Classification tree	Yes	✗	No

(continued)

TABLE IX (*Continued*)

Authors	Cat	Testing level	Software category	Behavioral and structural models	Tools	Steps complexity	NFR[a] testing
Crichton et al. (2001)	C	System	OO	System model (UML classes, object, statechart diagrams) and test directives (UML object and Statechart diagrams), intermediate format	ND	✓	No
Dai-Zhe et al. (2004)	C	Integration	Embedded system	UML interaction, activity, and statechart diagrams	ND	✗	Efficiency
Dalal et al. [5]	B	System	Not defined	Requirements described in AETGSpec	Yes	✓	No
Dan and Aichernig (2005)	D	System	Not defined	RSL specification	Yes	✗	No
Darmaillacq et al. (2008)	D	System	Not defined	Failure model	ND	✗	Security
Deng et al. (2004)	A	System and Regression	OO	UML use cases, classes, statechart, sequence, collaboration, and activity diagrams	Yes	△	No
Dias and Vieira (2000)	D	Integration	OO	Statechart diagram	Yes	△	No
Donat (1997)	B	System	Not defined	Requirements specification	Yes	✗	No
Dulz and Zhen (2003)	C	Integration	Not defined	UML annotated sequence diagram and MCUM (Markov Chain Usage Model)	Yes	✓	No
Edwards (2000)	B	Integration	OO	Control-flow graph	ND	✗	No
El-Fakih et al. (2008)	D	System	Not defined	Extended finite state machine	ND	△	No
Ernits et al. (2006)	D	System	Not defined	UPPAL models	Yes	△	No

Reference		Test level	Domain	Model			
Fraser and Wotawa (2007)	D	Unit	Not defined	NuSMV models	Yes	✓	No
Friedman et al. (2002)	B	System	Concurrent system	Finite state machine	Yes	✓	No
Gallagher and Offutt (2006)	D	Integration	OO	Component flow graph	Yes	✓	No
Gargantini (2007)	D	System	Not defined	Abstract state machine	Yes	✗	No
Gargantini and Heitmeyer (1999)	B	System	Not defined	SCR specification (software cost reduction)	Yes	✓	No
Gargantini et al. (2009)	A	System	Embedded system	Abstract state machine	Yes	✗	Efficiency
Garousi et al. (2006)	C	System (Stress Testing)	Distributed system	UML classes, sequence, context diagrams, Net deployment and modified interaction overview, control-flow model, Net interconnectivity tree, Net traffic standard, and inter-SD restrictions	ND	△	Efficiency and Reliability
Gnesi et al. (2004)	C	System	OO	UML statechart diagram and IOLTS (transitions labeled by input/output-pairs)	ND	✓	No
Gross et al. (2005)	C	Integration	OO	U2TP (UML 2.0 Testing Profile) and TTCN-3 (Testing and Test Control Notation)	ND	✓	No
Guo et al. (2005)	B	System	Not defined	Finite state machine	ND	✗	No
Gutierrez et al. (2008)	A	System	Not defined	UML use cases and activity diagrams	Yes	✓	No
Hagar and Bieman (1996)	B	System	Safety-critical system	Anna specification	Yes	✗	No
Hanna and Munro (2007)	B	System	Web service	Formal Abstraction model of XML schema	Yes	✓	No

(continued)

TABLE IX   (Continued)

Authors	Cat	Testing level	Software category	Behavioral and structural models	Tools	Steps complexity	NFR[a] testing
Hartman and Nagin (2004)	A	System	Distributed system	Combination of UML statecharts, classes, object Diagrams, and XML File	Yes	✓	No
Hartmann et al. (2000)	C	Integration and Unit	OO	UML statechart diagram and graph	Yes	✓	No
Hasling et al. (2008)	A	System	Medical system	UML use cases, classes, activities, package, and sequence	Yes	✓	No
Hayes and Sankar (1994)	D	Unit	Embedded system	Model in TDD (test-data description)	ND	✓	No
Hessel and Pettersson (2007)	B	System	Embedded system	Communication Net in extended finite state machine	Yes	✓	No
Hierons et al. (2009)	B	System	Not defined	Failure model in stochastic finite state machine	ND	✓	Efficiency
Hong et al. (2000)	B	System	Not defined	Statechart diagram and extended finite state machine	Yes	✓	No
Howe et al. (1997)	B	System	Embedded system	Specification in LISP	Yes	X	No
Hsia et al. (1997)	B	System	Not defined	Finite state machine based on scenarios, Scenarios Tree	Yes	X	No
Hungar et al. (2003)	B	System	Telecommunication system	Finite automata	Yes	X	No
Ipate and Holcombe (2005)	B	Unit	OO	X stream machines, finite state machine	ND	X	No

Jategaonkar et al. (1998)	B	System	Reactive system	Finite state machine	Yes	▲	Security
Jeannet et al. (2007)	B	System	Reactive system	Specifications in input/output symbolic transition systems (ioSTS)	Yes	✗	No
Jia et al. (2008)	A	System	Web application	UML activity diagram	Yes	✓	Usability
Jia (1993)	B	System	Not defined	Abstract Data Types (ADT)	ND	✓	No
Jourdan et al. (2006)	B	System	Sun workstation using Solaris Sparc 5.8	Extended finite state machine	Yes	✓	No
Jurjens (2008)	A	System	Safety-critical system	UMLsec models	Yes	✓	Security
Kahsai et al. (2008)	B	System	Product line	Specification in CSP-CASL	Yes	✗	No
Kandl et al. (2007)	B	System	Embedded system	NuSMV model	Yes	✗	Security
Kansomkeat and Rivepiboon (2003)	A	System	OO	UML statechart diagram and test flow graph	ND	✓	No
Kaplan et al. (2008)	A	System	OO	UML classes, use cases, and object diagrams	Yes	✓	No
Katara and Kervinen (2007)	B	System	Embedded system	Use case and LTS	ND	✓	No
Kervinen et al. (2005)	B	System	Embedded system	Test model	Yes	✗	No
Kim et al. (1999)	C	Unit	OO	UML statechart diagram and extended finite state machine	ND	✓	No
Kissoum and Sahnoun (2007)	D	Unit	Distributed system	InterElement requirements diagram, Petri nets	Yes	✗	No
Kissoum and Sahnoun (2008)	C	Unit	Distributed system	UML sequence diagram	Yes	✗	No
Koo and Mishra (2008)	D	Unit	Embedded system	Finite state machine	ND	✗	No

(continued)

TABLE IX (*Continued*)

Authors	Cat	Testing level	Software category	Behavioral and structural models	Tools	Steps complexity	NFR[a] testing
Koopman et al. (2007)	B	System	Web application	Extended finite state machine	Yes	X	Usability
Koopman and Plasmeijer (2006)	B	System	Reactive system	Extended finite state machine	Yes	X	No
Korel et al. (2002)	D	Regression	Not defined	Extended finite state machine	ND	⚠	No
Korel et al. (2007)	D	Unit	Not defined	Extended finite state machine	ND	✓	No
Kwang and Eun (2007)	A	System, Integration	OO	UML use cases, classes, sequences diagrams, OCL, and MM-Path	ND	✓	No
Lallali et al. (2008)	B	Unit	Web service	BPEL models	Yes	X	Efficiency
Leathrum and Liburdy (1996)	B	System	Not defined	Specification in ADA	Yes	X	No
Legeard et al. (2004)	D	System	Critical system	Formal specification (B or Z)	Yes	✓	No
Leung and Wong (2000)	D	System	OO	Classes graph	ND	✓	No
Li et al. (2007)	B	System	Real-time system	Intermediate format	Yes	X	Security
Li et al. (2007)	A	System	Web application	Navigational model describing user inputs validation	Yes	✓	Usability
Liang (2005)	D	Regression and Unit	OO	Specifications in TCOZ	Yes	✓	Efficiency
Lihua et al. (2004)	D	Regression	Not defined	Finite state machine and regression testing specification	Yes	✓	No
Linzhang et al. (2004)	A	System	OO	UML activity diagram	Yes	✓	No

Reference		Level	Domain	Model			
Liu et al. (2001)	D	System	Web application	Web application test model and object relation diagram	ND	△!	No
Liu et al. (2002)	D	Unit	OO	Finite state machine	Yes	X	No
Liuying and Zhichang (1999)	A	System	OO	UML statechart diagram and finite state machine	Yes	✓	No
Lucio et al. (2005)	A	System	OO	UML classes diagram (Fondue), UML collaboration and statechart diagrams, and OCL operations	ND	△!	No
Lund and Stølen (2006)	A	System	Not defined	UML sequence diagram	ND	X	No
Mandrioli et al. (1995)	B	System	Critical and real-time system	Software specification in TRIO (Tempo Reale ImplicitO)	Yes	✓	Efficiency
Massicotte et al. (2007)	C	Integration	Aspect-oriented	UML collaboration diagram	Yes	✓	No
Massink et al. (2006)	C	System	Concurrent system	UML statechart diagram	ND	X	No
Masson et al. (2007)	B	System	Smart card	System formal model functional	Yes	X	Security
Memon (2007)	B	System	Information system	Flow-event model	Yes	✓	Usability
Memon et al. (2000)	B	System	OO	GUI specification	Yes	X	No
Merayo and Nunez (2008)	B	System	Real-time system	Extended finite state machine	ND	X	Efficiency
Meyer and Sandfoss (1998)	A	System (GUI)	Not defined	UML use cases + operational profile—Test Engineering Model	Yes	X	No
Mikucionis et al. (2004)	B	System	Embedded and real-time system	Finite automata	Yes	X	Efficiency
Mingsong et al. (2006)	A	System	Java programs	UML activity diagram	Yes	△!	No

(continued)

TABLE IX   (*Continued*)

Authors	Cat	Testing level	Software category	Behavioral and structural models	Tools	Steps complexity	NFR[a] testing
Misailovic et al. (2007)	D	System	Not defined	Directed acyclic graph	Yes	✓	No
Morasca et al. (1996)	B	System and Integration	Critical-time system	Module specification in TRIO+ language	ND	✗	Efficiency
Murphy et al. (2009)	B	System	OO	Model in JML	Yes	✓	No
Murray et al. (1998)	D	Unit	OO	Finite state machine and test graph	Yes	✗	No
Murthy et al. (2006)	A	System	Not defined	UML extended statechart diagram, extended CTGM	Yes	✓	No
Nachmanson et al. (2004)	D	System	Nondeterministic system	Directed graph	Yes	△	No
Naslavsky et al. (2007)	A	System	OO	UML classes and sequence diagram, control-flow model, and inheritance model	Yes	✓	No
Nebut and Fleurey (2006)	A	System	OO embedded system	UML use cases, sequence diagrams, and simulation model	Yes	△	No
Nilson et al. (2004)	D	System	Concurrent and real-time system	Temporal automata with task model	Yes	✗	Efficiency
Offutt and Liu (1999)	B	System and Unit	Critical system	Condition data flow diagram (CDFD) in SOFL (Structured Object-Oriented Formal Language)	ND	✓	No
Offutt and Abdurazik (1999)	A	System	OO	UML statechart diagram	Yes	✓	Efficiency

Reference		Level	Application domain	Model			
Offutt et al. (2003)	A	System	OO	UML statechart diagram and specification graph	Yes	X	No
Okika et al. (2006)	D	System	Embedded system	Models in *Testing and Test Control Notation* (TTCN-3)	Yes	X	No
Olimpiew and Gomaa (2005)	A	System	Product line	Features Model, UML Use Cases Diagram, Static (classes) and Dynamic (statecharts and object) Models, component-based software architectural model	ND	✓	No
Paiva et al. (2005)	B	System	System in .NET	Finite state machine	Yes	X	No
Paradkar (2004)	B	System	Interactive system	Finite state machine	ND	X	No
Paradkar (2004)	D	System	Reactive system	Operational Model (SALT—Specification and Abstraction Language for Testing) and extended finite state machine	Yes	✓	No
Paradkar et al. (1997)	D	System	Real-time system	Cause–effect graph	ND	X	No
Paradkar et al. (2007)	B	System	Web service	IOPEs models	Yes	✓	No
Pari-Salas et al. (2007)	B	System	Not defined	System/component behavioral model and attack model	Yes	X	Security
Parissis and Ouabdesselam (1996)	B	System	Reactive system	Environment specification and security properties	Yes	X	Security
Parissis and Vassy (2001)	B	System	Synchronous and reactive system	Simulation state machine	Yes	X	Security

(continued)

TABLE IX (Continued)

Authors	Cat	Testing level	Software category	Behavioral and structural models	Tools	Steps complexity	NFR[a] testing
Peraire et al. (1998)	D	Unit	OO embedded system	Specification in CO-OPN/2	Yes	✗	No
Popovic and Velikic (2005)	B	System	System in Java and C++	Not defined	Yes	✗	No
Popovic and Kovacevic (2007)	B	System	Reactive system	Stress operational profile model	Yes	✗	No
Poston (1994)	B	System	OO	OMT function model	Yes	✓✓	No
Pretschner et al. (2008)	B	System	Not defined	Access policies	ND	✓✓	Security
Pretschner et al. (2001)	B	System	Reactive and embedded system	System structure, state transition and data type diagrams, and message sequence charts	Yes	✓	Efficiency
Prowell (2003)	D	Integration	Systems in C	System usage model in Markov Chain	Yes	✗	No
Rajappa et al. (2008)	B	System	Real-time system	Directed graph	ND	✓	No
Reuys et al. (2005)	A	System	OO	UML activity, use cases, and sequence diagrams	Yes	✓	No
Reza et al. (2008)	A	System	Web application	UML statechart diagram	Yes	✓✓	Usability
Richardson et al. (1992)	D	System	Reactive system	In the case study, RTIL (Real Time Interval Logic) and Z specification	ND	⚠	Efficiency and Security
Richardson and Wolf (1996)	D	Integration	Not defined	CHAM (CHemical Abstract Machine)	ND	✓	No
Riebisch et al. (2002)	A	System	OO	UML use cases and state-chart diagrams, graph and usage model	Yes	✓	No

Reference	Type	Testing level	System type	Model/specification	Automated	Support	Quality attribute
Robinson-Mallett et al. (2008)	B	Integration	Distributed and real-time system	Test models in Markov chain	Yes	✗	No
Rocha and Martins (2008)	C	Integration	COTS	UML activity diagram	Yes	✓	No
Rumpe (2003)	A	System	OO	UML object and sequence diagrams, OCL	ND	✗	Efficiency
Rutherford and Wolf (2003)	D	Unit and Integration	OO distributed system	System description in XML	Yes	✓	No
Sakurai et al. (2008)	B	System	Safety-critical system	Customized formal model	Yes	✗	Efficiency
Santos-Neto et al. (2008)	A	System	OO information system	UML classes and state-chart diagrams	Yes	✓	Efficiency and Usability
Satpathy et al. (2007)	B	System	Not defined	Specification in B Language	ND	✗	No
Satpathy et al. (2005)	D	System	OO	State coverage graph (B) and specification in PROLOG	Yes	✓	No
Satpathy et al. (2008)	B	System	Embedded system	State flow graph	Yes	✗	No
Scheetz et al. (1999)	C	Integration	OO	UML classes and state-chart diagrams + OCL	Yes	△	No
Schroeder et al. (2003)	B	System	Not defined	Directed graph, data models	Yes	✗	No
Seifert (2008)	C	System	Embedded system	UML statechart diagram	Yes	✓	No
Shu and Lee (2007)	B	System	Safety-critical system	Extended finite state machine	Yes	▲	Security
Sinha and Paradkar (2006)	D	Integration	Web service	WSDL-S and extended finite state machine	ND	✓	No
Sinha and Smidts (2006)	B	System	Not defined	Specifications in HaskellDB, extended finite state machine	Yes	✗	No
Sokenou (2006)	C	Integration and Unit	OO	UML sequence diagram, protocol state, and OCL	ND	✓	No

(continued)

TABLE IX (Continued)

Authors	Cat	Testing level	Software category	Behavioral and structural models	Tools	Steps complexity	NFR[a] testing
Song et al. (2008)	B	System	Web application	Navigational model On-the-fly and finite state machine	ND	✓	Security
Stobie (2005)	B	System	Any category	Finite state machine and Abstract State Machine Language	Yes	✓	No
Stocks and Carrington (1996)	D	Unit	Not defined	Test template, describing inputs and valid results	Yes	✓	No
Tahat et al. (2001)	B	System and Regression	Distributed and embedded system	Requirements expressed in textual format and SDL (Specification Description Language), Extended finite state machine	ND	✓	No
Tan et al. (2004)	B	System	Not defined	Software specification in LTL (linear temporal logic)	Yes	✓	Security and Efficiency
Tomita and Sakamura (1999)	D	Integration	Operational system	Deterministic finite state machine	Yes	✗	No
Traore (2003)	A	System	OO	UML statechart, classes, and sequence diagrams	Yes	⚠	No
Vaysburg et al. (2002)	D	System	Not defined	Extended finite state machine, static and dynamic dependency graph	ND	✗	No
Vieira et al. (2006)	A	System (GUI)	Not defined	UML use cases + activity and classes diagrams	Yes	⚠	No
Vilkomir and Bowen (2006)	D	System	Safety-critical system	Specification in Z notation	ND	✗	No

Reference		Level	Domain	Model/Notation	Tool		NFR
Voigt et al. (2007)	C	System	Not defined	UML statechart diagram	ND	△	No
Wang and Huang (2008)	D	Unit	Web service	OWL-S requirement models	Yes	✓	No
Watanabe and Sakamura (1996)	D	Integration	Real-time system	Specification in Z notation using finite state machine	ND	✗	No
Weber et al. (1994)	B	System	Avionic control system	Dynamic and static model	ND	✗	No
Whalen et al. (2006)	B	System	Embedded system	LTL properties	ND	✗	No
Wimmel and Jürjens (2002)	B	System	Concurrent, reactive, and safety-critical system	Propositional logic, structure diagram, autofocus system model	Yes	✗	Security and Efficiency
Wu et al. (2003)	C	Integration	Component-based system	UML collaboration, sequence, or statechart	ND	✓	No
Xie et al. (2006)	D	Unit	OO	Object State Abstract machine	Yes	✗	No
Xu and Xu (2006)	D	Integration	Aspect-oriented	State model (Aspect-oriented programming)	ND	✓	No
Yan et al. (2004)	A	System	Distributed and Safety-Critical System	UML use cases and sequence diagrams, expressions, Markov Chain	ND	✓	Reliability
Yao and Wang (2004)	B	System	Not defined	RPTA specifications	ND	✗	No
Yu et al. (2003)	B	System	Not defined	Classification Tree	Yes	✗	No
Zander et al. (2005)	C	System	Distributed system	UML 2.0 testing profile, testing and test control notation	Yes	✗	No
Zheng et al. (2008)	A	Unit	OO	UML interaction and classes diagrams	Yes	✓	No
Zhou et al. (2008)	C	Integration	OO	UML classes, sequence diagrams	ND	✓	No

[a] NFR, nonfunctional requirements.

techniques have been invited to take part in this study [20]. In total, 34 experts participated in this survey, what represents a sample's confidence level about 85% considering the initial population using the formula described in Ref. [21]. They answered about which attributes should be used to characterize MBT techniques and what could be the relevance of each attribute to select MBT techniques for software projects. In this survey, it has been identified 25 characterization attributes (a sublist of the fields presented in Table II), described in Table X with their respective relevance level for the selection of MBT techniques.

Crossing the MBT techniques' characteristics with the software project's characteristics and requirements, software engineers can make the decision regarding which techniques to apply to a software project easily, contributing for improving the final product quality.

The selection of software technologies (e.g., processes, products, techniques, methods, and tools that can be used to support the software development) for a

TABLE X
MBT TECHNIQUES' CHARACTERIZATION ATTRIBUTES

Characterization attributes	Relevance level for the MBT techniques selection (%)
Behavioral/structural model used for test generation	83.48
Test cases generation criteria	72.57
Testing coverage criteria	74.79
Inputs required to be used	72.54
Limitations/restrictions to be used	69.96
Software quality characteristics the technique is able to evaluate	68.30
Testing level	69.70
Type of testing technique	69.89
Software execution platform	55.85
Software development paradigm	55.85
Programming language of systems that can be evaluated	55.85
Results generated by the technique	69.70
Supporting tool's name	63.74
Costs associated to the supporting tool	63.74
Supporting tool's execution platform	63.74
Types of failures that can be revealed	48.80
Use of intermediate models	54.47
Test modeling technology	52.54
Complexity level of nonautomated steps	46.58
Type of experimental evaluation	47.43
Needs of external tools	49.96
List of automated and nonautomated steps	47.48
Existence of a traceability mechanism	34.39
Skills required to be used	33.00
Existence of a model checker	18.71

software project is a complex task that may influence directly on the development process's effectiveness and consequently the software's quality [14]. According to Bertolino [22], the definition of which techniques would be best suited to support a software development task is still an open question requiring more investigation. As more information is provided to support this decision, as easier will be the selection process, reducing the risk of inappropriate choices that may result in a negative effect for the software quality.

The main challenges regarding this issue should be to understand and decide for the selection of technologies more adequate for a specific task in a software project. In this context, several aspects may influence on this decision, such as technical knowledge, testing team background about these technologies and project domain, software project schedule, effort and costs associated to the technologies usage, external software organization political aspects, among others.

For some tasks in the software development process, including software testing, the combination of two or more software technologies with similar characteristics and goals may introduce improvements for the software process effectiveness and, consequently, in the testing activity and final product quality. In the context of software testing and MBT, the combination of techniques may result in improvements in the testing coverage and software quality. However, it is necessary to perform a feasibility analysis regarding the use of more than one MBT technique, because this scenario may introduce risks concerned with the increasing of testing effort and cost, what may make unfeasible the testing activity in a software project [23].

In the technical literature, there are some approaches to support the selection of general software technologies [24] or to specific software development activities, like requirements elicitation techniques ([25], [38], [39]). Among these approaches, none of them provides support to the combined selection of more than one software technology for the same software project, that is, they just provide support to the individual selection of software technologies. Moreover, because of their specific characteristics, they are not able to support the selection of testing or MBT techniques, the focus of this chapter. However, other three approaches supporting the selection of MBT techniques were identified at the technical literature and they are summarized below.

- Vegas and Basili [14]

Approach supporting the selection of general testing techniques, named *Characterization Schema*. In this approach, testing techniques attributes are characterized and stored in a repository. A catalog of testing techniques to support selection can be generated from this repository accordingly the target software project. The approach proposed by Vegas and Basili [14] was based on selection strategies applied to other technological areas such as components reuse, and it was adapted for software testing. The positive aspects of this approach include to make available knowledge regarding the techniques and to simplify the selection of testing techniques for a software project. However, its characterization attributes are generic, what makes difficult its adaptation for subcategories of testing techniques, such as MBT. Another possible restrictive aspect of this approach would be regarding the non availability of combined selection of testing techniques for those software projects demanding it. Therefore, this scenario may introduce risks for a software project using this approach to select MBT techniques due the lack of specific information regarding MBT.

- Wojcicki and Strooper [37]

Approach supporting the selection of Verification and Validation (V&V) techniques that evaluates the combination of such techniques with the purpose of:

1. maximizing the techniques completeness, represented by the types of defects/failures revealed by the selected techniques, and;
2. minimizing the effort, represented by metrics like defects detection effort (in minutes) and defects detection effectiveness (number of defects per minute).

This approach introduces a process for the selection of V&V techniques composed of three activities (Preselection, Maximize completeness, and Minimize effort) using a matrix representing the relationship between types of defects/failures revealed by the techniques and their effort. This matrix is filled step-by-step using metrics and subjective data collected in a software organization. The main advantage of this approach is its simplicity to analyze the combination of V&V techniques for a software project. Moreover, it uses cost-efficiency metrics; therefore each software organization can apply its own set of metrics using the approach.

- Dias-Neto and Travassos [36]

Porantim is an approach to support the selection of MBT techniques for a software project. It represents an evolution of the previously described characterization schema for testing techniques [14].

There are three main differences provided by this selection approach. Firstly, the characterization attributes (and their categories) for the testing technique were updated with specific MBT characteristics, making *Porantim* a specific selection approach for the context of MBT techniques. Secondly, a selection process was introduced to guide the testing team during the MBT techniques selection task. This process is responsible for suggesting which MBT techniques would be best suited for a software project by using an indicator called adequacy level to suggest the percentage of adequacy between the software project and MBT technique characteristics. And finally, after the selection of MBT techniques, it produces an estimate regarding the impact of the selected MBT techniques on some variables of the software testing process (e.g., software project requirements' coverage, modeling effort, and testing team members to be allocated to the software project).

Table XI presents a summary of the main characteristics of the testing techniques selection approaches published at the technical literature and cited in this section. The characteristics considered in this summary were

- *Scope*: is the approach applied to the selection of which software technologies?

- *Based on measurement*: does the approach provide information supporting the selection based on the use of metrics collected from the software technologies or projects?

- *Based on adequacy*: does the approach provide information supporting the selection based on the adequacy between the software technology and the software project where it would be applied to?

- *Based on impact*: does the approach provide information supporting the selection based on a possible impact of the software technologies in the development process?

- *Technologies suggestion*: does the approach formally suggest/indicate which software technologies are best suited to the software project from any predefined criteria?

TABLE XI
CHARACTERIZATION OF SOFTWARE TECHNOLOGIES SELECTION APPROACHES

Selection approach	Vegas and Basili	Wojcicki and Strooper	Dias-Neto and Travassos
Scope	Testing techniques	Verification and validation techniques	Model-based testing techniques
Based on measurement	NO	YES	NO
Based on adequacy	YES	NO	YES
Based on impact	NO	YES	YES
Technologies suggestion	Provides a catalog of techniques	Suggests the best suited techniques	Suggests the best suited combination of techniques
Technologies combination	Only individual selection	Combined selection	Combined selection
Supporting tool	YES	Not found	YES

- *Technologies combination*: does the approach analyze the combination of two or more software Technologies and their influence on the activity to be performed? That is, does it provide support to the combined selection of software technologies?
- *Supporting tool*: is there any support tool to use the selection approach?

4. Challenges in Using MBT Techniques in Software Projects

After identifying the available MBT techniques in the technical literature and knowing how they can be selected to be used in software projects, one challenge would be to understand the implications of using MBT techniques in software projects.

The next subsections describe risk factors associated to the use of MBT techniques. Besides, some mechanisms to mitigate their influence in software projects are also suggested. We believe this information may be useful for software organizations making decisions regarding the application of MBT in their projects.

4.1 Risk Factors Associated to the Use of MBT Techniques in Software Projects

Usually, the MBT techniques related papers describe evaluations of those techniques performed for small examples and directed to a specific scenario defined by their developers, most of the time not inserted into a complete software project. However, in real software projects, the testing activity is just one of the several activities to be executed throughout the software development process and it cannot be isolated from the other ones. Moreover, the testing activity must attend the restrictions imposed by the software project planning, such as schedule, costs, resources, or team availability.

Based on this scenario, we have identified, in the technical literature, 12 risk factors [26] that can support the impact understanding of using MBT in software projects. For their description, it will be illustrated the scenarios where these risk factors may influence, a description of their impact in a software project, their origin in the technical literature, and the testing process activities influenced by these risk factors. It can be observed that some of these risk factors are exclusive to the use of MBT techniques and others concerned with all types of testing strategies. These risk factors indicate scenarios included in the testing process not in scope of a MBT technique, but that need to be managed, as they may make unfeasible test cases generation for a software project.

The 12 risk factors were categorized according to their influence to the testing process activities, listed below:

- *Test Planning*: activity performed by the test manager. It is responsible for the definition of test goals, scope, and items, test schedule and team planning, and selection of testing techniques to be used in the software project.
- *Test Design*: activity performed by the test designer. It is responsible for detailing the testing techniques for each software quality characteristic to be evaluated, and the identification and specification of test cases and procedures.
- *Test Execution*: activity performed by the tester. It is responsible for the execution of test procedures as planed and designed, and reporting of incidents occurred during the tests execution.
- *Test Results Analysis*: activity performed by the test manager. It is responsible for summarizing the test results and elaboration of a test report to be sent to the development team for debugging or to the customer for deployment.
- *Test Control*: activity performed by the test manager. It is responsible for monitoring the schedule, tasks, changes in the process, and risks associated to the testing process.

4.1.1 Factor 1: Quality Assurance of Artifacts Used by the MBT Technique for Test Generation

Scenario	Success of testing is directly associated with the artifacts quality received as inputs for the building of behavior/ structural models used for test generation. These artifacts must be reviewed prior to their use in order to obtain a satisfactory quality level before constructing models for test generation.
Impact	Constructing models from incomplete, inconsistent, or wrong software artifacts may result in the generation and execution of inappropriate tests to evaluate the software characteristics. In this case, even when using the most adequate MBT technique, it will not be possible to ensure the software quality.
References in the literature	Dalal et al. [5], Horstmann et al. [27], Pretschner et al. [28], and Utting et al. [29]
Impacted activities	

- *Test Planning*: the selection of MBT techniques to be used, the test costs, schedule, and effort planning and testing team allocation.
- *Test Design*: the choice of tests generation criteria for a MBT technique.

4.1.2   Factor 2: Efficient Mechanism to Provide the Right Artifacts to be Used as Inputs by the MBT Technique

Scenario	The testing team should always have access to the current software artifacts version used as inputs by a MBT technique. Testers need to be notified if any change occurs in the software artifact, supporting the execution of regression testing.
Impact	The use of old software artifacts versions may influence the testing quality as the generated test cases set may be prepared to test a nonexisting software product, which may contribute for problems during the testing activities.
References in the literature	Santos-Neto et al. [30]
Impacted activities	• *Test Planning*: test costs, schedule, and effort planning. • *Test Design*: the choice of tests generation criteria for a MBT technique.

4.1.3   Factor 3: Strategy for Resources Allocation and Testing Schedule Planning

Scenario	The software testing process guides the effective and efficient planning of testing activities, resources, budget, and scheduling. It must always be in accordance with the software project planning. However, the skills and complexity levels required to use each MBT technique are different, possibly affecting the testing team, budget, and

	schedule definition in the software project. Therefore, the testing planning should consider the particularities of each MBT technique.
Impact	Imprecise or wrong planning may affect the testing quality, resulting in extra testing effort. For instance, one technique requires more effort to construct the models and a capable professional of using a particular modeling language; another one may require more effort to transform its models and a capable professional of working with a specific programming language and software domain, and so on.
References in the literature	Bernard et al. [31] and Utting et al. [29]
Impacted activities	• *Test Planning*: test costs, schedule, and effort planning. • *Test Control*: the strategies for resource allocation and schedule definition impact in how the testing process can be controlled.

4.1.4 Factor 4: Strategy for the Selection of MBT Techniques

Scenario	It has been acknowledged that one of the most important decision-making and harder tasks in the software testing process is the selection of which technique(s) to use in a software project. This is not different with MBT techniques. Different features must be observed when performing this task, such as the test coverage or software quality characteristics that need to be evaluated.
Impact	MBT techniques have limitations that may not make feasible their use in some software projects. The combination of MBT techniques may be an interesting solution, but it needs to be carefully planned as it can increase the efforts required in the software project.
References in the literature	Clarke [32], Dalal et al. [5], Juristo et al. [2], Bernard et al. [31], Blackburn et al. [33], Utting et al. [29], Dias-Neto and Travassos [36]

Impacted activities	• *Test Planning*: the selection of MBT techniques to be used in the software project. • *Test Design*: the test design is directly associated to the MBT techniques selected for a software project.

4.1.5   Factor 5: Strategy Adopted for the Behavioral/Structural Model Construction

Scenario	The existence of a behavioral/structural model represents the main requirement to use MBT techniques. However, these techniques do not consider the variables related to cost, effort, or strategy to build the software model used for test generation. These variables depend on several factors, such as the software modules that should be tested, the coverage level desired for each module, the number of software models used by the MBT technique to represent the software behavior/structure, whether the model is shared by developers and testers, or if it is exclusive for testing, among others.
Impact	The effort, cost, and strategy adopted for software model construction directly affect the testing quality. Additional effort requires additional time and resources for a software project. The tester must analyze which modules are more critical and require higher coverage level, and how to prioritize the software model construction aiming at attending the desired coverage level. Sometimes the effort and cost to build the software models may make unfeasible the use of a specific MBT technique in a software project.
References in the literature	Dalal et al. [5], Pretschner et al. [28], and Utting et al. [29]
Impacted activities	• *Test Planning*: the strategy adopted for the software model construction impacts in the definition of test costs, schedule, and effort, and the testing team allocation, because it is adequate to select professionals familiarized with the modeling notation to be used. • *Test Design*: during this activity the software models are built, for in the future to be used for test cases generation.

4.1.6   Factor 6: Strategy Adopted for the Test-Generation Criteria Selection

Scenario	MBT techniques usually allow the use of several test-generation criteria to be used. The choice of which one to use in a software project must be based on the effort and cost to build and execute test cases, the total number of generated test cases, and mainly on the test coverage level. Different software modules may require different test coverage levels, which makes the choice of the test generation criteria an important and difficult task.
Impact	Inappropriate choices of test generation criteria may make unfeasible the test cases generation and/or execution according to the test schedule and budget defined for a software project, impacting on the final product quality.
References in the literature	Utting et al. [29] and Santos-Neto et al. [30]
Impacted activity	• *Test Design*: the test cases identification and generation activities are impacted by the selected test generation criteria.

4.1.7   Factor 7: Tracking and Impacting Analysis of Changes in Software Specification

Scenario	One of the main MBT techniques' characteristics is the automated support for test case generation. In the case of evolution of the software specification, these techniques usually consider a new software model that is already developed to regenerate test cases, regardless the effort to analyze the impact of these changes and to update the software model. However, it is necessary to analyze which changes had been made in the software specification and what could be their impact in the test cases set before constructing a new software model. This scenario suggests the use of a change tracking mechanism.

Impact	The lack of a change tracking mechanism makes the impact analysis a complex task. This type of analysis is also essential to support new effort and cost estimates for test case updating activities (model evolution, test case regeneration, and execution).
References in the literature	Dalal et al. [5], Utting et al. [29], and Santos-Neto et al. [30]
Impacted activities	• *Test Planning*: in this, activity should be identified the test items that during the test design would be associated with test cases by a traceability mechanism. • *Test Design*: in this, activity should be generated test cases that need to be associated with test items by a traceability mechanism. • *Test Control*: in this, activity should be identified the changes between two different versions of a test model.

4.1.8 Factor 8: Test Suit Evolution After Changes in the Software Specification

Scenario	After identifying the software specification changes (described in risk factor # 7), the test suit must be updated. In this case, evolving the software model represents the first task aimed at the test suit updating. However, the MBT techniques do not explain how to update their models or what could be the effort or how feasible could be to perform this task. They usually consider a new software model is ready to regenerate test cases which may introduce risks to a project.
Impact	Not having an adequate effort estimation to update a model used by a MBT technique directly affects regression testing quality results. Moreover, this estimate is very useful because in some situations the effort to update a model may be higher than building a new one.
References in the literature	Dalal et al. [5], Utting et al. [29], and Santos-Neto et al. [30]

Impacted activities	• *Test Design*: after the identification of changes in the test model and their impact on the test cases set, the test models need to be updated, a new test cases set should be generated, and the traces between test items and test cases should be updated.
	• *Test Control*: it should be performed an impact analysis regarding the changes in the test models, evaluating whether it would be necessary to construct new models or just updating them.

4.1.9   Factor 9: Manual Inclusion of Extra Test Cases

Scenario	Eventually, it could be necessary to manually include test cases to evaluate specific software features or characteristics not covered by the test cases set generated by a MBT technique. This facility is very important to allow extending the test coverage and consequently testing quality.
Impact	If this facility is not available in the test environment the software evaluation will be restricted to the test suit generated by the selected MBT technique(s), which may be limited or may not cover a desired software feature, decreasing the testing quality. A solution in this case could be the combination of different MBT techniques. However, it may introduce more effort in the testing process.
References in the literature	Dalal et al. [5] and Santos-Neto et al. [30]
Impacted activities	• *Test Design*: test cases must be identified and generated. Moreover, it is necessary to record the traces between the test cases and the test items they can evaluate.
	• *Test Execution*: automated and manual test cases are executed, and their results should be recorded.

4.1.10   Factor 10: Test Generation and Execution Process Control

Scenario	The testing team should always receive information on the current testing process stage and its results. It is important to control the dependency among the testing process activities. Moreover, the need for a new test trial could be easily identified and executed.
Impact	Not following the planned testing process may result in delays in the testing schedule, and affect the testing quality.
References in the literature	Dalal et al. [5], Utting et al. [29], and Santos-Neto et al. [30]
Impacted activities	• *Test Planning, Design, Execution, and Results Analysis*: the test manager should manage the execution of all testing process activities, including their execution date, spent effort, responsibility, and results. • *Test Control*: a set of information should be provided to support the controlling of test cases generation and execution process using MBT techniques.

4.1.11   Factor 11: Tracking of Failures Revealed by MBT Techniques

Scenario	Testing reveals failures. It is important to record these failures and associate them with the test cases responsible for their identification. This failure tracking should support testing control and further evaluation of the MBT techniques using, for example, a causal-analysis approach [34].
Impact	The lack of a failure tracking mechanism working together with the MBT technique can make testing control and management inefficient because relevant historical information on the MBT techniques in previous software projects will be lost. Keeping the usage history is essential for the continuous improvement of the effort, cost, and coverage level estimative mechanisms associated with the use of a MBT technique.
References in the literature	Utting et al. [29] and Santos-Neto et al. [30]

Impacted activities	• *Test Execution*: failures revealed in the software must be identified and reported.
	• *Results Analysis*: it summarizes the failures identified during the test execution, grouping this information to extract measures regarding the performance of a MBT technique and their test generation criteria.
	• *Test Control*: it should monitor the identified failures until they can be fixed by the development team. Moreover, in this, activity is performed the failure traceability to identify their origin (test cases that revealed each failure and test items where the failure was exposed).

4.1.12   Factor 12: Evaluation of MBT Techniques and Their Test Selection Criteria

Scenario	The evaluations of MBT techniques and their test selection criteria are very important in a software organization. It can simplify their estimation and make it more precise, and also support the selection of MBT techniques for future software projects.
Impact	The MBT technique performance evolves throughout its use in different software projects. Not managing this evolution may make the estimative mechanism null or useless; rendering the criteria used to select techniques and test generation criteria inefficient.
References in the literature	Horstmann et al. [27] and Santos-Neto et al. [30]
Impacted activities	• *Test Planning*: it needs to consider information regarding the MBT techniques evaluation in previous software projects to support the decision-making regarding which MBT techniques to use in a new software project.
	• *Results Analysis*: it should group information regarding performance, effort, effectiveness, efficiency of a MBT technique, and their test generation criteria. Moreover, this is the moment to evaluate a MBT technique by the testing team using, for instance, an evaluation form similar to a *postmortem* analysis [35] regarding the testing process.

4.2   Mitigating the Risk Factors in Software Projects

The risk factors previously described can influence the testing process results in software projects using MBT techniques. As it has been illustrated, each risk factor is associated to one or more testing process activity. Based on this scenario, one possible contribution aiming at to mitigate these risk factors would be to provide mechanisms to support the conduction of the software testing process using MBT techniques.

In the next subsections, it will be presented suggestions of mechanisms aiming at to support the selection, use, and evaluation of MBT techniques in software projects according to the testing process activities.

4.2.1   Mechanisms Supporting Test Planning

At total, eight risk factors (Factors 1, 2, 3, 4, 5, 7, 10, 12) would influence the testing planning activity. These factors are associated, mainly, to decisions making regarding the quality of artifacts used as inputs by MBT techniques and selection of MBT techniques and the testing team to be allocated in a software project. Therefore, some mechanisms could be applied throughout the testing process to support the application of MBT techniques in a software project:

- Application of Verification and Validation (V&V) techniques such as peer-review or inspections to evaluate the different artifacts produced in the software development process. Thus, we could reduce the incidence of defects affecting the use of a MBT technique and, consequently, improving the testing quality.
- Integration of configuration management and test artifacts traceability mechanisms. Thus, the testing team would have simplified access to the current versions of the artifacts produced throughout the software development and testing process.
- Creation of a strategy supporting the selection of MBT techniques for software projects, suggesting the best suited MBT techniques according to the characteristics and particularities of a software project. In the Section 3.4, we presented three approaches that can be used for the selection of MBT techniques for a software project: *Porantim* [36], Characterization Schema [14], and Based on Completeness/Effort Matrix [37].
- Creation of a mechanism supporting the selection of testing team members to be allocated for a software projects according to the characteristics and particularities of the software project and the MBT techniques selected for it. The selection approach *Porantim* [36] supports this decision.

4.2.2   Mechanisms Supporting Test Design

The test design activity is the moment where the models used by a MBT technique for test generation are developed. The risk factors (1, 2, 4, 5, 6, 7, 8, 9, 10) concerned with this activity are associated, mainly, to quality assurance of the artifacts used to construct the test models, strategy adopted to construct the test models, choice of test generation criteria, and definition of the test cases final set.

Therefore, the mechanisms supporting this testing process activity could be

- Creation of a strategy supporting the choice of test generation criteria for each model used by a MBT technique, providing different combinations of criteria to support the decision-making.

- Mechanism making possible to include and execute extra test cases, that is, test cases not generated by the selected MBT techniques and that were not included *a priori* in the test suit, allowing the increasing of testing coverage.

- Creation of a mechanism to support the traceability between the elements composing the software development artifacts (e.g., software requirements use cases, components, classes, etc.) and testing process elements (test cases and procedures). This mechanism would support several activities, such as test failures debugging, evaluation of MBT techniques and their test generation criteria, and impact analysis of changes in the software specification for the current test cases set.

4.2.3   Mechanisms Supporting the Test Execution

The use of the MBT strategy in software projects makes the test execution activity almost fully automated (risk factors 9, 10, 11). The manual interference in this activity is reduced to a minimum. Therefore, the mechanism supporting this activity should also be automated and it consists in collecting of testing process metrics to support future evaluations of MBT techniques and their test generation criteria. The main interference could be the definition or suggestion of which metrics should be collected according to the software project characteristics and process.

4.2.4   Mechanisms Supporting the Test Results Analysis

During the analysis of test results, the focus should be to evaluate the selected MBT techniques and their test generation criteria (risk factors 10, 11, 12). To support this task, it could be necessary to create mechanisms similar to those applied in the testing process *postmortem* analysis, evaluating metrics obtained throughout the testing process and interacting with the project's testing team to get their opinion regarding the use of MBT techniques in the software project.

4.2.5 Mechanisms Supporting Test Control

The test control must be performed throughout all testing process activities aiming at to support several tasks, such as assuring the activities execution on schedule, monitoring of testing team tasks and the current status of the testing process, comparing the results of different test rounds, and supporting the decision regarding when to stop the tests execution (risk factors 3, 7, 8, 10, 11). Most of the tasks associated to test control are not influenced by the testing strategy (e.g., MBT, specification-based, or code-based) used in a software project. However, some additional tasks are introduced when the MBT strategy is applied. Therefore, the mechanisms supporting this testing process activity could be

- Impact analysis of changes in the software specification and their impact on the test cases set. This mechanism should be used before the evolution of the test models, and it should present indicators and estimates regarding what information need to be updated in the test models, which test cases shall be updated, and the effort to update the test models.
- After the use of the mechanism previously described, the next step should be to provide support for the regression testing, supporting the selection of new test generation criteria, and generation/execution of a new test cases set.

The next section will present the conclusions and some future perspectives regarding the MBT field.

5. Conclusions and Future Perspectives

5.1   Final Considerations

MBT and the behavior of MBT techniques have been important investigation areas in the software engineering field for years. There is a possible explanation for this: the quality of a software product is dependent on the test set applied to evaluate it, and therefore, as discussed in this chapter, MBT is observed to be a feasible and efficient strategy to conduct software testing.

The high number of MBT techniques available with different characteristics, the lack of technical knowledge regarding them, the risks associated with their use, and the absence of a central repository containing information concerned with MBT techniques make the application of such testing techniques in a software project a hard task for software engineers. Table XII summarizes the relationship between the risk factors identified in Section 4.1 and the testing process activities.

This chapter presented a discussion regarding the MBT field, describing several relevant aspects that can support the MBT technology transferring from academia to the industry. In this context, this chapter presented:

- The main concepts concerned with this area of research, allowing the understanding of this testing strategy;
- The test cases generation process according to MBT strategy, making possible to identify what are the needed steps when performing a MBT process;

TABLE XII
RISK FACTORS X IMPACT ON TESTING PROCESS ACTIVITIES

Risk factors	Impact on testing process activities				
	Test planning	Test design	Test execution	Results analysis	Test control
1. Quality assurance of artifacts used by MBT techniques for test generation	✓	✓			
2. Efficient mechanism to provide the right artifacts to be used as inputs by the MBT technique	✓	✓			
3. Strategy for resource allocation and testing schedule planning	✓				✓
4. Strategy for the selection of MBT techniques	✓	✓			
5. Strategy adopted for the behavioral/ structural model construction	✓	✓			
6. Strategy adopted for the test generation criteria selection		✓			
7. Tracking and impacting analysis of changes in software specification	✓	✓			✓
8. Test suit evolution after changes in the software specification		✓			✓
9. Manual inclusion of extra test cases		✓	✓		
10. Test generation and execution process control	✓	✓	✓	✓	✓
11. Tracking of failures revealed by MBT techniques			✓	✓	✓
12. Evaluation of MBT techniques and their test selection criteria	✓			✓	

- The possible benefits that can be obtained with the application of MBT in software projects, highlighting the advantages and drawbacks in the use of this testing strategy;
- The characterization through a secondary study and analysis of 219 MBT techniques available in the technical literature until 8/2009;
- Suggestion of three approaches and strategies that can be used to support software engineers in the selection of best suited MBT techniques for software projects;
- Finally, a set of 12 risk factors that may influence on the MBT strategy use in software projects, including possible mechanisms to mitigate the impact of these risk factors aiming at to obtain success during the application of MBT.

5.2   Future Perspectives

The results described in this chapter, besides the regular reader interested on the testing area, were intended to be also useful for two different types of software engineers: researchers working with MBT and practitioners who are trying to apply MBT in their software projects.

- *MBT researcher's perspective*

Under the perspective of a researcher working with MBT, the results provided in this chapter may contribute for future research in the field, because these data can be deeply analyzed to contextualize research on MBT described in the technical literature. Therefore, this information may present scenarios on software engineering not covered by MBT techniques that require more investigation, including:

- ○ Analysis of the limitation of the software models used to represent the software behavior/structure;
- ○ Conduction of experimental studies to obtain more evidence regarding the effort, effectiveness, and scalability of MBT techniques for different software domains;
- ○ To enlarge the investigation about NFR categories not enough evaluated by the MBT techniques;
- ○ To enlarge the investigation regarding software execution platforms not enough covered by MBT techniques.

- *MBT practitioner's perspective*

Under the perspective of practitioners trying to apply MBT in their software projects, the results provided in this chapter may contribute for the understating of risks, challenges, and limitations of using MBT in software projects, including:

- Skills/background required to use a MBT technique in a software project;
- Context where each MBT technique would be more adequate;
- Limitation to use a MBT technique in a software project;
- Effectiveness and scalability of MBT techniques in similar software projects;
- Tools available to use a MBT technique.

The MBT field is continuously evolving. Therefore, it would be important to re-execute periodically the systematic review presented in Section 3 aiming at to keep it updated, because it can represent the body of knowledge regarding MBT techniques. It is also very important to incentive experience reports describing the use of different MBT techniques *in loco*. Thus, software engineers can generate more and better evidences regarding the performance and scalability of MBT techniques and the effective benefits in the use of this testing strategy.

Finally, we hope this chapter presented information that can be useful for researchers and practitioners, contributing for the dissemination of the MBT strategy.

ACKNOWLEDGMENTS

This research has been developed into the context of projects CNPq 475459/2007-5 and 302469/2007-9 - Experimental Software Engineering and e-Science, FAPERJ, and FAPEAM. We thank SCR/USA (Marlon Vieira and Rajesh Subramanian) by providing the initial insights and infrastructure for the starting point of this research.

Category	Title	Authors	Source	Year
D	A case for test-code generation in model-driven systems	Rutherford and Wolf	GPCE	2003
A	A case study for generating test cases from use cases	Gutierrez et al.	ICRCIS	2008
B	A choice relation framework for supporting category-partition test case generation	Chen et al.	IEEE Transactions on Software Engineering	2003
D	A formal approach for functional and structural test case generation in multiagent systems	Kissoum and Sahnoun	AICCSA	2007
B	A formal approach to requirements-based testing in open systems standards	Leathrum and Liburdy	International Conference on Requirements Engineering	1996
D	A framework for specification-based class testing	Liu et al.	ICECCS	2002
D	A framework for specification-based testing	Stocks and Carrington	IEEE Transactions on Software Engineering	1996
D	A generalized model-based test generation method	Bonifacio	SEFM	2008
D	A generic model-based test case generator	Popovic and Velikic	ECBS	2005
B	A global algorithm for model-based test-suite generation	Hessel et al.	Electronic Notes in Theoretical Computer Science	2007
B	A holistic approach to test-driven model checking	Belli and Guldali	International conference on Innovations in Applied Artificial Intelligence	2005
C	A method for model-based test harness generation for component testing	Rocha and Martins	Journal of the Brazilian Computer Society	2008
A	A method for the automatic generation of test suites from object models	Cavarra et al.	ACM Symposium on Applied computing	2003
B	A method of generating massive virtual clients and model-based performance test	Kim	QSIC	2005
A	A methodology and a framework for model-based testing	Lucio et al.	Lecture Notes in Computer Science	2005
A	A model-based testing technique to test Web applications using statecharts	Reza et al.	ITNG	2008

	Title	Author	Venue	Year
B	A model-based statistical usage testing of communication protocols	Popovic et al.	Workshop on Engineering of Computer Based Systems	2006
A	A model-driven validation & verification environment for embedded systems	Gargantini et al.	ISIES	2008
B	A model-to-implementation mapping tool for automated model-based GUI testing	Paiva et al.	ICFEM	2005
B	A new approach to test-case generation based on real-time process algebra (RTFA)	Yao and Wang	Canadian Conference on Electrical and Computer Engineering	2004
C	A practical approach to UML-based derivation of integration tests	Basanieri and Bertolino	QWE	2000
C	A recursive colored Petri Nets semantics for AUML as base of test-case generation	Kissoum and Sahnoun	AICCSA	2008
D	A specification-based adaptive test case generation strategy for open operating system standards	Watanabe and Sakamura	ICSE	1996
C	A State-based approach to integration testing for object-oriented programs	Ali et al.	Technical Report of Carleton University	2005
B	A statistical approach to model-based robustness testing	Popovic and Kovacevic	Workshop on Engineering of Computer Based Systems	2007
A	A subset of precise UML for model-based testing	Bouquet et al.	AMOST	2007
B	A test sequence selection method for statecharts	Hong et al.	Software Testing Verification & Reliability	2000
D	A theory of specification-based testing for object-oriented software	Barbey et al.	EDCC	1996
A	A transition-based strategy for object-oriented software testing	Traore	ACM Symposium on Applied computing	2003
A	A UML-based approach to system testing	Briand and Labiche	Technical Report of Carleton University	2002
B	Action refinement in conformance testing	Van Der Bijl et al.	Lecture Notes in Computer Science	2005
D	Adding natural relationships to simulink models to improve automated model-based testing	Boden and Busser	AIAA/IEEE Digital Avionics Systems Conference	2004
D	ADLscope: an automated specification-based unit testing tool	Chang and Richardson	ASE	1998

(continued)

Appendix A (*Continued*)

Category	Title	Authors	Source	Year
B	Aiding modular design and verification of safety-critical time-triggered systems by use of executable formal specifications	Sakurai et al.	ISHASE	2008
B	An approach for specification-based test-case generation for Web services	Hanna and Munro	AICCSA	2007
B	An approach to detecting domain errors using formal specification-based testing	Chen and Liu	Asia-Pacific Software Engineering Conference	2004
D	An approach to integration testing based on data flow specifications	Chen et al.	Lecture Notes in Computer Science	2005
D	An automated testing experiment for layered embedded C code	Chetali and Nguyen	Journal on Software Tools for Technology Transfer	2009
A	An automatic execution system for Web functional test based on modeling user's behavior	Jia et al.	ISISE	2008
A	An evaluation of a model-based testing method for information systems	Santos-Neto et al.	Symposium on Applied Computing	2008
B	An event-flow model of GUI-based applications for testing	Memon	Software Testing Verification and Reliability	2007
D	An explorative journey from architectural tests definition down to code tests execution	Bertolino et al.	ICSE	2001
B	An extension of the Classification-Tree method for embedded systems for the description of events	Conrad and Krupp	Electronic Notes in Theoretical Computer Science	2006
D	An overview of Lutess: a specification-based tool for testing synchronous software	du Bousquet and Zuanon	ASE	1999
D	Analyzing software architectures with Argus-I	Vieira et al.	ICSE	2000
D	Application of system models in regression test suite prioritization	Korel et al.	ICSM	2008
D	Applying conventional testing techniques for class testing	Chung et al.	IEEE Computer Society's International Computer Software & Applications Conference	1996

	Title	Authors	Venue	Year
A	Applying use case methodology to SRE and system testing	Meyer and Sandfoss	STAR West Conference	1998
C	Architecting fault tolerance with exception handling: verification and validation	Brito et al.	Journal of Computer Science and Technology	2009
C	Aspects-classes integration testing strategy: an incremental approach	Massicotte et al.	Lecture Notes in Computer Science	2006
B	Automated boundary test generation from JML specifications	Bouquet et al.	Lecture Notes in Computer Science	2006
B	Automated formal verification and testing of C programs for embedded systems	Kandl et al.	ISORC	2007
B	Automated functional conformance test generation for semantic Web services	Paradkar et al.	ICWS	2007
A	Automated generation of statistical test cases from UML state diagrams	Chevalley and Fosse	COMPSAC	2005
A	Automated large-scale simulation test-data generation for object-oriented software systems	Zheng et al.	ISDPE	2007
D	Automated test case generation for programs specified by relational algebra queries	Tsai et al.	IEEE Transactions on Software Engineering	1990
B	Automated test oracles for GUIs	Memon et al.	ACM SIGSOFT international symposium on Foundations of software engineering	2000
B	Automated testing from object models	Poston	Communications of the ACM	1994
D	Automated testing of classes	Buy et al.	ISSTA	2000
C	Automated TTCN-3 test case generation by means of UML sequence diagrams and Markov chains	Beyer et al.	ATS	2003
B	Automated validation test generation	Weber et al.	DASC	1994
C	Automated, contract-based user testing of commercial-off-the-shelf components	Briand et al.	ICSE	2006
A	Automated-generating test case using UML statecharts diagrams	Kansomkeat and Rivepiboon	SAICSIT	2003

(continued)

Appendix A *(Continued)*

Category	Title	Authors	Source	Year
D	Automatic extraction of abstract-object-state machines from unit-test executions	Xie et al.	ICSE	2006
B	Automatic generation of model-based tests for a class of security properties	Masson et al.	AMOST	2007
C	Automatic model-based generation of parameterized test cases using data abstraction	Calame et al.	Electronic Notes in Theoretical Computer Science	2007
A	Automatic test case generation for UML activity diagrams	Mingsong et al.	AST	2006
C	Automatic test generation on a (U)SIM smart card	Bigot et al.	Lecture Notes in Computer Science	2006
A	Automatic test generation: a use case-driven approach	Nebut and Fleurey	IEEE Transaction Software Engineering	2006
D	Automatic testing from formal specifications	Satpathy et al.	Lecture Notes in Computer Science	2007
B	Automatic timed test case generation for Web services composition	Lallali et al.	ECOWS	2008
D	Automatic validation of Java page flows using model-based coverage criteria	Alava et al.	ICSAC	2006
D	Automatically testing interacting software components	Gallagher and Offutt	AST	2006
B	Automating formal specification-based testing	Donat	International Joint Conference CAAP/FASE on Theory and Practice of Software Development	1997
A	Automating impact analysis and regression test selection based on UML designs	Briand et al.	ICSM	2002
D	Automating software module testing for FAA certification	Santhanam	ACM SIGAda International Conference on Ada	2001
A	Automation of GUI testing using a model-driven approach	Vieira et al.	AST	2006

D	Black-box testing using flowgraphs: an experimental assessment of effectiveness and automation potential	Edwards	Software Testing Verification and Reliability	2000
B	Boundary coverage criteria for test generation from formal models	Kosmatov et al.	ISSRE	2004
D	Combining algebraic and model-based test case generation	Dan and Aichernig	Lecture Notes in Computer Science	2005
B	Combining behavior and data modeling in automated test case generation	Schroeder et al.	QSIC	2003
B	Combining test case generation for component and integration testing	Benz	AMOST	2007
C	Conformance testing based on UML state machines: automated test case generation, execution, and evaluation	Seifert	Lecture Notes in Computer Science	2008
B	Constructing multiple unique input/output sequences using metaheuristic optimization techniques	Guo et al.	IEE Proceedings Software	2005
D	Controlling test case explosion in test generation from B formal models	Legeard et al.	Software Testing, Verification & Reliability'	2004
B	Coverage metrics for requirements-based testing	Whalen et al.	ISSTA	2006
D	Coverage-directed test generation with model checkers: challenges and opportunities	Devaraj et al.	COMPSAC	2005
B	Data abstraction and constraint solving for conformance testing	Calame et al.	APSEC	2005
D	DeepTrans—a model-based approach to functional verification of address translation mechanisms	Adir et al.	4th International Workshop on Microprocessor Test and Verification	2003
B	Dependence analysis in reduction of requirement-based test suites	Vaysburg et al.	International Symposium on Software Testing and Analysis	2002
B	Derivation of tests from timed specifications according to different coverage criteria	Merayo and Nunez	ICONS	2008

(continued)

Appendix A (*Continued*)

Category	Title	Authors	Source	Year
D	Deriving test plans from architectural descriptions	Bertolino et al.	ICSE	2000
A	Deriving tests from UML 2.0 sequence diagrams with neg and assert	Lund and Stølen	AST	2006
D	Design and implementation of Triveni: a process-algebraic API for threads + events	Colby et al.	International Conference on Computer Languages	1998
D	Designing fault injection experiments using state-based model to test a space software	Ambrosio et al.	Lecture Notes in Computer Science	2007
D	Developing a TTCN-3 test harness for legacy software	Okika et al.	AST	2006
B	Development of a framework for automated systematic testing of safety-critical embedded systems	Kandl et al.	WISES	2006
D	Distributed software testing with specification	Chang et al.	IEEE Computer Society's International Computer Software & Applications Conference	1990
B	Domain-specific test case generation using higher ordered typed languages for specification	Sinha and Smidts	University of Maryland at College Park	2005
B	Efficient software test case generation using genetic algorithm–based graph theory	Rajappa et al.	ICETET	2008
B	Employing user profiles to test a new version of a GUI component in its context of use	Memon	Software Quality Journal	2006
B	Environment behavior models for scenario generation and testing automation	Auguston et al.	A-MOST	2005
B	Evaluating several path-based partial dynamic analysis methods for selecting black-box-generated test cases	Chan and Yu	QSIC	2004
D	Extended finite state machine based test derivation driven by user defined faults	El-Fakih et al.	ICST	2008

	Title	Authors	Venue	Year
B	Extending EFSMs to specify and test timed systems with action durations and time-outs	Merayo et al.	IEEE Transactions on Computers	2008
B	Extending Stream X-machines to specify and test systems with time-outs	Merayo et al.	SEFM	2008
D	Extending test templates with inheritance	Murray et al.	ASWEC	1997
A	Formal test generation from UML models	Buchs et al.	Lecture Notes in Computer Science	2006
C	Formal test-case generation for UML statecharts	Gnesi et al.	IEEE ICECCS	2004
D	Formally testing fail-safety of electronic purse protocols	Jurjens and Wimmel	ASE	2001
B	From faults via test purposes to test cases: on the fault-based testing of concurrent systems	Aichernig and Delgado	9th International Conference on Fundamental Approaches to Software Engineering {FASE}	2006
D	From MC/DC to RC/DC: formalization and analysis of control-flow testing criteria	Vilkomir and Bowen	Formal Aspects of Computing	2006
D	From Object-Z specifications to ClassBench test suites	Carrington et al.	Journal of Software Testing Verification and Reliability	2000
B	Fully automatic testing with functions as specifications	Koopman and Plasmeijer	Lecture Notes in Computer Science	2006
B	Generating functional test cases in-the-large for time-critical systems from logic-based specifications	Morasca et al.	ISSTA	1996
D	Generating regression tests via model checking	Lihua et al.	COMPSAC	2004
B	Generating test cases for real-time systems from logic specifications	Mandrioli et al.	ACM Transactions on Computer Systems	1995
C	Generating test cases from an OO model with an AI planning system	Scheetz et al.	ISSRE	1999
B	Generating test cases from class vectors	Leung et al.	Journal of Systems and Software	2003
A	Generating test cases from UML activity diagram based on Gray-box method	Linzhang et al.	APSEC	2004
B	Generating test data from SOFL specifications	Offutt and Liu	Journal of Systems and Software	1999

(continued)

Appendix A *(Continued)*

Category	Title	Authors	Source	Year
A	Generating test data from state-based specifications	Offutt et al.	Journal of Software Testing, Verification and Reliability	2003
C	Generating test sequences from UML sequence diagrams and state diagrams	Sokenou	Informatik Forschung und Entwicklung	2006
B	Generating test suites for software load testing	Avritzer and Weyuker	International Symposium on Software testing and analysis	1994
D	Generating tests from EFSM models using guided model checking and iterated search refinement	Ernits et al.	Lecture Notes in Computer Science	2006
A	Generating tests from UML specifications	Offutt and Abdurazik	UML	1999
B	Generating, selecting, and prioritizing test cases from specifications with tool support	Yu et al.	QSIC	2003
B	HOTTest: a model-based test design technique for enhanced testing of domain-specific applications	Sinha et al.	ACM Transactions on Software Engineering and Methodology	2006
B	Identification of categories and choices in activity diagrams	Chen et al.	QSIC	2005
D	Improving design dependability by exploiting an open model-based specification	Tomita and Sakamura	IEEE Transactions on Computers	1999
C	Improving state-based coverage criteria using data flow information	Briand et al.	Technical Report of Carleton University	2004
D	Improving test suites via operational abstraction	Harder et al.	ICSE	2003
B	Improving Web application testing with user session data	Elbaum et al.	ICSE	2003
B	In-parameter-order: a test generation strategy for pairwise testing	Lei and Tai	IEEE International High-Assurance Systems Engineering Symposium	1998
C	Integration of ''components'' to test software components	Bertolino et al.	Electronic Notes in Theoretical Computer Science	2003
B	Integration of specification-based and CR-based approaches for GUI testing	Chen et al.	AINA	2005

C	Introducing a reasonably complete and coherent approach for model-based testing	Bertolino et al.	Electronic Notes in Theoretical Computer Science	2005
A	ISDGen: an automated simulation data generation tool for object-oriented information systems	Zheng et al.	ICSC	2007
D	JUMBL: a tool for model-based statistical testing	Prowell	Annual Hawaii International Conference on System Sciences	2003
D	Korat: automated testing based on Java predicates	Boyapati et al.	ISSTA	2002
A	Less is more: a minimalistic approach to UML model-based conformance test generation	Kaplan et al.	ICST	2008
B	Lessons learned from automating tests for an operations support system	Fecko and Lott	Software—Practice & Experience	2002
D	Lutess: a specification-driven testing environment for synchronous software	du Bousquet et al.	ICSE	1999
B	Making model-based testing more agile: a use case-driven approach	Katara and Kervinen	Lecture Notes in Computer Science	2007
B	Mastering test generation from smart card software formal models	Bouquet et al.	Lecture Notes in Computer Science	2005
D	MaTeLo—statistical usage testing by annotated sequence diagrams, Markov chains, and TTCN-3	Dulz and Zhen	International Conference on Quality Software	2003
B	Message confidentiality testing of security protocols—passive monitoring and active checking	Shu and Lee	Lecture Notes in Computer Science	2006
D	Model-based regression test reduction using dependence analysis	Korel et al.	ICSM	2002
B	Model-based testing in evolutionary software development	Pretschner et al.	RSP	2001
B	Model-based testing in practice at Microsoft	Stobie	Electronic Notes in Theoretical Computer Science	2005
A	Model-based testing of system requirements using UML use case models	Hasling et al.	ICST	2008

(continued)

Appendix A   (Continued)

Category	Title	Authors	Source	Year
C	Model-based built-in tests	Gross et al.	Electronic Notes in Theoretical Computer Science	2005
B	Model-based formal specification directed testing of abstract data types	Jia	COMPSAC	1993
D	Model-based functional conformance testing of Web services operating on persistent data	Sinha and Pardkar	TAV-WEB	2006
A	Model-based security testing using UMLsec. A case study	Jurjens	Electronic Notes in Theoretical Computer Science	2008
B	Model-based security vulnerability testing	Pari-Salas et al.	ASWEC	2007
B	Model-based specification and testing applied to the ground-based midcourse defense (GMD) system: an industry report	Lakey	A-MOST	2005
B	Model-based test case generation for smart cards	Philipps et al.	Electronic Notes in Theoretical Computer Science	2003
D	Model-based test prioritization heuristic methods and their evaluation	Korel et al.	AMOST	2007
B	Model-based test selection for infinite-state reactive systems	Jeannet et al.	Lecture Notes in Computer Science	2007
A	Model-based testing and maintenance	Deng et al.	*ICMSE*	*2004*
A	Model-based testing for applications derived from software product lines	Olimpiew and Gomaa	A-MOST	2005
B	Model-based testing for real: the inhouse card case study	Pretschner et al.	International Journal on Software Tools for Technology Transfer (STTT)	2001
A	Model-based testing from UML Models	Bernard et al.	Informatik Forschung und Entwicklung	2006
B	Model-based testing in practice	Dalal et al.	ICSE	1999
B	Model-based testing of a highly programmable system	Dalal et al.	International Symposium on Software Reliability Engineering	1998
A	Model-based testing of object-oriented systems	Rumpe	Formal Methods for Components and Objects	2003
B	Model-based testing of thin-client Web applications and navigation input	Koopman et al.	Lecture Notes in Computer Science	2007

C	Model-based testing with UML applied to a roaming algorithm for Bluetooth devices	Zhen et al.	Journal of Zhejiang University Science	2004
B	Model-based tests for access control policies	Pretschner et al.	ICST	2008
B	Modeling requirements for combinatorial software testing	Lott et al.	A-MOST	2005
B	Modeling Web browser interactions and generating tests	Song et al.	CIS	2008
B	Models for synchronous software testing	Lakehal et al.	International Workshop on Model, Design and Validation	2004
D	Module documentation based testing using gray-box approach	Baharom et al.	ITSim	2008
B	Mutation-based testing criteria for timeliness	Nilsson et al.	COMPSAC	2004
C	On testing UML statecharts	Massink et al.	Journal of Logic and Algebraic Programming	2006
B	On the complexity of generating optimal test sequences	Boyd and Ural	IEEE Transactions on Software Engineering	1991
D	On the correctness of upper layers of automotive systems	Botaschanjan et al.	Formal Aspects of Computing	2008
B	On the effect of test-suite reduction on automatically generated model-based tests	Heimdahl et al.	ASE	2007
B	On the effectiveness of mutation analysis as a black-box testing technique	Murnane and Reed	ASWEC	2001
B	On the integration of design and test: a model-based approach for embedded systems	Pfaller et al.	AST	2006
B	Online testing with model programs	Veanes et al.	ESEC/FSE	2005
A	Ontology-based test modeling and partition testing of Web services	Bai et al.	ICWS	2008
B	Optimal strategies for testing nondeterministic systems	Lev Nachmanson	ISSTA	2004
D	Parallel test generation and execution with Korat	Misailovic et al.	ESEC/FSE	2007

(continued)

Appendix A (*Continued*)

Category	Title	Authors	Source	Year
D	Parameterized unit tests	Tillmann and Schulte	ESEC/FSE-13	2004
D	PKorat: parallel generation of structurally complex test inputs	Siddiqui and Khurshid	ICST	2009
B	Plannable test selection criteria for FSMs extracted from operational specifications	Paradkar	ISSRE	2004
D	Play to test	Blass et al.	Formal Approaches to Software Testing	2005
C	Polymorphism sequence diagrams test data automatic generation based on OCL	Zhou et al.	ICYCS	2008
D	Practical approach to specification and conformance testing of distributed network applications	Kuliamin et al.	Lecture Notes in Computer Science	2005
B	Probe: a formal specification-based testing system	Amayreh and Zin	International Conference on Information Systems	1999
B	Projected state machine coverage for software testing	Friedman et al.	ISSTA	2002
B	ProTest: an automatic test environment for B specifications	Satpathy et al.	Electronic Notes in Theoretical Computer Science	2005
B	Randomized directed testing (REDIRECT) for simulink/Stateflow models	Satpathy et al.	EMSOFT	2008
D	Redundancy based test-suite reduction	Fraser and Wotawa	Lecture Notes in Computer Science	2007
D	Regression testing of classes based on TCOZ specification	Liang	ICECCS	2005
D	Requirement model-based mutation testing for Web service	Wang and Huang	NWeSP	2008
B	Requirement-based automated black-box test generation	Tahat et al.	COMPSAC	2001
B	Requirements traceability in automated test generation: application to smart card software validation	Bouquet et al.	A-MOST	2005
B	Requirements-based monitors for real-time systems	Peters and Parnas	IEEE Transactions on Software Engineering	2002

C	Revisiting strategies for ordering class integration testing in the presence of dependency cycles—an investigation of graph-based class integration test order strategies	Briand et al.	Technical Report of Carleton University	2002
A	Rigorous vertical software system testing in IDE	Kwang and Eun	SERA	2007
D	SALT—an integrated environment to automate generation of function tests for APIs	Paradkar	ISSRE	2000
D	Security policy testing using vulnerability exploit chaining	Darmaillacq	ICSTW	2008
D	Software architecture analysis based on statechart semantics	Dias and Vieira	International Workshop on Software Specification and Design	2000
D	Software testing at the architectural level	Richardson and Wolf	ISAW-2 and Viewpoints	1996
B	Specification-based test sequence generation with propositional logic	Wimmel et al.	Software Testing Verification and Reliability	2000
D	Specification-based class testing with ClassBench	Murray et al.	Asia Pacific Software Engineering Conference	1998
D	Specification-based compaction of directed tests for functional validation of pipelined processors	Koo and Mishra	CODES	2008
A	Specification-based regression test selection with risk analysis	Chen et al.	CASCON	2002
B	Specification-based test generation for security-critical systems using mutations	Wimmel and Jürjens	International Conference on Formal Methods and Software Engineering	2002
D	Specification-based test oracles for reactive systems	Richardson et al.	ICSE	1992
B	Specification-based testing for real-time avionic systems	Biberstein and Fitzgerald	IEE Colloquium on Applicable Modelling, Verification and Analysis Techniques for Real-Time Systems	1999
B	Specification-based testing for real-time reactive systems	Alagar et al.	TOOLS	2000

(continued)

Appendix A (*Continued*)

Category	Title	Authors	Source	Year
B	Specification-based testing for software product lines	Kahsai et al.	ICSEFM	2008
C	Specification-based testing method using testing flow graphs	Voigt et al.	ICSEA	2007
B	Specification-based testing of reactive software: a case study in technology transfer	Jagadeesan et al.	Journal of Systems and Software	1998
B	Specification-based testing of reactive software: tools and experiments-experience report	Jagadeesan et al.	ICSE	1997
B	Specification-based testing of synchronous software	Parissis and Ouabdesselam	Symposium on the Foundations of Software Engineering	1996
B	Specification-based testing using cause–effect graphs	Paradkar et al.	Annals of Software Engineering	1997
B	Specification-based testing with linear temporal logic	Tan et al.	IRI	2004
D	Specifying and testing software components using ADL	Hayes and Sankar	Techinical Report at Sun Microsystems	1994
D	State-based incremental testing of aspect-oriented programs	Xu and Xu	AOSD	2006
D	State-based testing of integration aspects	Xu and Xu	WTAOP	2006
B	Statechart testing method for aircraft control systems	Bogdanov and Holcombe	Software Testing Verification & Reliability	2001
B	Strategies for automated specification-based testing of synchronous software	Parissis and Vassy	ASE	2001
D	Structural specification-based testing with ADL	Chang et al.	ISSTA	1996
D	Structural specification-based testing: automated support and experimental evaluation	Chang and Richardson	ESEC	1999
B	Symbolic model-based test selection	Jeron	Electronic Notes in Theoretical Computer Science	2009
B	Synthesis of scenario based test cases from B models	Satpathy et al.	Lecture Notes in Computer Science	2006

	Title	Authors	Venue	Year
B	Systematic model-based testing of embedded control software: the MB³/T approach	Conrad et al.	ICSE	2004
B	Telecommunication software validation using a synchronous approach	du Bousquet et al.	ASSET	1998
B	Test case generation as an AI Planning problem	Howe et al.	ASE	1997
B	Test case generation from formal models through abstraction refinement and model checking	Satpathy, M., Ramesh	AMOST	2007
C	Test cases generation from UML state diagrams	Kim et al.	IEE Software	1999
D	Test generation and execution for security rules in temporal logic	Darmaillacq et al.	ICSTW	2008
B	Test generation from security policies specified in Or-BAC	Li et al.	ICSAC	2007
D	Test input generation for Java containers using state matching	Visser et al.	ISSTA	2006
D	Test input generation with Java PathFinder	Visser et al.	ISSTA	2004
A	Test ready UML statecharts models	Murthy et al.	SCESM	2006
D	Test selection for object-oriented software based on formal specifications	Peraire et al.	International Conference on Programming Concepts and Methods	1998
A	Test selection from UML statecharts	Liuying and Zhichang	TOOLS	1999
B	Test-suite reduction based on dependence analysis	Jourdan et al.	Lecture Notes in Computer Science	2006
D	Test template framework: a specification-based testing case study	Stocks and Carrington	ISSTA	1993
D	Test templates: a specification-based testing framework	Stocks and Carrington	ICSE	1993
B	Test-based model generation for legacy systems	Hungar et al.	ITC	2003
D	TestEra: specification-based testing of Java programs using SAT	Khurshid and Marinov	ASE	2004
A	Testing agile requirements models	Botaschanjan et al.	Journal of Zhejiang University Science	2004
B	Testing finite state machines presenting stochastic time and time-outs	Merayo et al.	Lecture Notes in Computer Science	2007

(continued)

Appendix A (*Continued*)

Category	Title	Authors	Source	Year
B	Testing from a stochastic timed system with a fault model	Hierons et al.	Journal of Logic and Algebraic Programming	2009
B	Testing of concurrent programs based on message sequence charts	Chung et al.	International Symposium on Software Engineering for Parallel and Distributed Systems	1999
B	Testing real-time embedded software using UPPAAL-TRON: an industrial case study	Larsen et al.	EMSOFT	2005
B	Testing security properties of protocol implementations—a machine learning based approach	Shu and Lee	ICSCS	2007
B	Testing times: on model-driven test generation for nondeterministic real-time systems	Brinksma, E.	ACSD	2004
B	Testing Web applications by modeling with FSMs	Andrews et al.	Systems and Modeling	2005
B	Test-suite reduction for model-based tests: effects on test quality and implications for testing	Heimdahl and George	ASE	2004
C	TestUml: user-metrics driven Web applications testing	Bellettini et al.	SAC	2005
A	The AGEDIS tools for model-based testing	Hartman and Nagin	ISSTA	2004
B	Thoroughness of specification-based testing of synchronous programs	Parissis and Vassy	ISSRE	2003
D	TinMan—a test derivation and management tool for specification-based class testing	Murray et al.	TOOLS	1999
B	Toward a more efficient way of generating test cases: class graphs	Leung and Wong	Asia-Pacific Conference on Quality Software	2000
C	Toward a tool supporting integration testing of aspect-oriented programs	Massicotte et al.	Journal of Object Technology	2007
C	Toward automated support for deriving test data from UML statecharts	Briand et al.	Technical Report of Carleton University	2004

B	Toward integration of use case modeling and usage-based testing	Regnell et al.	Journal of Systems and Software	2000
B	Toward model-based generation of self-priming and self-checking conformance tests for interactive systems	Paradkar	Information and Software Technology	2004
D	Toward modularized verification of distributed time-triggered systems	Botaschanjan et al.	Lecture Notes in Computer Science	2006
A	Toward traceability of model-based testing artifacts	Naslavsky	AMOST	2007
C	Traffic-aware stress testing of distributed systems based on UML models	Garousi et al.	ICSE	2006
B	T-UPPAAL: online model-based testing of real-time systems	Mikucionis et al.	ASE	2004
B	T-VEC: a tool for developing critical systems	Blackburn and Busser	COMPASS	1996
B	T-VECTM product summary		Workshop on Industrial Strength Formal Specification Techniques	1998
C	UML-based integration testing	Hartmann et al.	ISSTA	2000
C	UML-based integration testing for component-based software	Wu et al.	ICCBSS	2003
A	UML-based statistical test case generation	Riebisch et al.	NetObjectDays	2002
B	Use case-based testing of product lines	Bertolino and Gnesi	ESEC and FSE-11	2003
B	Use case-driven test for object-oriented system	Choi	Software Engineering and Applications	2001
B	Using artificial life techniques to generate test cases for combinatorial testing	Shiba et al.	International Computer Software and Applications Conference	2004
B	Using communication coverage criteria and partial model generation to assist software integration testing	Robinson-Mallett et al.	Software Quality Journal	2008
B	Using formal methods to derive test frames in category-partition testing	Ammann and Offutt	COMPASS	1994
B	Using formal specifications as test oracles for system-critical software	Hagar and Bieman	ACM SIGAda Ada Letters	1996

(continued)

Appendix A (Continued)

Category	Title	Authors	Source	Year
B	Using JML runtime assertion checking to automate metamorphic testing in applications without test oracles	Murphy et al.	ICST	2009
D	Using model checking to generate fault detecting tests	Gargantini	Lecture Notes in Computer Science	2007
B	Using model checking to generate tests from requirements specifications	Gargantini and Heitmeyer	ESEC/FSE-7	1999
C	Using UML collaboration diagrams for static checking and test generation	Abdurazik and Offutt	International Conference of UML	2000
C	Using UML for automatic test generation	Crichton et al.	ASE	2001
B	Using Z specifications in category-partition testing	Amla and Ammann	COMPASS	1992
A	Verification of requirements for safety-critical software	Carpenter	SIGAda	1999
A	Web application model recovery for user input validation testing	Li et al.	ICSEA	2007
B	White on black: a white-box-oriented approach for selecting black-box-generated test cases	Chen et al.	Asia-Pacific Conference on Quality Software	2000

REFERENCES

[1] C. Kaner, Exploratory testing, in: Quality Assurance Institute Worldwide Annual Software Testing Conference, Florida Institute of Technology, Orlando, FL, 2006 November.

[2] N. Juristo, A.M. Moreno, S. Vegas, Reviewing 25 years of testing technique experiments, Emp. Softw. Eng.: An Int. J. 9 (1) (2004) 7–44 (March).

[3] W. Perry, Effective Methods for Software Testing, third ed., Wiley, New York, 2006.

[4] G. Myers, The Art of Software Testing, Wiley, New York, 1979.

[5] S. Dalal, A. Jain, N. Karunanithi, J. Leaton, C. Lott, G. Patton, B. Horowitz, Model-based testing in practice, in: Proceedings of the 1999 International Conference on Software Engineering (ICSE'99), May 1999, pp. 285–294.

[6] A.C. DIAS-NETO, Selection of Model-Based Testing Techniques, Systems Engineering and Computer Science Program. Doctoral Thesis, COPPE. Federal University of Rio de Janeiro, November 2009 (in Portugese).

[7] J. Biolchini, P.G. Mian, A.C. Natali, G.H. Travassos, Systematic Review in Software Engineering: Relevance and Utility, 2005. Available at http://www.cos.ufrj.br/uploadfiles/es67905.pdf Technical Report ES-679/05, PESC-COPPE/UFRJ.

[8] C.V. Ramamoorthy, S.F. HO, W.T. Chen, On the automated generation of program test data, IEEE Trans. Softw. Eng. SE-2 (4) (1976) 293–300 (December).

[9] T.S. Chow, Testing software design modeled by finite-state machines, IEEE Trans. Softw. Eng. SE-4 (1978) 178–187 (March).

[10] M. Utting, B. Legeard, Practical Model-Based Testing: A Tools Approach, Morgan-Kaufmann, San Francisco, CA, 2007. ISBN-13: 978-0-12-372501-1.

[11] A. Pretschner, Model-based testing, in: Proceedings of 27th International Conference on Software Engineering, (ICSE'05), 2005, pp. 722–723.

[12] M. Prasanna, S.N. Sivanandam, R. Venkatesan, R. Sundarrajan, Survey on automatic test case generation, Acad. Open Internet J. 15 2005. Available at http://www.acadjournal.com/2005/v15/part6/p4/.

[13] A.C. Dias-Neto, R. Subramanyan, M. Vieira, G.H. Travassos, S. Forrest, Improving evidence about software technologies: a look at model-based testing, IEEE Softw. 25 (3) (2008) 10–13 (May).

[14] S. Vegas, V. Basili, A characterization schema for software testing techniques, Emp. Softw. Eng. 10 (4) (2005) 437–466 (October).

[15] G.H. Travassos, P.S.M. Dos Santos, P.G.M. Neto, J. Biolchini, An environment to support large scale experimentation in software engineering, ICECCS 2008. 13th IEEE International Conference on, Eng. Complex Comput. Syst. (2008) 193–202 (March 31–April 3, 2008).

[16] B. Beizer, Black-Box Testing: Techniques for Functional Testing of Software and Systems, Wiley, New York, 1995.

[17] R.V. Binder, Testing Object-Oriented Systems: Models, Patterns, and Tools, Addison-Wesley, Boston, MA, 1999.

[18] A.C. Dias-Neto, R. Subramanyan, M. Vieira, G.H. Travassos, A survey on model-based testing approaches: a systematic review, in: Proceedings of the 1st ACM international Workshop on Empirical Assessment of Software Engineering Languages and Technologies (WEASELTech'07): Held in Conjunction with the 22nd IEEE/ACM International Conference on Automated Software Engineering (ASE) 2007 (Atlanta, Georgia), 2007, pp. 31–36. http://doi.acm.org/10.1145/1353673.1353681 (November).

[19] G.C. Roman, A taxonomy of current issues in requirements engineering, IEEE Comput. 18 (4) (1985) 14–22.

[20] A.C. Dias-Neto, G.H. Travassos, Surveying on model based testing approaches characterization attributes, in: No: International Symposium on Empirical Software Engineering and Measurement (ESEM'08), Kaiserslautern, Germany, October 2008.

[21] M. Hamburg, Basic statistics: a modern approach, J. R. Stat. Soc. Ser. A (Gen.) 143 (1) 1980 (2a Ed).

[22] A. Bertolino, Guide to the knowledge area of software testing. Software engineering body of knowledge, IEEE Comput. Soc. 2004. http://www.swebok.org (February).

[23] T. Menzies, D. Owen, B. Cukic, Saturation effects in testing of formal models, in: 13th International Symposium on Software Reliability Engineering (Issre'02), Washington, DC, vol. 15, 2002.

[24] V.R. Basili, H.D. Rombach, Support for comprehensive reuse, Softw. Eng. J. 6 (5) (1991) 303–316 (September).

[25] A. Birk, Modeling the application domains of software engineering technologies, in: Proceedings of the 12th International Conference on Automated Software Engineering (Formerly: Kbse). Automated Software Engineering. IEEE Computer Society, Washington, DC, 1997, p. 291.

[26] A.C. Dias-Neto, G.H. Travassos, Model-based testing approaches selection for software projects. Information and Software Technology, AST'08 special edition, 2009.doi:10.1016/j. infsof.2009.06.010 (July).

[27] M. Horstmann, W. Prenninger, M. El-Ramly, Case studies. Model-Based Testing—A Tutorial Volume, Springer LNCS 3472, 2005, pp. 439–461.

[28] A. Pretschner, W. Prenninger, S. Wagner, C. Kuhnel, M. Baumgartner, B. Sostawa, R. Zolch, T. Stauner, One evaluation of model-based testing and its automation, in: Proc. ICSE'05, 2005, pp. 392–401.

[29] M. Utting, A. Pretschner, B. Legeard, A Taxonomy of Model-Based Testing, Department of Computer Science, University of Waikato, Hamilton, New Zealand, 2006, Technical report 04/2006.

[30] P. Santos-Neto, R. Resende, C. Pádua, Requirements for information systems model-based testing methods, in: ACM Symposium on Applied Computing (ACM SAC), Seoul. Proceedings of the 22nd ACM Symposium on Applied Computing (ACM SAC), Software Engineering Track (SE), 2007.

[31] E. Bernard, B. Legeard, X. Luck, F. Peureux, Generation of test sequences from formal specifications: GSM 11.11 standard case-study, Softw. Pract. Exp. 34 (10) (2004) 915–948.

[32] J. Clarke, Automated test generation from behavioral models, in: Proc. 11th Software Quality Week, 1998.

[33] M. Blackburn, R. Busser, A. Nauman, Why model-based test automation is different and what you should know to get started, in: International Conference on Practical Software Quality and Testing, PSQT/PSTT'2004 East, EUA, Washington, DC, March 2004.

[34] D.N. Card, Learning from our mistakes with defect causal analysis, IEEE Softw. 15 (1) (1998) 56–63. http://dx.doi.org/10.1109/52.646883 (Jan).

[35] A. Birk, T. Dingsøyr, T. Stålhane, Postmortem: never leave a project without it, IEEE Softw. May–June (2002) 43–45. Special Issue on Knowledge Management in Software Engineering.

[36] A.C. Dias-Neto, G.H. Travassos, *Porantim*: an approach to support the combination and selection of model-based testing techniques, in: 4th Workshop on Automation of Software Test, Vancouver, May 2009.

[37] M.A. Wojcicki, P. Strooper, An iterative empirical strategy for the systematic selection of a combination of verification and validation technologies, in: Proceedings of the 5th International Workshop on Software Quality (May 20–26, 2007). International Conference on Software Engineering, 2007. http://dx.doi.org/10.1109/WOSQ.2007.4.

[38] N.A. Maiden, G. Rugg, ACRE: Selecting methods for requirements acquisition, Software Engineering Journal 11 (3) (1996) 183–192.

[39] G.N. Aranda, A. Vizcaino, A. Cechich, M. Piattini (2006), "Technology Selection to Improve Global Collaboration", In: International Conference on Global Software Engineering (ICGSE), Outubro, pp. 223–232.

Advances in Automated Model-Based System Testing of Software Applications with a GUI Front-End

ATIF M. MEMON

Department of Computer Science, University of Maryland, Maryland, USA

BAO N. NGUYEN

Department of Computer Science, University of Maryland, Maryland, USA

Abstract

Despite the ubiquity of software applications that employ a graphical-user interface (GUI) front-end, functional system testing of these applications has remained, until recently, an understudied research area. During "GUI testing," test cases, modeled as sequences of user input events, are created and executed on the software by exercising the GUI's widgets. Because each possible sequence of user events may potentially be a test case and today's GUIs offer enormous flexibility to end-users, in principle, GUI testing requires a prohibitively large number of test cases. Any practical test-case generation technique must sample the vast GUI input space. Existing techniques are largely manual, and hence extremely resource intensive. Several new automated model-based techniques have been developed in the past decade. All these techniques develop, either manually or automatically, a model of the GUI and employ it to generate test cases. This chapter presents the first detailed taxonomy of these techniques. A small GUI application is used as a running example to demonstrate each technique and illustrate its relative strengths and weaknesses.

ADVANCES IN COMPUTERS, VOL. 80
ISSN: 0065-2458/DOI: 10.1016/S0065-2458(10)80003-8

1. Introduction

As computers play an increasingly important role aiding end-users, researchers, and businesses in today's internetworked world, the class of software that has a graphical-user interface (GUI) front-end has become ubiquitous [1–3]. A GUI takes events (mouse clicks, selections, typing in text-fields) as input from users, and then changes the state of its widgets. GUIs have become popular because of the advantages this "event-handler architecture" offers to both developers and users [4–6]. From the developer's point of view, the event handlers may be created and maintained fairly independently; hence, complex system may be built using these loosely coupled pieces of code. From the user's point of view, GUIs offer many degrees of usage freedom, that is, users may choose to perform a given task by inputting GUI events in many different ways in terms of their type, number, and execution order.

Quality Assurance (QA) is becoming increasingly important for GUIs as their functional correctness may affect the quality of the entire system in which the GUI operates [7]. *Software testing* is a popular QA technique employed during software development and deployment to help improve its quality [8,9]. During software testing, test cases are created and executed on the software. One way to test a GUI is to execute each event individually and observe its outcome, thereby testing each event handler in isolation [10,11]. However, the execution outcome of an event handler may depend on its internal state, the state of other entities (objects, event handlers), and the external environment. Its execution may lead to a change in its own state or that of other entities. Moreover, the outcome of an event's execution may vary based on the sequence of preceding events seen thus far. Consequently, in GUI testing, each event needs to be tested in different states. GUI testing therefore involves generating and executing sequences of events [5,12].

The event-driven nature of GUIs creates several challenges for testing. One important challenge stems from the enormous space of possible event interactions with the GUI [13,14]. Because each possible event sequence (ES) may potentially be a test case, GUI testing, in principle, may require a prohibitively large number of test cases. Practical GUI testing techniques attempt to sample the vast input space of all possible sequences with the goal of detecting faults; for effective testing, it is important to sample this space carefully [15].

In practice, GUI testing is done in two ways. First, testers employ unit testing tools [13,16] such as *JFCUnit* [17], *Abbot* [18], *Pounder* [19], and *Jemmy Module* [20] to manually create unit test cases for GUIs. A unit test case consists of method calls to an instance of the class under test. Assertions are inserted in the test cases to determine whether the classes/methods executed correctly. The test cases are automatically executed on the GUI under test. Assertion violations are reported as failures. The parts of the GUI state space explored depend largely on the nature of the test cases. Because manual coding of test cases can be tedious, an alternative, which is the second popular technique, "captures" sequences of events that testers perform manually on the GUI. Hence, this technique treats a test case as a sequence of input events. These test cases can be "replayed" automatically on the GUI. Tools used for this "capture" and "replay" are called *capture/replay* tools [21,22]. As was the case with unit testing, the test-case creation is manual (in terms of the ES) and the tools facilitate only the execution of test cases. The "goodness" of the test cases depends on the tester's ability to obtain fault-exposing sequences [14,23].

The last decade has seen some advances in automated model-based GUI testing techniques. In this chapter, we provide a taxonomy of these techniques, which are shown in Table I. As the table shows, we discuss 16 techniques. All these techniques require the creation of a model of the software or its GUI, and algorithms to use the model to generate test cases. The techniques of interest to us employ six distinct models, shown in Column 1 of Table I; the "hierarchical" model uses a combination of these models organized in a hierarchy.

There are two important aspects of each technique that we discuss. First is the model that it employs. In some cases, the models are created manually; in others, they are derived in an automated manner. The second important aspect is the test-case generation approach, which, for some techniques is manual; but for most is automated. Figure 1 shows the set of techniques discussed in this chapter, partitioned along two dimensions: model creation (*manual, automated*) and test generation (*manual, automated*).

TABLE I
GUI TESTING TECHNIQUES DISCUSSED IN THIS CHAPTER

Model	Technique	Abbreviation	Section
State machine	Finite state machine	FSM	3.1.1
	Variable finite state machine	VFSM	3.1.2
	Complete interaction sequence	CIS	3.1.3
	Faulty complete interaction sequence	FCIS	3.1.4
Workflow	Event-flow graph	EFG	3.2.1
	Event interaction graph	EIG	3.2.2
	Feedback based	ESIG	3.2.3
	Faulty event sequence graph	FESG	3.2.4
Pre- and Postcondition	AI planning	AI	3.3
Event sequence	Genetic models	GA	3.4
Probabilistic	Probabilistic event-flow graph	PEFG	3.5
Combinatorial	Latin squares	LS	3.6.1
	Coverage arrays	CA	3.6.2
Hierarchical	Keyword-driven model	KW	3.7.1
	Hierarchical finite state machines	HFSM	3.7.2
	UML diagram-based	UML	3.7.3

Test generation \ Model creation	Manual	Automated
Manual	FSM, VFSM, CIS, FCIS,	
Automated	KW, FESG, AI, GA, PEFG, LS, CA, HFSM, UML	EFG, EIG, ESIG

FIG. 1. Technique taxonomy.

The remainder of this chapter presents these techniques. But first, we present a small GUI application that we use as a running example, to illustrate the important aspects of each technique, and its relative strengths and weaknesses.

2. Running Example of GUI Application Under Test

The simple running example application called "Radio Button Demo" is seen in Fig. 2. The GUI contains nine widgets labeled w_0 through w_8. A user can perform events on almost all the widgets (there is no event available on w_4). Table II shows

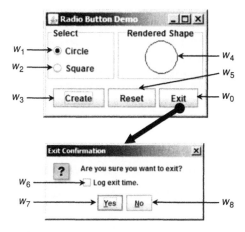

FIG. 2. The Radio Button Demo application.

TABLE II
EVENTS AVAILABLE ON EACH WIDGET

Widget	Event name
w_1	*circle*
w_2	*square*
w_3	*create*
w_5	*reset*
w_0	*exit*
w_6	*(un)check*
w_7	*yes*
w_8	*no*

the events associated with each widget. We note that in this simple example, each widget has at most one associated event. In a more complex GUI, a widget may have multiple associated events.

The application's functionality is very straightforward—the *initial state* has Circle (corresponding to w_1) selected, the Rendered Shape area (widget w_4) is empty, and the Reset button is disabled. Events are used to change the state of the GUI. Event *circle* sets the radio button to circle; if there is already a square in the Rendered Shape area, then the shape is immediately changed to a circle. Event *square* is similar to *circle*, except that it changes the shape to a square. Event *create* creates a shape in the Rendered Shape area according to current settings of w_1 and w_2. Event *reset* resets the entire software to its initial state. This event is only available when there is an existing shape. Event *exit* opens a modal "Exit Confirmation" window that contains widgets w_6, w_7, and w_8. This window blocks all widgets in the main window when it opens. Event *(un)check* changes the status of the check-box w_6 (originally unchecked) so that when it is checked the exiting time will be logged to a file before the application is terminated. Event *no* closes the window and moves focus back to the main window; and event *yes* closes the entire application.

The GUI of this application is simple, yet quite flexible. The numbers of 1-, 2-, 3-,4-, and 5-way unique ESs (and hence possible test cases) that may be executed in the initial state of the GUI are 4 (remember that the Exit Confirmation window is initially closed and w_5 is disabled), 17, 66, 253, and 798, respectively.

3. Test-Case Generation Techniques

This section presents an overview of all the techniques listed in Table I. The techniques are classified according to the underlying model used.

3.1   State Machines

Because GUIs are composed of objects (i.e., the widgets) that maintain state, in terms of widget properties (e.g., *Enabled, Caption, Width*) and their values (e.g., *TRUE, "Cancel"*, 20), many researchers have found it natural to model GUIs using state machines [10,14,24,25]. For example, the GUI shown in Fig. 2 starts in an "initial state" in which, among other widgets, widget w_3 is not selected and w_5 is disabled. If one were to model the state of the GUI as a set of triples (*widget, property, value*), the initial state could be represented as {..., (w_3, *Selected, FALSE*), (w_3, *Enabled, TRUE*), (w_5, *Enabled, FALSE*), ...}. As can be imagined, depending on how one models the state, such machines can get extremely large for nontrivial GUIs. In this section, we present several techniques that researchers have employed to control this state space explosion. Shehady et al. [24] use global variables, White et al. [25] focus on a part of the state machine, and Belli et al. [14] develop off-nominal test cases. We present these techniques in the following sections.

3.1.1   Finite State Machines

In this section, we present a generic approach to model the GUI as a finite state machine (FSM). Formally, a FSM can be represented as a quintuple FSM = (S, I, O, T, Φ), where S is the finite set of GUI states, I is the set of inputs, that is, events that may be performed on the GUI, O is the finite set of outputs, T is the transition function $S \times I \rightarrow S$ that specifies the next state as a function of the current state and input event, ϕ is the output function $S \times I \rightarrow O$ that specifies the resulting output from a transition.

For GUI testing, a tester is free to select certain aspects of the software to model in the state. For example, we choose to represent the state of the GUI using four of its elements: (1) *log*, which is 1 if w_6 is checked, 0 otherwise; (2) *exitWinOpen*, which is 1 if the Exit Confirmation window is open, 0 otherwise; (3) *created*, which is 1 if a shape is created, 0 otherwise; (4) *shape*, which is either *Circle* or *Square*.

We can then represent the state of the GUI using a length 4 vector consisting of the above four elements in the order specified above. For example, state S_{000C} is the initial state in which w_6 is unchecked, the exit confirmation window is closed, no shape is created at w_4, and the shape radio button for circle is set. Similarly, S_{111S} is the state in which w_6 is checked, the exit confirmation window is open, a shape is visible at w_4, and the shape radio button for square is set.

We use the above definition of GUI state to create an FSM. Figure 3 shows the FSM of the GUI of Fig. 2. Nodes in the graph represent states and edges represent transitions; there are two special states (shaded nodes) in the FSM: the initial state right after the software starts (S_{000C}), and the terminal state when the software has been terminated (S_t). Some of the state transitions are as follows: If the Create button has never been clicked, then the user can transit between S_{000x} states by selecting different radio button options (x represents any value of the corresponding state element, in this case x is either C or S). Once Create has been clicked, the GUI transits to a new state where the third state element turns from 0 is 1 (i.e., a new shape has been created). The user can transit back and forth between S_{x0xC} and S_{x0xS} by selecting different radio button options (x represents any value of the corresponding state element). However, the user cannot do the same for the pair (S_{01xC}, S_{01xS}) or S_{11xC} states because the Exit Confirmation window blocks all widgets in the main window.

Once the FSM has been created, test-case generation from an FSM is very intuitive. The test designer may start at the initial state, traverse edges of the FSM as desired, and record the transitions as events. For example, in Fig. 3, a test case could be: ⟨*square, circle, create, exit, (un)check, yes*⟩ which takes the software through states S_{000S}, S_{000C}, S_{001C}, S_{011C}, S_{111C}, and S_t.

Although FSMs are easy to create, they suffer from some major problems. First, they do not scale for large GUIs. Moreover, the states may not have any relationship to the structure of the GUI. Hence, they can be difficult to maintain. A new model called variable finite state machines (VFSMs), developed by Shehady et al. [24], presented in the following section, attempts to rectify some of these problems.

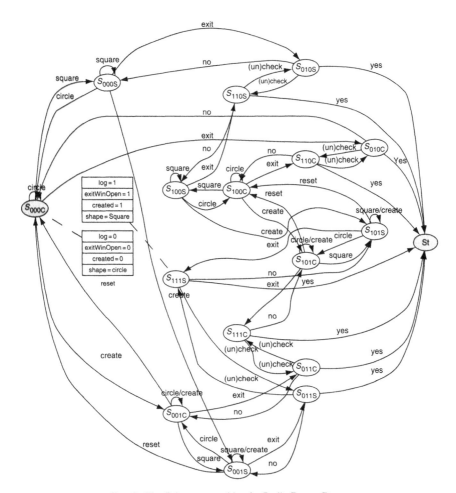

FIG. 3. The finite state machine for Radio Button Demo.

3.1.2 Variable Finite State Machines

Shehady et al. [24] use VFSMs for testing GUIs. The key difference between VFSMs and FSMs is that the former allow a number of global variables, each of which takes values from a finite domain. The values of the variables are used to compute the next state and the output in response to an input. Transitions may also modify the values of these variables. In principle, the space of GUIs that can be modeled using VFSMs is the same as those that can be modeled using FSMs.

Formally, a VFSM is represented as a 7-tuple $VFSM = (S, I, O, T, \Phi, V, \zeta)$, where S, I, O are similar to their counterparts in FSMs, $V = \{V_1, V_2, V_3, \ldots, V_n\}$ (each V_i is the set of values that the ith variable may assume) and n is the total number of variables in the VFSM. Let $D = S \times I \times V_1 \times V_2 \times \ldots \times V_n$ and $D_T \subseteq D$; T is the transition function $D_T \rightarrow S$ and Φ is a function $D_T \rightarrow O$. Hence, the current state of each of the variables affects both the next state and the output of the VFSM. ζ is the set of variable transition functions. At each transition, ζ is used to determine whether any of the variables' values have been modified. Each variable has an initial state at startup.

Figure 4 shows a VFSM of the Radio Button Demo's GUI. Each state is simply represented by a length 3 vector, that is, that specifies whether *log* needs to be maintained, the Exit Confirmation window is open, and the type of shape that has been selected.

The states have been simplified because the element *created* has been removed from the state. This information is now maintained in a variable V that can take values 0 and 1. Edges of the VFSM are annotated with predicates (shown in parenthesis placed before the edge label) and assignments to the variables (shown in square brackets

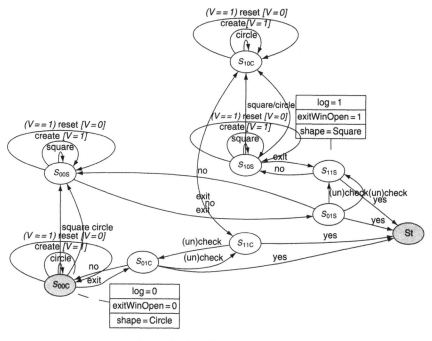

Fig. 4. Variable finite state machine.

placed after the edge label). Initially, V is set to 0. Transitions are taken depending on the outcome of the predicates. For example, the *reset* transition is taken from S_{00C} only if $V == 1$; once taken, it changes V to 0. Similarly, *create* changes V to 1.

The VFSM created is much more concise (it has nine states) than the original FSM in Fig. 3 (which has 17 states). This is because several states in the FSM are grouped and represented by a single state in the VFSM. VFSMs can be converted into their equivalent FSMs for test-case generation. The key idea is to fold the information of V and ζ into S and T. Given a VFSM's S and $V = \{V_1, V_2, \ldots, V_n\}$, the new FSM's set of states S_{eq} is obtained as $S_{eq} = \{S_i | S_i \in S \times V_1 \times V_2 \times V_3 \times \ldots \times V_n\}$, that is, this creates a set of states that combines the information of the states and the variables into one state. Similarly, the new FSM's transition function $T_{eq}: S_{eq} \times I \rightarrow S_{eq}$ may be created by combining the T and ζ functions of the VFSM. Since the range of T is S and the range of ζ is $V = \{V_1, V_2, \ldots, V_n\}$, S_{eq} is the Cartesian product of the two ranges; also T and S have the same domain.

3.1.3 Complete Interaction Sequences

Another approach to restrict the state space of a state machine is to employ software usage information. The method proposed by White et al. [25] focuses on a subset of interactions performed on the GUI. The key idea is to identify *responsibilities* for a GUI; a responsibility is a GUI activity that involves one or more GUI objects and has an observable effect on the surrounding environment of the GUI, which includes memory, peripheral devices, underlying software, and application software. For each responsibility, a *complete interaction sequence* (*CIS*), which is a sequence of GUI objects and selections that will invoke the given responsibility, is identified. Parts of the CIS are then used for testing the GUI.

The GUI testing steps for CIS are as follows.

1. Manually identify responsibilities in the GUI.
2. For each responsibility, identify its corresponding CIS.
3. Create an FSM for each CIS.
4. Apply transformations to the FSM to obtain a *reduced FSM*. These transformations include the following.
   a. Abstracting strongly connected components into a *superstate*.
   b. Merging CIS states that have structural symmetry.
5. Use the reduced FSM to test the CIS for correctness.

The two abstractions mentioned above (Steps 4a and 4b) are useful from a modeling point of view. They are described in more detail next.

Definition: A part of an FSM, called a *sub-FSM*, is a *strongly connected component* if for every pair $(S_1, S_2), S_1, S_2 \in S$, there exists a directed path from S_1 to S_2. Each such component is then replaced by a *superstate* and tested in isolation.

A sub-FSM has structural symmetry if the following conditions hold.

1. It contains states S_1 and S_2 such that S_1 has one incoming transition, S_2 has one outgoing transition, and a number of paths reach S_2 from S_1.
2. For each path in the sub-FSM, context (the path taken to get to S_1 from outside the sub-FSM) has no effect on the states/transitions or output.
3. No transition or state encountered after S_2 is affected by paths taken inside the sub-FSM.

Such a sub-FSM can be reduced into a superstate and tested in isolation.

Given a GUI, the test designer first reduces the FSM after applying the above transformations, thereby reducing the total number of states in the FSM. This results in smaller number of paths in the FSM, hence reducing the number of test cases. Without any loss of generality, each FSM is assumed to have a distinct start state and distinct terminal state.

As was the case before, a test is a path through the FSM. The test designer creates two types of tests: *design tests* that assume that the FSM is a faithful representation of the GUI's specifications and *implementation tests* that for each CIS, consider the possibility that potential transitions not described in the design may occur in the implementation.

For design tests, the test designer creates sufficient number of tests starting at the initial state and ending at the terminal state so that the following conditions hold:

- all distinct paths in the reduced FSM are executed; each time a path enters a superstate corresponding to a component, an appropriate test path of the component is inserted into the test case at that point,
- all the design subtests of each component are included in at least one test, which may require additional tests of the reduced FSM to satisfy this constraint.

The key idea of conducting implementation testing is to check all GUI events in the CIS to determine whether they invoke any new transitions in the reduced FSM. To implement the reduced FSM test, the test designer must construct sufficient test sequences starting at the initial state and stopping at the terminal state so that the following conditions hold:

- all the paths of the reduced FSM are executed, and
- all the implementation tests for each remaining component are included at least once.

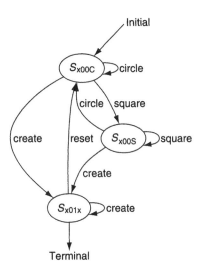

Fig. 5. FSM for the *create a new shape* responsibility.

By using the CIS concept, the test designer can test a GUI from various perspectives, each defined by the CIS. For example, in the Radio Button Demo application, the tester may design a "*create a new shape*" responsibility that involves four objects w_1, w_2, w_3, and w_5 (assuming that the Rendered Shape area is empty and the Exit Confirmation window is not open). Figure 5 shows an FSM for this responsibility where each node represents a GUI state and each edge represents a state transition. Note that the states in this FSM are abstract states representing several states in the FSM of Section 3.1.1. For example, S_{x00C} is an abstraction of all states where the Circle radio button is selected (x can be replaced by any value of the corresponding state element).

The sub-FSM consisting of the two states S_{x00C} and S_{x00S} is a strongly connected component. Thus, this sub-FSM can be tested in isolation and then replaced it by a superstate S_{x00x} (i.e., a shape is selected). To test the internal behaviors of the sub-FSM, the state sequence needed to be covered is $\langle S_{x00C}, S_{x01S} \rangle$; which is obtained by the ES $\langle square, circle \rangle$. With an assumption that the sub-FSM is well tested, the state sequence needed to test the reduced FSM is $\langle Initial, S_{x00x}, S_{x01x}, S_{x00x}, S_{x01x}, Terminal \rangle$. This sequence is then translated to an executable test case taking the GUI from the initial state to the terminal state: $\langle create, reset, create \rangle$.

3.1.4   Off-Nominal Finite State Machines

The three approaches discussed thus far generate test cases to test the GUI for legal ESs specified in the state machine model. However, the GUI might have been coded incorrectly to allow other sequences left unspecified in the state machine.

For example, in our Radio Button Demo GUI, does the GUI allow the user to click on the *reset* button when the application is launched, or after *reset* has been executed once? For example, is the sequence ⟨*reset, reset, reset*⟩ allowed?

The implicit assumption is that such off-nominal sequences are illegal and should not be allowed by the GUI. Belli et al. [14] argue that these sequences should also be tested in addition to the legal sequences. They augment the *CIS* approach to test the GUI system's robustness by generating such off-nominal test cases. The augmented model is called a *Faulty Complete Interaction Sequence (FCIS)*.

As was the case for the CIS, each FCIS can also be specified by an FSM. This FSM is constructed by the following steps:

1. Build the CIS and the corresponding FSM consisting of all legal sequences of user–system interactions. Each edge of the FSM is called an *Interaction Pair (IP)*.
2. Identify Faulty Interaction Pairs (FIPs) consisting of inputs that are not legal. These are all the "missing" IPs in the original FSM. Note that FIPs and IPs together define a complete FSM called the *Complete Finite State Automata* (CFSA).

Figure 6 shows an FSM of the FCIS corresponding to the CIS in Fig. 5. The solid lines in the graph represent the FIPs and the dotted lines represent the edges in the original CIS's FSM.

Test-case generation for a FCIS is straightforward. The tester can systematically design test cases for various undesired system behaviors by covering all possible FIPs. One way to do this is to select an untested FIP, that is, an edge in the FCIS, generate a

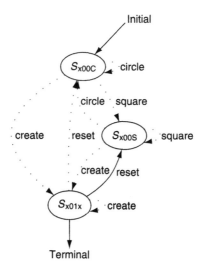

FIG. 6. Faulty complete interaction sequence—dotted edges are transitions in the CIS.

sequence of events from the FSM's start state to the first event in the selected edge, and prepend this sequence to the edge, creating a test case that will test the selected FIP. Once this is done for each FIP, all of them would be tested and covered.

As shown in Fig. 6, there is one FIP in the FSM: $\langle S_{x01x}, S_{x00S} \rangle$. By prefixing this FIP with the state sequence $\langle Initial, S_{x00C}, S_{x01x} \rangle$, we get a complete sequence in the CFSA to examine the illegal behavior: $\langle Initial, S_{x00C}, S_{x01x}, S_{x00S} \rangle$. The sequence can be translated to a test case which is a sequence of events starting at the initial state: $\langle create, reset \rangle$.

3.2 Workflows

Some researchers have used the GUI's business *workflow*, that is, a sequence of connected steps, for test-case generation. A typical GUI workflow is represented by a set of *events* (the steps) and some type of sequencing relationship between the events. In this section, we describe the Event-Flow Graph (EFG) model [26], a seminal work in this category. Then, we present two variants of this model: the Event Interaction Graph (EIG) [12] and the Event Semantic Interaction Graph [5]. Finally, we discuss the Faulty Event Sequence Graph [14], an off-nominal model for the workflow-based approach.

3.2.1 Event-Flow Graph

Intuitively, an EFG represents all possible ESs that may be executed on a GUI [26]. The graph nodes represent events in the GUI and the graph edges represent a sequencing relationship that shows the set of events that may be performed immediately after a given event. The concept of the EFG is similar to that of a control-flow or program-flow graph [27] that captures the flow of all possible executions of program statements, except that an EFG represents the flow of events, not code, in a GUI.

Definition: An EFG for a GUI G is formally defined as a triple $\langle \mathbf{V}, \mathbf{E}, \mathbf{B} \rangle$ where:

1. $\mathbf{V}$ is a set of vertices representing all the events in G. Each $v \in \mathbf{V}$ represents an event in G.

2. $\mathbf{E} \subseteq \mathbf{V} \times \mathbf{V}$ is a set of directed edges between vertices. Event e_j follows e_i (or equivalently $e_j = $ follows (e_i)) iff e_j may be performed immediately after e_i. An edge $(v_x, v_y) \in \mathbf{E}$ iff the event represented by v_y follows the event represented by v_x.

3. $\mathbf{B} \subseteq \mathbf{V}$ is a set of vertices representing *initial events* of G that are available to the user when the GUI is first invoked.

The EFG for the Radio Button Demo application is shown in Fig. 7. The events are shown as oval nodes. The shaded nodes are *initial events*, that is, they are available to the user when the GUI is first launched. The directed edges show the

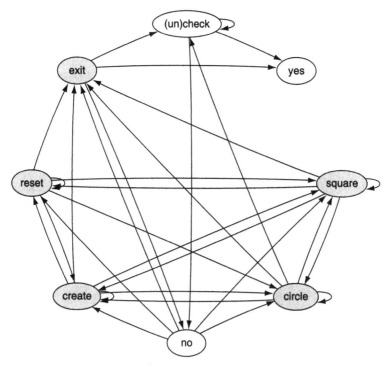

FIG. 7. Event-flow graph.

follows relationship between the events. For example, a user can click on the Yes button in the Exit Confirmation window either immediately after clicking on the Exit button or immediately after clicking on w_6; hence there is an edge from *exit* to *yes*, and from *(un)check* to *yes*. The user cannot click on the Yes button after the No button because *no* closes the dialog; there is no edge from *no* to *yes*. Similarly, there is neither an edge from *no* to *no* nor from *yes* to *yes*.

An approximation of the EFG for a GUI can be automatically obtained by a reverse engineering process called GUI ripping [28]. All events available in the GUI are automatically performed to open the hidden widgets and windows in a depth-first manner. During the GUI ripping process, the key attributes of each widget are captured (e.g., whether it opens a modal/modeless window, it opens a menu, it closes a window). These attributes are then used to automatically construct the EFG. Because such a process is unable to infer complex state-based relationships between the events, for example, one enables/disables the other, a tester has to manually check and edit it to obtain the final EFG.

Because the EFG captures all possible sequences of events that may be executed by a user on the GUI, any path in the EFG is a valid user-executed ES, and hence, a potential test case. Moreover, any graph traversal technique on the EFG can be used to yield test cases. Examples of some techniques that have been used in the past are *goal-directed search* [11], *random walk* [12], and *bounded breadth-first search* [29]. For example, a random walk of the EFG of Fig. 7 may yield the test case ⟨*square, square, circle, square, create, reset, exit, yes*⟩.

3.2.2   Event Interaction Graph

Because the EFG captures all possible ESs that may be executed on the GUI, the number of ESs that may be generated from an EFG becomes extremely large. In fact, the number grows exponentially with sequence length [26,30]. It is important to reduce this number for practical reasons. To address this issue, Xie et al. [29,31] conducted several empirical studies on the characteristics of test cases derived from the EFG model. The experiments showed that a large number of faults were detected by test cases that tested interactions between certain type of events which (1) close a modal window (*termination events*) and (2) interact with the underlying code (*system-interaction events*). Other events used to manipulate the GUI structure such as open or close menu/modeless windows, called *structural events*, are unlikely to reveal faults. One possible explanation for these results was that the code for structural events is usually simple and generated automatically by visual GUI-building tools; therefore, it is less likely to be faulty. Based on these results, a new model called the EIG was developed.

Intuitively, an EIG contains only *termination* and *system-interaction* events; anedge between two nodes in the EIG shows that one event might be executed after (not necessarily immediately after) the other along some execution path. Formally, EIG edges are defined by an `interacts-with` relation through the following definitions:

Definition: There is an *event-flow-path* from node n_x to node n_y iff there exists a (possibly empty) sequence of nodes n_j; n_{j+1}; n_{j+2}; $\ldots$; n_{j+k} in the EFG E such that $\{(n_x, n_j), (n_{j+k}, n_y)\} \subseteq edges(E)$ and $\{(n_{j+i}, n_{j+i+1}) \, for \, 0 \leq i \leq (k-1)\} \subseteq edges(E)$.

Definition: An event-flow-path $\langle n_1; n_2; \ldots; n_k \rangle$ is *interaction-free* iff none of $n_2, \ldots, n_{k-1}$ represents termination or system-interaction events.

Definition: A system-interaction (or termination) event e_x *interacts-with* system-interaction and termination event e_y iff there is at least one interaction-free event-flow-path from the node n_x (that represents e_x) to the node n_y (that represents e_y).

The EIG edges actually represent the above *interacts-with* relationship between the events. An EFG can be automatically transformed into an EIG by using

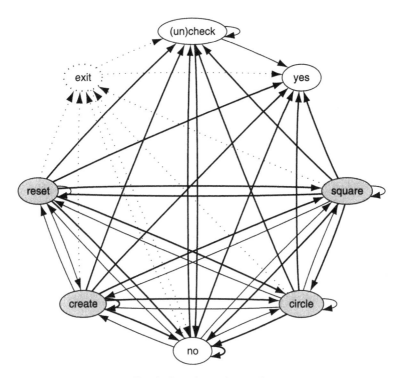

Fɪɢ. 8. Event interaction graph.

graph-rewriting rules (details are presented in Ref. [31]). The EIG for the Radio Button Demo application is shown in Fig. 8. Note that the EIG does not contain the window-opening *exit* event. The graph-rewriting rule used to obtain this EIG was to (1) delete *exit* because it is a window-open event, (2) for all remaining events e_x replace each edge (e_x, *exit*) with edge (e_x, e_y) for each occurrence of edge (*exit*, e_y), and (3) for all e_y, delete all edges (*exit*, e_y).

As was the case with EFGs, a test case in the EIG model is also a path in the EIG, starting with an initial event. One possible test case might be ⟨*square, square, circle, yes*⟩. Because EIG nodes do not represent events to open or close menus/windows, the sequences obtained from the EIG may not be executable. For example, the test case ⟨*square, square, circle, yes*⟩ will not execute because *yes* is not available for execution after *circle*. For this reason, at execution time, other events needed to reach the EIG events are automatically inserted using the original EFG. During test-case execution, the EIG test case above will be expanded to ⟨*square, square, circle, exit, yes*⟩.

3.2.3   Event Semantic Interaction Graph

Although the EIG model is smaller than the EFG, it is still a dense graph and suffers from the same problems as does the EFG—the number of generated ESs grows exponentially with length. In more recent work, Yuan et al. [5] create a sparse graph, where events are connected by edges only if they were shown to influence each other's execution behavior. Consider the Radio Button Demo example. The top-left GUI in Fig. 9 shows the *initial state* (S_0) of the application. After an event *square* is executed, the GUI changes its state to the one shown in the top-right (*square*(S_0)). In this state, the Square radio button is selected. Starting from S_0, one can execute another event (*create*) and obtain the state shown in the bottom-left (*create*(S_0)); a circle is created by clicking the Create button. If, however, the sequence ⟨*square, create*⟩ is executed in S_0, a new state (*create*(*square*(S_0))), shown in the bottom-right is obtained; a square has been created. This execution is equivalent to the execution of event *create* in the state *square* (S_0). The event *square* clearly influences the event *create*. We say that event *square* "interacts with" event *create*, and should be tested together to check for interaction problems.

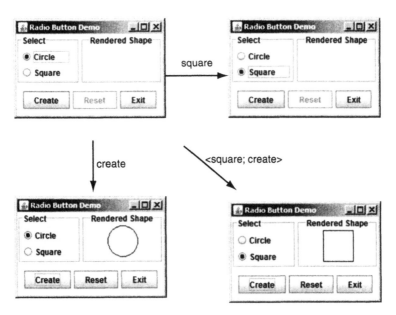

FIG. 9. Event semantic interaction example.

The main idea behind observing GUI run-time states and using them to determine which events to test together can also be justified by examining the code of event handlers. For example, the event handlers for *square* and *create* share two variables `created`, which indicates if a shape is created, and `currentShape`, which specifies the current selected shape; *create* sets `created` to TRUE and influences *square*'s flow of control; *square* sets `currentShape` to a square, which *create* uses as a parameter to create a shape; hence, it is not surprising that they influence each other's execution.

The example illustrated in Fig. 9 is just one case of how the GUI state may be used to pinpoint interactions between event handlers. Yuan et al. formally define six cases that describe (as evaluative predicates) situations in which two events, called e_1 and e_2, interact, that is, e_1 influences e_2. In these six cases, e_1 and e_2 are system-interaction events in modeless windows; this situation is referred as *Context 1*.

Case 1:

$$\mathcal{P}_{1(1)}(e_1, e_2) = \exists w \in W, \ p \in P_w, \ v \in V_p, \ v' \in V_p,$$
$$\text{s.t.}((v \neq v') \wedge ((w, p, v) \in \{S_0 \cap e_1(S_0) \cap e_2(S_0)\}) \wedge ((w, p, v') \in e_2(e_1(S_0))))$$

there is at least one widget w with property p with initial value v (hence the triple (w, p, v) is in S_0), which is not affected by the individual events e_1 or e_2 (the triple is also in $e_1(S_0)$ and $e_2(S_0)$); however, it is modified when the sequence $\langle e_1, e_2 \rangle$ is executed, that is, the value of w's property p changes from v to v'.

Case 2:

$$\mathcal{P}_{2(1)}(e_1, e_2) = \exists w \in W, \ p \in P_w, \ v \in V_p, \ v' \in V_p, \ v'' \in V_p,$$
$$\text{s.t.}((v \neq v') \wedge (v' \neq v'') \wedge ((w, p, v) \in \{S_0 \cap e_2(S_0)\}) \wedge ((w, p, v') \in e_1(S_0))$$
$$\wedge ((w, p, v'') \in e_2(e_1(S_0))))$$

there is at least one widget w with property p that has an initial value v, which is not modified by the event e_2; it is modified by e_1; however, it is modified differently by the sequence $\langle e_1, e_2 \rangle$.

In our running example, widget w_4, in the GUI's initial state, is not modified by event *square*, that is, it remains empty; it is modified by event *create*, that is, a circle is shown; however, w_4 is modified differently by the sequence $\langle create, square \rangle$. Hence, Case 2 applies to *create* and *square*.

Case 3:

$$\mathcal{P}_{3(1)}(e_1, e_2) = \exists w \in W, \ p \in P_w, \ v \in V_p, \ v' \in V_p, \ v'' \in V_p,$$
$$\text{s.t.}((v \neq v') \wedge (v' \neq v'') \wedge ((w, p, v) \in \{S_0 \cap e_1(S_0)\}) \wedge ((w, p, v') \in e_2(S_0))$$
$$\wedge ((w, p, v'') \in e_2(e_1(S_0))))$$

there is at least one widget w with property p that has an initial value υ, which is not modified by the event e_1; it is modified by e_2; however, it is modified differently by the sequence $\langle e_1, e_2 \rangle$. Note that this case is different from Case 2 because the ES remains the same, that is, e_1 is executed before e_2.

In our running example, widget w_4, in the GUI's initial state, is not modified by event *square*, that is, it remains empty; it is modified by event *create*, that is, a circle is shown; however, w_4 is modified differently by the sequence $\langle square, create \rangle$. Hence, Case 3 applies to *square* and *create*.

Case 4:

$$\mathcal{P}_{4(1)}(e_1, e_2) = \exists w \in W, \; p \in P_w, \; v \in V_p, \; v' \in V_p, \; v'' \in V_p, \; \bar{v} \in V_p,$$
$$\text{s.t.}((v \neq v') \wedge (v \neq v'') \wedge (v'' \neq \bar{v}) \wedge ((w,p,v) \in S_0) \wedge ((w,p,v') \in e_1(S_0))$$
$$\wedge ((w,p,v'') \in e_2(S_0)) \wedge ((w,p,\bar{v}) \in e_2(e_1(S_0))));$$

there is at least one widget w with property p that has an initial value υ, which is modified by individual events e_1 and e_2; however, it is modified differently by the sequence $\langle e_1, e_2 \rangle$.

The above four cases handle widgets that persist across the four states being considered, that is, S_0, $e_1(S_0)$, $e_2(S_0)$, and $e_2(e_1(S_0))$. In many cases, event execution "creates" new widgets, for example, by opening menus; the next case handles newly created widgets.

Case 5:

$$P_{5(1)}(e_1, e_2) = \exists w \in W, p \in P_w, v \in V_p, v' \in V_p,$$
$$\text{s.t.}((v \neq v') \wedge ((w,p,v) \in e_x(S_0)) \wedge ((w,p,v) \notin S_0) \wedge ((w,p,v') \in e_2(e_1(S_0))));$$

there is at least one *new* widget w with property p and value υ in $e_x(S_0)$, that is, it was created by event e_x (either e_1 or e_2) but did not exist in state S_0; it was created by the sequence $\langle e_1, e_2 \rangle$ but with a different value for some property.

A common occurrence of event interaction in GUIs is enabling/disabling widgets, which may be modeled as the widget's ENABLED property being set to TRUE or FALSE.

Case 6:

$$\mathcal{P}_{6(1)}(e_1, e_2) = \exists w \in W, \; \text{ENABLED} \in P_w, \; \text{TRUE} \in V_{\text{ENABLED}}, \; \text{FALSE} \in V_{\text{ENABLED}},$$
$$\text{s.t. } (((w, \text{ENABLED}, \text{FALSE}) \in S_0) \wedge ((w, \text{ENABLED}, \text{TRUE}) \in e_1(S_0)) \wedge \text{EXEC}(e_2, w));$$

there exists at least one widget w that was disabled in S_0 but enabled by e_1. Event e_2 is performed on w, represented by a predicate $\text{EXEC}(e_2, w)$.

In our running example, *create* enables *reset*; hence Case 6 applies.

If multiple cases apply, then one of the case numbers is used. Due to the specific ordering of the events in the sequence $\langle e_1, e_2 \rangle$, the ESI relationship is not symmetric. As demonstrated earlier, for our `Radio Button Demo` application: *square* → *create*, *create* → *square*, and *create* → *reset*.

Once all of the cases have been implemented, the feedback-based process execution is straightforward. The steps of the execution are as follows.

1. The seed suite consisting of all two-way interactions $\langle e_x, e_y \rangle$ between GUI events is executed on the software in state S_0; these test cases are simple enumerations of all EIG edges. All events e_y are also executed in S_0. The state information $e_x(S_0)$, $e_y(S_0)$, $e_y(e_x(S_0))$ is collected and stored.
2. The above predicates are evaluated for each pair of system-interaction events in the EIG that are either (1) directly connected by an edge (Context 1) or (2) connected by a path that does not contain any intermediate system-interaction events (contexts 2 and 3), that is, there is at least one termination event that closes a modal window on this path. If one of the predicates evaluates to TRUE, the two events are ESI-related.

Once all the ESIs in a GUI have been identified, a graph model called the ESI graph (ESIG) is created. The ESIG contains nodes that represent events; a directed edge from node n_x to n_y shows that there is an ESI relationship from the event represented by n_x to the event represented by n_y. Figure 10 shows the ESIG of the Radio Button Demo GUI. The solid lines are ESIG edges; for comparison, we also show the EFG edges (dotted lines) and EIG edges (dashed lines).

As was the case for EFGs and EIGs, the ESIG may be traversed using different graph traversal algorithms to generate test cases. For our example ESIG in Fig. 10, two test cases are $\langle create, reset \rangle$ and $\langle square, create, square, create, reset \rangle$.

3.2.4 Off-Nominal Event Graph

Belli et al. develop a technique to generate off-nominal test cases using the GUI's workflow [14]. They define the workflow as an Event Sequence Graph (ESG).

Definition: An *ESG* = (V, E) is a directed graph where $V \neq \emptyset$ is a finite set of vertices (nodes), $E \subseteq V \times V$ is a finite set of arcs (edges), and $\Xi, \Gamma \subseteq V$ are finite sets of distinguished vertices with $\xi \in \Xi$ and $\gamma \in \Gamma$ called entry nodes and exit nodes, respectively, wherein $\forall \upsilon \in V$ there is at least one sequence of vertices $< \xi, \upsilon_0, \ldots, \upsilon_k >$ from each $\xi \in \Xi$ to $\upsilon_k = \upsilon$ and one sequence of vertices $\langle \upsilon_0, \ldots, \upsilon_k \rangle$ from $\upsilon_0 = \upsilon$ to each $\gamma \in \Gamma$ with $(\upsilon_i, \upsilon_{i+1}) \in E$, for $i = 0, \ldots, k-1$ and $\upsilon \neq \xi, \gamma$.

Intuitively, the ESG is similar to the EFG, except that there is a notion of exit nodes in an ESG. Such a workflow allows the definition of an ES.

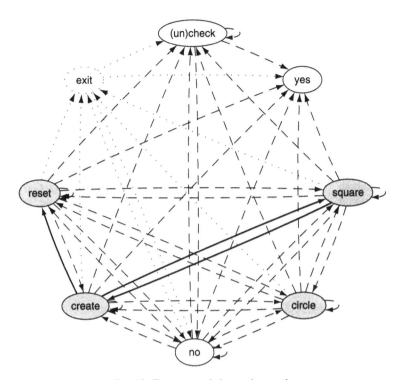

Fɪɢ. 10. Event semantic interaction graph.

Definition: Let V and E be as defined above. Then any sequence of vertices $\langle v_0, \ldots, v_k \rangle$ is called an ES if $(v_i, v_{i+1}) \in E$, for $i = 0, \ldots, k$.

This definition is used to define a complete event sequence (CES) in the ESG.

Definition: An ES is a complete ES (or, it is called a CES), if $\alpha(\text{ES}) = \xi \in \Xi \hat{A} A$ is an entry and $\beta(\text{ES}) = \gamma \in \Gamma$ is an exit.

where α and β are manually defined functions used to determine the entry and exit vertex of an ES.

These above definitions allow the formal definition of an off-nominal test case (or faulty event sequence, FES) based on the ESG.

Definition: For an ESG $= (V, E)$, its completion is defined as $\widehat{\text{ESG}} = (V, \hat{E})$ with $\hat{E} = V \times V$.

Definition: The inverse (or complementary) ESG is then defined as $\overline{\text{ESG}} = (V, \bar{E})$ with $\bar{E} = \hat{E} \setminus E$.

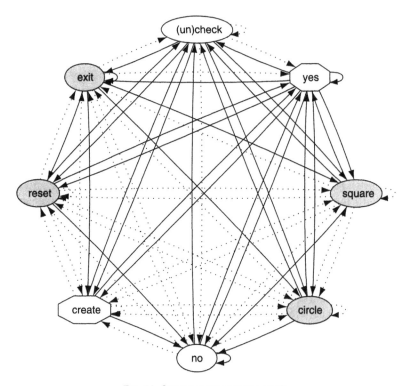

Fɪɢ. 11. Inverse event sequence graph.

Figure 11 shows the inverse ESG of the Radio Button Demo GUI. The dotted edges are ESG (EFG) edges. The oval shaded nodes represent initial events while the octagon nodes represent exit events.

The solid edges in Fig. 11 are the ones that are absent from the ESG. More formally, they represent *faulty event pairs* (FEPs).

Definition: Any edge of the $\overline{\text{ESG}}$ is a FEP for the ESG.

Definition: Let $ES = v_0, \ldots, v_k$ be an ES of length $k + 1$ of an ESG and $FEP = \langle v_k, v_m \rangle$ a FEP of the corresponding *ESG*. The concatenation of the ES and FEP then forms a FES $= \langle v_0, \ldots, v_k, v_m \rangle$.

Such an FES can be used as an off-nominal test case. An example of such a test case for our running example is $\langle square, circle, reset, no \rangle$. The pair (*reset, no*) should not be executable because of the Exit Confirmation modal dialog.

3.3   Pre- and Postcondition Models

In an approach presented by Memon et al. [26], the test designer models the GUI in terms of pre- and postconditions for each event. The test designer then identifies commonly used tasks for the GUI; these are then input to the test-case generator. The generator employs the pre- and postconditions and specifications to generate ESs to achieve the tasks.

The motivating idea behind this approach is that GUI test designers will often find it easier to specify typical user goals than to specify sequences of GUI events that users might perform to achieve those goals. The software underlying any GUI is designed with certain intended uses in mind; thus the test designer can describe those intended uses. However, it is difficult to manually obtain different ways in which a user might interact with the GUI to achieve typical goals. Users may interact in idiosyncratic ways, which the test designer might not anticipate. Additionally, there can be a large number of ways to achieve any given goal, and it would be very tedious for the GUI tester to specify even those ESs that s/he can anticipate. The test-case generator described in this section uses AI planning to generate GUI test cases for commonly used tasks using a GUI model based on pre- and postconditions of all GUI events.

The test-case generation process is partitioned into two phases, the *setup* phase and *plan-generation* phase. In the first step of the setup phase, the GUI is used to identify planning operators, which are used by the planner to generate test cases. By using knowledge of the GUI, the test designer defines the pre- and postconditions of these operators. During the second or plan-generation phase, the test designer describes scenarios (tasks) by defining a set of initial and goal states for test-case generation. Finally, the AI planning system generates a test suite for the tasks using the plans. The test designer can iterate through the plan-generation phase any number of times, defining more scenarios and generating more test cases.

Formally, a planning problem $P(\Lambda, D, I, G)$ is a 4-tuple, where Λ is the set of operators; D is a finite set of objects, I is the initial state, and G is the goal state. Note that an operator definition may contain variables as parameters; typically an operator does not correspond to a single executable action but rather to a family of actions, one for each different instantiation of the variables. The solution to a planning problem is a plan: a tuple $\langle S, O, L, B \rangle$ where S is a set of plan steps (instances of operators, typically defined with sets of preconditions and effects), O is a set of ordering constraints on the elements of S, L is a set of causal links representing the causal structure of the plan, and B is a set of binding constraints on the variables of the operator instances in S. Each ordering constraint is of the form $S_i < S_j$ (read as ''S_i before S_j'') meaning that step S_i must occur sometime before step S_j (but not necessarily immediately before). Typically, the ordering constraints

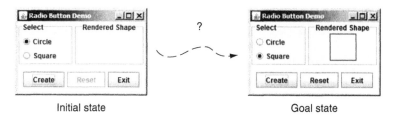

Fɪɢ. 12. A task specification.

induce only a partial ordering on the steps in S. Causal links are triples $< S_i, c, S_j >$, where S_i and S_j are elements of S and c represents a proposition that is the unification of an effect of S_i and a precondition of S_j. Note that corresponding to this causal link is an ordering constraint, that is, $S_i < S_j$. The reason for tracking a causal link $< S_i, c, S_j >$ is to ensure that no step "threatens" a required link, that is, no step S_k that results in c can temporally intervene between steps S_i and S_j.

For the Radio Button Demo application, one possible *task* may be to create a square shape for w_4. This task is shown in Fig. 12. Even with this simple application, there are several ways to perform this task. In fact, there are an infinite number of ways—in principle, a user can click on the Square radio button an arbitrary number of times. This task is input to the planner by describing the state of all the widgets in the initial and goal states.

Together with a specification of all pre- and postconditions of the events, the task is used by the planner to output the plan shown in Fig. 13(A). As mentioned above, most AI planners produce *partially ordered* plans, in which only some steps are ordered with respect to one another. The plan in Fig. 13(A) is one such plan. The ordering constraints are shown as edges and also explicitly stated in Fig. 13(B).

A total-order plan can be derived from a partial-order plan by adding ordering constraints, induced by removing threats. Each total-order plan obtained in such a way is called a linearization of the partial-order plan. A partial-order plan is a solution to a planning problem if and only if every consistent linearization of the partial-order plan meets the solution conditions. Figure 13(C) shows the two linearizations of the plan; each of these linearizations can be used as a test case.

3.4 ES-Based Models

Because GUI test cases are sequences of events, Kasik et al. [32] manipulate such sequences of events to obtain new test cases. Their approach is based on genetic algorithms.

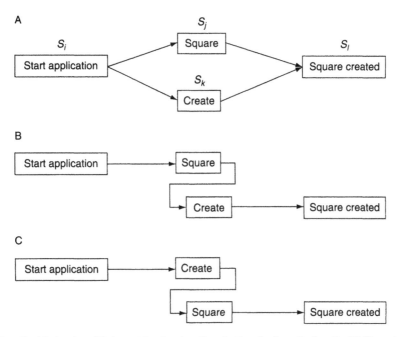

FIG. 13. AI planning. (A) A partial-order plan. $S_i < S_j$; $S_i < S_k$; $S_k < S_l$; $S_j < S_l$. (B) The ordering constraints in the plan. (C) The two linearization.

The key motivation behind using genetic algorithms is that there is a need to test the GUI from the perspective of different groups of users, for example, experts and novice users. Unsophisticated and novice users often exercise GUI applications in ways that the designer, the developer, and the tester did not anticipate. An expert user or tester usually follows a predictable path through an application to accomplish a familiar task. The developer knows where to probe, to find the potentially problematic parts of an application. Consequently, applications are well tested for state transitions that work well for predicted usage patterns but become unstable when given to novice users. Novice users follow unexpected paths in the application, causing program failures. Such failures are difficult to predict at design and testing time.

One approach to test the GUI for novice interactions is to release the software to a small community for beta testing. However, this approach is expensive and time-consuming. Kasik et al.'s approach generates test cases that mimic a novice user. The key idea behind this approach is that expert users take short paths through an application's GUI, using shortcuts when available and perform their tasks quickly. Novice users, on the other hand, take longer, exploratory paths to complete a task and gradually build better ways as they learn more about the application. It is challenging to automatically generate these paths for GUI testing.

In its simplest form, a genetic algorithm manipulates a table of random numbers; each row of the table represents a gene. The individual elements of a row (gene) contain a numeric genetic code and are called *alleles*. Allele values start as numbers that define the initial genetic code. The genetic algorithm lets genes that contain "better" alleles survive to compete against new genes in subsequent generations.

The basic genetic algorithm is as follows:

- Initialize the alleles with valid numbers.
- Repeat the following until the desired goal is reached:
  - Generate a *score* for each gene in the table.
  - Reward the genes that produce the best results by replicating them and allowing them to live in a new generation. All others are discarded using a *death rate*.
  - Apply two operators, mutation and crossover, to create new genes.

For GUIs testing, the ES is represented by a gene, each element being an event. The primary task of setting up the genetic algorithm is to set the death rates, crossover styles, and mutation rates so that novice behavior is generated. Also, to use genetic algorithms to generate meaningful interactions mimicking novice users, a clear and accurate specification of both the user interface dialog and the program state information is needed. The state information controls the legality of specific dialog components and the names of a legal command during an interaction. Without access to the state information, the generator may produce many meaningless input events.

For our running example, the Radio Button Demo GUI, an expert might use ⟨*square*, *create*⟩ to create a square. The genetic algorithm may convert this sequence into the longer sequence ⟨*circle, create, square, create*⟩, thereby mimicking a novice user.

3.5 Probabilistic Models

As seen in this chapter, there are several techniques to generate GUI test cases based on a model of the GUI. In practice, a GUI test designer may use a mix of these techniques to obtain several test suites. The test designer is faced with two significant challenges:

- *Overlaps in test suites:* As can be imagined, many of these techniques often overlap in what they test. A test designer who uses two or more GUI testing techniques may waste valuable resources testing and retesting the same parts of the GUI. Ideally, the test designer would like to consolidate all the test suites and obtain one suite that minimizes overlaps.

- *Large number of short tests and few long tests:* The sheer size of the individual suites presents practical problems for test execution. Because each test case requires significant overhead in terms of *setup* and *teardown*, having a large number of short tests is inefficient. Ideally, the test designer would like to obtain longer sequences that combine the strengths of individual short-sequence suites.

Consider for example, the three test suites shown in Fig. 14, each generated using a different technique. It may be expensive to execute and maintain all these test cases. Brooks et al. [33] employ a probabilistic model of the GUI to combine these suites.

The probabilistic model is based on the EFG model. The model contains a collection of R paths through the EFG called $r_1, r_2, \ldots, r_R$. Each path r_i where $1 \le i \le R$, consists of a sequence of n events in addition to *INIT* and *FINAL*:

$$r_i = INIT, x_1, x_2, \ldots, x_n, FINAL;$$
$$\forall_j e_j \in \{e_1, e_2, \ldots, e_{n-1}\} \wedge$$
$$follows(e_{j+1}, e_j)$$

where $x_1, x_2, \ldots, x_n$ and $e_1, e_2, \ldots, e_{n-1}$ are events in the EFG, r_i denotes a path, and each path r_i contains only events with a *follows* relationship between them. Valid paths can also be formed by the concatenation of two paths, for example, r_a and r_b, provided the first event of r_b *follows* the last event of r_a in the EFG.

Let count(e_i) return the number of times event e_i occurs in the paths $r_1, r_2, \ldots, r_R$. The prior probability that a randomly selected event from any of $r_1, r_2, \ldots, r_R$ is e_i is:

$$P(e_i) = \frac{\text{count}(e_i)}{\Sigma_{j=1}^{E} \text{count}(e_j)}.$$

Now, count(e_i) and the prior probability calculation are extended from single events to sequences of events. Let s be a length-S subsequence of some path through the EFG (not necessarily in $r_1, r_2, \ldots, r_R$):

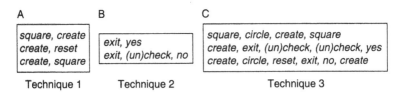

A	B	C
square, create create, reset create, square	exit, yes exit, (un)check, no	square, circle, create, square create, exit, (un)check, (un)check, yes create, circle, reset, exit, no, create
Technique 1	Technique 2	Technique 3

FIG. 14. Example test cases.

$$s_i = x_1, x_2, \ldots, x_s$$
$$\forall_j e_j \in \{INIT, e_1, e_2, \ldots, e_{n-1}, FINAL\} \wedge$$
$$follows(e_{j+1}, e_j).$$

The prior probability that a randomly selected, length-S subsequence from any of $r_1, r_2, \ldots, r_R$ turns out to be s is

$$P(s) = \frac{\text{count}(s)}{\Sigma_{s_i \in \text{subs}(S)} \text{count}(s_i)},$$

where count(s) returns the number of times s occurs as a subsequence of $r_1, r_2, \ldots, r_R$ and subs(S) is the set of all length-S subsequences in $r_1, r_2, \ldots, r_R$.

Given that s immediately precedes e_i, the conditional probability of e_i is

$$P(e_i|s) = \frac{P(s_1, s_2, \ldots, s_S, e_i)}{\Sigma_{j=1}^{E} P(s_1, s_2, \ldots, s_S, e_j)}.$$

Note that $P(e_i|s)$ can be thought of as $P(e_i)$ when s has length 0. This is not the same as $P(e_i|INIT)$, which is the probability that event e_i is the first event in the sequence, occurring immediately after $INIT$. Rather, $P(e_i|s)$ is the probability of e_i given *no information* about the events that precede it.

A *probabilistic EFG* (PEFG) is created by annotating each event (node) in the EFG with a table containing the event's prior probability and its probability conditioned on each subsequence in $\{r_1, r_2, \ldots, r_R\}$ up to some maximum subsequence length, or history, H.

Figure 15 shows the PEFG obtained for the test suites of Fig. 14. Column 2 of each table associated with every node shows the probability of executing the event associated with the node after the length 2 sequence shown in Column 1 of the table. For example, the entry for node (*un*)*check* corresponding to row *exit, (un)check* is 0.5. This is because the subsequence *exit, (un)check* appears twice in the original test suites. Once *exit, (un)check* has been executed, there is a 0.5 probability that the next event will be (*un*)*check*. These probabilities can be used to generate ESs. One example sequence is ⟨*INIT, exit, (un)check, FINAL*⟩. The resulting test case is ⟨*exit, (un)check*⟩.

3.6 Combinatorial Interaction Models

Software system faults are not only caused by individual components working in isolation but also caused by the interactions between them [34,35]. In its basic form, GUI interaction testing consists of testing for interactions between all GUI

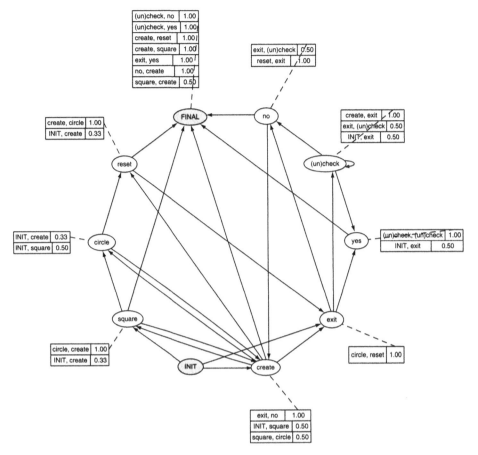

FIG. 15. Probabilistic event-flow graph with history $H = 2$.

components and their selections. However, since the number of GUI components is often huge, the number of tests required to cover the combinational interactions grows large very quickly [5]. Several combinational interaction models have been proposed to model GUI component interactions and reduce the number of test cases. This section presents two combinatorial models used for test-case generation—a *Latin square* to cover *pair-wise* interactions [30] and a *Covering Array* to cover *multiway* interactions with an arbitrary coverage strength [15].

3.6.1 Latin Squares

White [30] proposes the use of Latin squares to model the GUI inputs and generate test cases. He identifies two ways in which GUI interactions can arise: statically and dynamically (or a combination of both). Static interactions are restricted to one screen whereas dynamic interactions move from one screen to another to perform events on GUI objects. White makes the assumption that it is enough to test pair-wise interactions of GUI events. Similar assumptions have led to success in finding errors efficiently for conventional software [36].

The concept of Latin square is used to maintain the pair-wise interaction coverage while keeping the number of test cases minimized.

Definition: A *Latin square*, of order n, is a matrix of n symbols in an $n \times n$ cells, arranged in n rows and n columns, such that every symbol exactly once in each row and once in each column.

Definition: A pair of Latin squares $A = (a_{ij})$ and $B = (b_{ij})$ are *orthogonal* iff the ordered pairs (a_{ij}, b_{ij}) are distinct for all i and j. In other words, when superimposed on each other, the ordered elements pairs of two orthogonal squares created in each cell cover all n^2 pairs.

Given k factors $F_1, F_2, \ldots, F_k$, where each factor is a GUI component from which selections are made. The GUI inputs are modeled as follow:

- Reorder k factors by cardinality: $|F_1| \geq |F_2| \geq \ldots \geq |F_k|$.
- Construct $k-2$ orthogonal Latin squares with size n, where n is the cardinality of $|F_1|$.

To test k GUI components with maximum n level, we need $k-2$ orthogonal Latin squares. The cell entries of the superimposed square represent $k-2$ components in the test and the row and column indices represent the additional two components. Since the generated triples (*row index, column index, cell entry*) are unique, the pair-wise coverage requirement is guaranteed.

The original model proposed by White only considered menu items. Because our running example does not have menus, we cannot use this approach to test our example GUI.

3.6.2 Covering Arrays

Yuan et al. [15] use *covering arrays* [26] to generate test cases. The key motivation behind using covering arrays is to generate longer sequences that are systematically sampled at a particular coverage strength. This approach is a generalization of the Latin square discussed in the previous section; a fundamental difference is that in covering arrays, the coverage strength is not limited to two-way interactions. Furthermore, the use of covering arrays allows fine control over the location of each event in the test case.

Definition: A *covering array CA(N; t, k, υ)* is an $N \times k$ array on $υ$ symbols with the property that every $N \times t$ subarray contains all ordered subsets of size t of the $υ$ symbols *at least* once. In other words, any subset of t-columns of this array will contain all t-combinations of the symbols.

Constructing a covering array with a minimal number of rows is an optimization problem. There are both mathematical algorithms [37] as well as computational techniques such as greedy [35] and meta-heuristic search [36] for this problem.

This test-case generation technique leverages covering arrays to keep the number of test cases minimized while maintaining a required t-way coverage is between GUI events. A GUI is taken as input and first partitioned into different parts. Then, for each GUI part, a covering array is constructed to cover all events inside it. The output of this process is a set of covering arrays for all GUI partitions. Each array row becomes a GUI test case.

For our example `Radio Button Demo` application, we first partition the events into different groups. For example, the three events *(un)check*, *yes*, and *no* in the `Exit Confirmation` window can form the "Exit" group. Suppose we are interested in two-way coverage (i.e., test all possible two-way interactions shown in Fig. 16(A)) such that each event occupies all four positions in a length 4 sequence. If we used exhaustive enumeration, we need $3 \times 3 \times 3 \times 3 = 81$ test cases. Formulating the problem as a covering arrays *CA(N; 2, 4, 3)*, Fig. 16(B), the number of rows is only nine, each of which becomes a test case.

A

| 1. ⟨yes, yes⟩ |
| 2. ⟨yes, no⟩ |
| 3. ⟨yes, (un)check⟩ |
| 4. ⟨no, no⟩ |
| 5. ⟨no, (un)check⟩ |
| 6. ⟨no, yes⟩ |
| 7. ⟨(un)check, (un)check⟩ |
| 8. ⟨(un)check, yes⟩ |
| 9. ⟨(un)check, no⟩ |

B

yes	yes	yes	yes
yes	(un)check	(un)check	no
yes	no	no	(un)check
no	yes	(un)check	(un)check
no	(un)check	no	yes
no	no	yes	no
(un)check	yes	no	no
(un)check	(un)check	yes	(un)check
(un)check	no	(un)check	yes

FIG. 16. Two-way covering and covering array. (A) 2 way covering. (B) Covering array: CA(9; 2, 4, 3).

3.7   Hierarchical Models

All of the testing techniques discussed thus far use a single model of the GUI. However, using only one model may be impractical for a large GUI. Several researchers have addressed this problem by modeling the GUI at multiple levels of abstraction. The GUI is broken down into different components and modeled hierarchically. We now discuss three such hierarchies, namely Keyword-driven hierarchy [38], Hierarchical finite state machines (HFSM) [39], and UML diagram-based hierarchy [40].

3.7.1   Keyword-Driven Models

Keyword-driven testing [41] is a script-based testing technique widely used in Industry. This technique divides the test-case generation process into two phases: test plan and test implementation. In the test plan phase, the test designers design test cases using high-level activities called *action words*. In the test implementation phase, the test engineers transform the action words into executable events called *keywords*. To avoid ambiguities, the selected keywords are unique.

The idea behind using abstract test cases, that is, those that contain high-level action words, is that domain experts, without any implementation skills, can easily design test cases using only the action words. This step can be done early, even before the system implementation has been started. The abstract test cases are also easier to comprehend; test maintenance is also more efficient.

Inspired by the keyword-driven testing technique, Antti et al. [38] propose a GUI testing model using Label Transition Systems (LTS). A LTS is a state machine whose transition names are taken from an alphabet. Formally, a LTS is defined as:

Definition: A LTS is a quadruple $(S, \Sigma, \Delta, \hat{s})$ where S is a set of states, Σ is a set of actions (alphabet), $\Delta \subseteq S \times \Sigma \times S$ is a set of transitions, and $\hat{s} \in S$ is an initial state.

A GUI is modeled using two sets of LTSs corresponding to the two levels of abstraction in the keyword-driven approach. The LTSs for the action word level are called *action machines* and the LTSs for the keyword level are called *refinement machines*. The action machines provide an overview of the system while each refinement machine describes GUI navigation for certain parts of the GUI.

Figure 17(A) presents an action machine $\mathcal{A}$ for the `Radio Button Demo` application GUI. The labels in this machine represent the action words. Figure 17(B) is a refinement machine for the main window. The labels in this machine are keywords describing the actual GUI events.

These machines are automatically composed of an executable LTS by a parallel composition operator defined as follows.

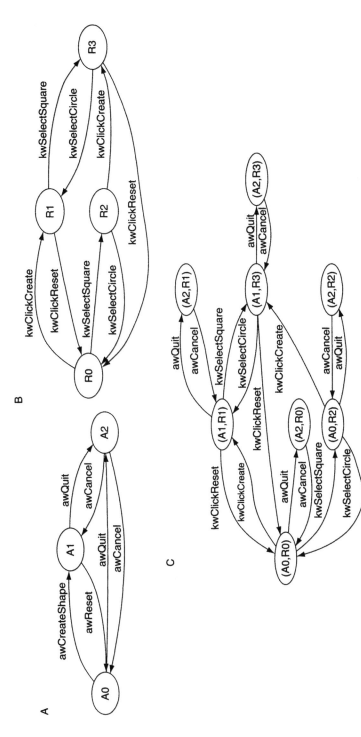

FIG. 17. Label transition systems. (A) Action machine $\mathcal{A}$. (B) Refinement machine $\mathcal{R}$. (C) Parallel composition $\mathcal{C}$.

Definition: $\|_R(\mathcal{L}_1, \ldots, \mathcal{L}_n)$ is the *parallel composition* of n LTSs according to rules R where LTS $\mathcal{L}_i = (S_i\Sigma_i, \Delta_i, \hat{s}_i)$ if let Σ_R be a set of resulting actions and $\lor$ be a "pass" symbol such that $\forall i : \lor \notin \Sigma_i$. The rule set $R \subseteq (\Sigma_1 \cup \{\lor\}) \times \cdots \times (\Sigma_n \cup \{\lor\}) \times \Sigma_R$. Now $\|_R(\mathcal{L}_1, \ldots, \mathcal{L}_n) = (S, \Sigma, \Delta, \hat{s})$ where:

- $S = (S_1 \times \cdots \times S)n$
- $\Sigma = \{a \in \Sigma_R \mid \exists a_1, \ldots, a_n : (a_1, \ldots, a_n, a) \in R\}$
- $((s_1, \ldots, s_n), a, (s_i', \ldots, s_n')) \in \Delta$ if and only if there is $(a_1, \ldots, a_n, a) \in R$ such that for every i $(1 < i < n)$
  - $(s_i, a_i, s_i' \in \Delta$ or
  - $a_i = \lor$ and $s_i = s_i'$
- $\hat{s} = \langle \hat{s}_1, \ldots, \hat{s}_n \rangle$

A rule in a parallel composition associates an array of actions (or "pass" symbol $\lor$) of input LTSs to an action in the resulting LTS. The action is the result of the synchronous execution of the actions in the array. If there is a $\lor$ instead of an action, the corresponding LTS will not participate in the synchronous execution described by the rule.

Let us assume that the following composition rules are given:

$$R = \{(1) \ \langle awCreateShape, kwClickCreate, kwClickCreate \rangle$$
$$(2) \ \langle awCreateShape, kwSelectCircle, kwClickCircle \rangle$$
$$(3) \ \langle awCreateShape, kwSelectSquare, kwClickSquare \rangle$$
$$(4) \ \langle awReset, kwClickReset, kwClickReset \rangle$$
$$(5) \ \langle awCancel, \lor, awCancel \rangle$$
$$(6) \ \langle awQuit, \lor, awQuit \rangle \}$$

Figure 17(C) shows the composition machine $\mathcal{C}$ synthesized using the above rules. As we can see, the states in $\mathcal{C}$ are a combination (product) of $\mathcal{A}$'s states and $\mathcal{R}$'s states. By applying rules (1)–(4), two action words *awCreateShape* and *awReset* are refined to the corresponding keywords in $\mathcal{C}$. However, the action words *awCancel* and *awQuit* still remain unchanged. The rules (5) and (6) only copy them from $\mathcal{A}$ to $\mathcal{C}$. To refine these action words, we need other refinement machines and composition rules.

After the composition machine is created, the test-case generation is straightforward. Each path in the composition machine will become a GUI test case, which is a sequence of keywords. For our example, one possible test case might be $\langle kwClickCreate, kwSelectSquare, kwSelectCircle, kwClickReset \rangle$ which translates to $\langle create, square, circle, reset \rangle$.

3.7.2 Hierarchical Finite State Machines

Paiva et al. [39] use the hierarchy of GUI dialogs to create a hierarchical state-machine model for testing. In particular, the GUI is modeled as a hierarchy of FSMs whose vertices can either represent single states or groups of states in the original FSM. The model consisting of these FSMs is called a HFSM.

The hierarchy is based on GUI dialogs. Consider a GUI represented by k dialogs $D_1, D_2, \ldots, D_k$ which manipulate a set of variable V: $V = \{v_1, \ldots, v_{|V|}\}$. From the complete FSM of the application, the tester manually specifies the state machine F_i for each dialog D_i. Given the FSM_{Di} for a dialog D_i, it is possible to deduce the variables manipulated that dialog. A variable v_i is *written* by (or is affected by) a dialog D if there is a transition in FSM_D that changes the value of v_i. A variable v_i is *read* by (or influences the behavior of) a dialog D if at least one of the following conditions holds:

1. there are two transitions T and T' in FSM_D and a variable v_k in V (not necessarily $i \neq k$) such that (i) the source states of T and T' are different only in the value of v_i, (ii) T and T' have the same triggering action (name and arguments), (iii) the destination states of T and T' have different values of v_k, and (iv) at least one of the transitions (say T) changes the value of v_k,
2. there are two states S and S' and a transition T with source S in FSM_D such that (i) S and S' are different only in the value of v_i, (ii) there is no transition T' with source S' and the same action as T.

Let $PFSM_{Di}$ be the projection of FSM_{Di} onto the variables manipulated by dialog D_i then we can use $PFSM_{Di}$ to describe the internal behaviors of D_i. Also from $PFSM_{Di}$, it is possible to reconstruct FSM_{Di} by taking the union of the instances of $PFSM_{Di}$ for all possible combinations of variable values that are not manipulated by it.

Using the notation of PFSMs, the original state machine can be organized into a three-level HFSM:

1. The *top level* is an abstract FSM representing the relationships between independent dialogs.
2. The *intermediate level* is a set of projected FSMs representing internal behaviors for each dialog.
3. The *bottom level* is a complete FSM representing the behaviors of the entire GUI.

Considering the `Radio Button Demo` application, and its GUI states represented by a length 4 vector {*log, exitWinOpen, created, shape*} as done in Section 3.1.1, a tester may specify a sub-FSM for the main window (dialog D_{Main}) to include all states where *exitWinOpen* is set to 0 and the transitions between them. The other states make up the sub-FSM for the `Exit Confirmation` window (dialog D_{Exit}). Figure 18(C) shows the complete FSM (*bottom level*) for the application. The states are organized into two regions (enclosed by dashed lines) corresponding to two sub-FSMs. Note that the same full FSM was previously shown in Section 3.1.1, except that its layout has changed.

We can infer that *created* and *shape* are two variables manipulated by D_{Main} while *log* is the only variable manipulated by D_{Exit}. Neither D_{Main} nor D_{Exit} manipulates

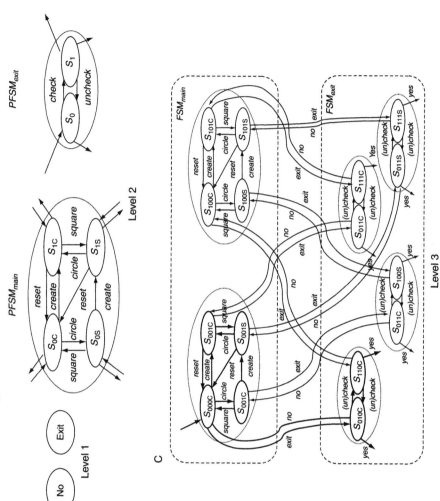

Fig. 18. Hierarchical finite state machine (self-loops are omitted to increase the readability).

exitWinOpen. Using this analysis, the *top level* and *the intermediate level* of the HFSM can be constructed as shown in Fig. 18(A) and (B).

Two dialogs are *independent* if the set of variables written by one dialog is disjoint from the set of variables manipulated (read or written) by the other. In this case, instead of testing the complete FSM, we need to consider only their PFSMs individually. In other words, those dialogs do not need to be tested every time if there is a change on variables that they do not depend on. To test a dialog D, the variables not manipulated by D are fixed to a particular value and the test cases are generated using the PFSM of D.

Applying this strategy to test the `Radio Button Demo`'s GUI, we first realize that D_{Main} and D_{Exit} are two independent dialogs. So we can test D_{Main} by fixing $log = 0$ (*exitWinOpen* is already fixed) and generate test case in the $PFSM_{Main}$. Similarly, to test D_{Exit} we fix $created = 0$ and $shape = C$. Two transiting actions *exit* and *no* also need to be tested once by fixing $created = 0$, $shape = C$, and $log = 0$. Instead of testing all possible paths of the FSM in Fig. 18(C), we now only need to examine those in bold.

3.7.3   UML Diagram-based

As seen in previous sections, using formal models to represent GUIs makes it possible to systematically generate and analyze test cases. However, these models are often not intuitive, causing difficulties for test designers who are not familiar with formal Computer Science concepts. Paiva et al. [40] builds another visual layer on top of formal models to assist testers. The GUI is modeled using familiar UML notations and then automatically translated to the underlying formal model by tools. More specifically, the formal model is a set of FSMs which are encoded in a specification language called Spec# (an extension of the C# programming language) [42].

The GUI behaviors are specified by four UML diagrams: *use case diagrams*, *activity diagrams*, *class diagrams*, and *state machine diagrams*. These diagrams are enriched with additional stereotypes to enable automatic transformation from the visual forms to Spec# code.

Use case diagrams provide an overview of the main functionalities and features of the GUI application. They describe the scenarios in which the GUI is used. The use case diagrams are used to support other UML diagrams. However, there is no formal Spec# code directly generated from these diagrams. Figure 19 shows a use case diagram one might design for the `Radio Button Demo` example. The diagram consists of three main use case *Edit shape*, *Reset*, and *Exit* corresponding to three main scenarios the user may interact with the GUI.

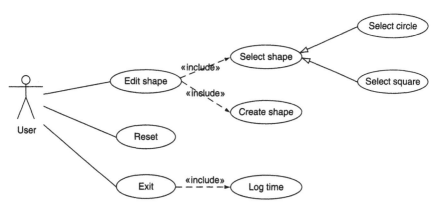

Fɪɢ. 19. Use case diagram.

Activity diagrams describe the business logic of use cases. The conditions and steps in the diagrams are directly encoded in Spec# syntax. Besides the user steps, they may have parameters that correspond to user inputs, pre/postconditions (describing use case intent), and assertions. *Class diagrams* describe the static structure of the GUI. Each top-level window is modeled as an object. The state variables are represented by class variables, while the interactive controls are represented by class methods. *State machine diagrams* describe the dynamic reactive behaviors of the GUI. The diagrams show GUI states at different levels of abstraction, the user actions available at each state, their effects on the GUI states, and the sequences of user actions. Each state of the state machine can be formalized by a Boolean condition on the state variables. Each transition has a triggering event that is the call of a method representing a user action. The transitions may additionally have pre- and postconditions on state variables and method parameters. A set of rules is developed to translate the state machine diagrams into the Spec# code. After the formal specifications (e.g., Spec# code) are generated for all UML diagrams, an analyzer tool (e.g., Spec Explorer) is used to analyze the formal models and generate test cases for each diagram accordingly.

4. Conclusions

GUIs are by far the most popular means used to interact with software today. Unfortunately, the state-of-the-practice in GUI testing has not kept pace with the rapidly evolving GUI technology. In practice, GUI testing is largely manual, often resulting in inadequate testing. There have been several research efforts to improve GUI testing. This chapter presented some of the recent advances in automated model-based GUI testing. It also provided the first detailed taxonomy of these techniques. A small GUI application was used as a running example to demonstrate each technique.

In its very fundamental form, the goal of GUI testing is to determine whether the GUI executes as expected, as documented in the specifications, or as required by the intended user. This definition is very broad and may encompass factors such as testing the GUI's usability, correctness, and performance. Since GUI testing is a multifaceted problem, no one technique can be used for GUI testing; in fact, in practice, a collection of techniques are almost always used.

Finally, the GUI interaction testing problem can be viewed as a search problem with the state space of the GUI being the search space and the objective of the search to find errors. Since the number of events that a user may perform on the GUI at any given time is very large, the search space is extremely large (even infinite in most cases). Exhaustively traversing the search space is impractical in such cases. The field of GUI testing remains ripe for the application of upcoming areas of research, such as search-based software engineering.

ACKNOWLEDGMENTS

This work was partially supported by the US National Science Foundation under NSF grants CNS-0855055, CCF-0447864 and the office of Naval Research grant N00014-05-1-0421.

REFERENCES

[1] B.A. Myers, User interface software tools, ACM Trans. Comput. Hum. Interact. 2 (1) (1995) 64–103.

[2] M. Grechanik, D.S. Batory, D.E. Perry, Integrating and reusing GUI-driven applications, in: ICSR-7: Proceedings of the 7th International Conference on Software Reuse, Springer-Verlag, London, UK, 2002, pp. 1–16.

[3] B. Shneiderman, C. Plaisant, M. Cohen, S. Jacobs, Designing the User Interface: Strategies for Effective Human–Computer Interaction, Addison-Wesley, Boston, MA, 2009.

[4] M.B. Dwyer, V. Carr, L. Hines, Model checking graphical user interfaces using abstractions, in: ESEC '97/FSE-5: Proceedings of the 6th European SOFTWARE ENGINEERING Conference held Jointly with the 5th ACM SIGSOFT International Symposium on Foundations of Software Engineering, Springer-Verlag New York, New York, NY, 1997, pp. 244–261.

[5] X. Yuan, A.M. Memon, Generating event sequence-based test cases using GUI runtime state feedback, IEEE Trans. Softw. Eng. 36 (2009) 81–95.

[6] J. Chen, Formal modelling of Java GUI event handling, in: ICFEM '02: Proceedings of the 4th International Conference on Formal Engineering Methods, Springer-Verlag, London, UK, 2002, pp. 359–370.

[7] P. Ammann, J. Offutt, Introduction to Software Testing, Cambridge University Press, New York, NY, 2008.

[8] M.J. Harrold, Testing: a roadmap, in: ICSE '00: Proceedings of the Conference on The Future of Software Engineering, ACM, New York, NY, 2000, pp. 61–72.

[9] S. McConnell, Best practices: daily build and smoke test, IEEE Softw. 13 (4) (July 1996) 143–144.

[10] S. Esmelioglu, L. Apfelbaum, Automated test generation, execution, and reporting, in: Proceedings of Pacific Northwest Software Quality Conference, IEEE Press, Portland, Oregon, 1997.

[11] A.M. Memon, M.E. Pollack, M.L. Soffa, Hierarchical GUI test case generation using automated planning, IEEE Trans. Softw. Eng. 27 (2) (2001) 144–155.

[12] A.M. Memon, Q. Xie, Studying the fault-detection effectiveness of GUI test cases for rapidly evolving software, IEEE Trans. Softw. Eng. 31 (10) (2005) 884–896.

[13] L. White, H. Almezen, N. Alzeidi, User-based testing of GUI sequences and their interactions, in: ISSRE '01: Proceedings of the 12th International Symposium on Software Reliability Engineering, IEEE Computer Society, Washington, DC, 2001, p. 54.

[14] F. Belli, C.J. Budnik, L. White, Event-based modelling, analysis and testing of user interactions: approach and case study, Softw. Test. Verif. Reliab. 16 (1) (2006) 3–32.

[15] X. Yuan, M. Cohen, A.M. Memon, Covering array sampling of input event sequences for automated GUI testing, in: ASE '07: Proceedings of the Twenty-Second IEEE/ACM International Conference on Automated Software Engineering, ACM, New York, NY, 2007, pp. 405–408.

[16] M. Finsterwalder, Automating acceptance tests for GUI applications in an extreme programming environment, in: Proceedings of the 2nd International Conference on eX-treme Programming and Flexible Processes in Software Engineering, May 2001, pp. 114–117.

[17] Introduction to jfcUnit, http://jfcunit.sourceforge.net, 2009.

[18] Abbot framework for automated testing of Java GUI components and programs, http://jfcunit.sourceforge.net, 2009.

[19] Pounder Java GUI testing utility, http://pounder.sourceforge.net, 2009.

[20] Jemmy module, https://jemmy.dev.java.net, 2009.

[21] J.H. Hicinbothom, W.W. Zachary, A tool for automatically generating transcripts of human–computer interaction, in: Proceedings of the Human Factors and Ergonomics Society 37th Annual Meeting, 1993, p. 1042, vol. 2 of SPECIAL SESSIONS: Demonstrations.

[22] Marathon integrated testing environment, http://www.marathontesting.com, 2009.

[23] M. Grechanik, Q. Xie, C. Fu, Maintaining and evolving GUI-directed test scripts, in: ICSE '09: Proceedings of the 2009 IEEE 31st International Conference on Software Engineering, IEEE Computer Society, Washington, DC, 2009, pp. 408–418.

[24] R.K. Shehady, D.P. Siewiorek, A method to automate user interface testing using variable finite state machines, in: Proceedings of The Twenty-Seventh Annual International Symposium on Fault-Tolerant Computing (FTCS'97), IEEE Press, Washington/Brussels/Tokyo, June 1997, pp. 80–88.

[25] L. White, H. Almezen, Generating test cases for GUI responsibilities using complete interaction sequences, in: Proceedings of the International Symposium on Software Reliability Engineering, Oct. 8–11, 2000, pp. 110–121.

[26] M.B. Cohen, P.B. Gibbons, W.B. Mugridge, C.J. Colbourn, Constructing test suites for interaction testing, in: ICSE '03: Proceedings of the 25th International Conference on Software Engineering, IEEE Computer Society, Washington, DC, 2003, pp. 38–48.

[27] F.E. Allen, Control flow analysis, SIGPLAN Not. 5 (7) (1970) 1–19.

[28] A. Memon, I. Banerjee, A. Nagarajan, GUI ripping: reverse engineering of graphical user interfaces for testing, in: WCRE '03: Proceedings of the 10th Working Conference on Reverse Engineering, IEEE Computer Society, Washington, DC, 2003, p. 260.

[29] Q. Xie, A.M. Memon, Designing and comparing automated test oracles for GUI-based software applications, ACM Trans. Softw. Eng. Methodol. 16 (1) (2007) 4.

[30] L. White, Regression testing of GUI event interactions, in: Proceedings of the International Conference on Software Maintenance (Washington), Nov. 4–8, 1996, pp. 350–358.

[31] Q. Xie, A.M. Memon, Using a pilot study to derive a GUI model for automated testing, ACM Trans. Softw. Eng. Methodol. 18 (2) (2008) 1–35.

[32] D.J. Kasik, H.G. George, Toward automatic generation of novice user test scripts, in: CHI '96: Proceedings of the SIGCHI Conference on Human Factors in Computing Systems, ACM, New York, NY, 1996, pp. 244–251.

[33] P.A. Brooks, A.M. Memon, Automated GUI testing guided by usage profiles, in: ASE '07: Proceedings of the Twenty-Second IEEE/ACM International Conference on Automated Software Engineering, ACM, New York, NY, 2007, pp. 333–342.

[34] R.C. Bryce, C.J. Colbourn, M.B. Cohen, A framework of greedy methods for constructing interaction test suites, in: ICSE '05: Proceedings of the 27th International Conference on Software Engineering, ACM, New York, NY, 2005, pp. 146–155.

[35] D.M. Cohen, S.R. Dalal, M.L. Fredman, G.C. Patton, The AETG system: an approach to testing based on combinatorial design, IEEE Trans. Softw. Eng. 23 (7) (1997) 437–444.

[36] D.M. Cohen, S.R. Dalal, A. Kajla, G.C. Patton, The automatic efficient test generator (AETG) system, in: Proceedings of the Fifth International Symposium on Software Reliability Engineering, IEEE Computer Society Press, Monterey, CA, 1994, pp. 303–309.

[37] A. Hartman, Software and hardware testing using combinatorial covering suites, in: Graph Theory, Combinatorics and Algorithms: Interdisciplinary Applications, 2005, pp. 327–366.

[38] A. Kervinen, M. Maunumaa, T. Pakkonen, M. Katara, Model-based testing through a GUI, in: Proceedings of the 5th International Workshop on Formal Approaches to Testing of Software (FATES 2005), Springer, Berlin, 2006, pp. 16–31, number 3997 in Lecture Notes in Computer Science.

[39] A. Paiva, N. Tillmann, J. Faria, R. Vidal, Modeling and testing hierarchical GUIs, in: Proceedings of the 12th International Workshop on Abstract State Machines (ASM 2005), Paris, France. Springer Inc., March 8–11, 2005.

[40] A. Paiva, J. Faria, R. Vidal, Towards the integration of visual and formal models for GUI testing, Electronic Notes Theor. Comput. Sci. 190 (2) (2007) 99–111.

[41] H. Buwalda, Action figure, STQE Mag. 2003.

[42] M. Barnett, K. Leino, W. Schulte, The Spec# programming system: an overview, Lect. Notes Comput. Sci. 3362 (2005) 49–69.

Empirical Knowledge Discovery by Triangulation in Computer Science

RAVI I. SINGH

*Department of Electrical and Computer Engineering,
The University of Alberta, Edmonton, Alberta, Canada*

JAMES MILLER

*Department of Electrical and Computer Engineering,
The University of Alberta, Edmonton, Alberta, Canada*

Abstract

No one will disagree that solid empirical facts must be acquired from a series of studies. What constitutes a proper fundamental structure for such a series of studies is an unsettled issue. However, we are finally starting to see triangulation from other disciplines emerge as a serious contender to the traditional framework of replication for such studies. We start with two sample problems from Computer Science that are in need of frameworks other than those provided by one-shot studies or replication. Using these to open the topic of triangulation, we see that the mixed methods of triangulation also have room for researcher acumen. A working example of triangulation is looked at where researchers were able to derive more findings with triangulation than without it. The expected outcome of triangulation is convergence, but although it happens occasionally, it is hardly the norm. We move onto an example of triangulation in Software Engineering and basic frameworks that exist. Lastly, we take a look at how triangulation can help with setting goals by providing an established framework to move deliberation ahead.

ADVANCES IN COMPUTERS, VOL. 80
ISSN: 0065-2458/DOI: 10.1016/S0065-2458(10)80004-X

163

1. Introduction

Computer Science is a young discipline [1,2] and is therefore yet to establish norms in a number of philosophical areas. One such area is with regard to the limits of objectification or quantification and their impact on the limits of producing generalized knowledge from such observations. As a young discipline, it is normal to fill these gaps in the norms by "borrowing" ideas from other disciplines. However, it is common to "borrow" ideas without necessarily considering all the options and without explicitly stating the requirements that the idea must achieve. This paper argues that quantification has serious limitations in Computer Science, especially when human subjects are part of the endeavor. This, in turn, requires us to look for frameworks that embrace these limitations when seeking to generate empirically derived facts or factoids.

Keep in mind that there is no silver bullet on the path to the uncovering of knowledge [3]. It is not expected that Computer Science be made as regimented as electrical or mechanical engineering [4]. That being said, it would be easy to adopt an attitude of pessimism when reviewing the literature on empirical knowledge research in Computer Science. The findings of this paper, however, lead one to believe that a healthy skepticism is in order instead [3].

So what are some of these limitations and how have other disciplines gotten around them? One is that Computer Science in general seems more in line with

Simon's [5] "sciences of the artificial" than "sciences of the natural" in that it is knowledge about artificial objects and phenomena [5,6].

Simon also considers Cognitive Science to be a science of the artificial [7]. Yet, in a literature review, there are numerous examples where mixed quantitative and qualitative methods have been used in cognitive science research to investigate new ideas [8]. Since Cognitive Science also contains artificial objects and phenomena, why cannot similar methods be used in Computer Science?

The topic is design centric; and practitioners spend a considerable amount of time, exploring different avenues for a solution. Many of these avenues will prove fruitless; others will yield a solution. However, this highly nonlinear, opportunistic behavior [9] clearly causes significant performance variations within and between practitioners. The simplistic top-down design approach of Computer Science works well only in special case well-structured problems where "the designer already knows the correct decomposition" [6,9].

Take note that Guindon is a cognitive psychologist. While at first glance, it may be natural to consider design as a cognitive activity, there are a number of situational, organizational, and social interactions to be considered as well. The authors proceed to make a case for "cognitive ethnography" stating that "it is especially well suited to addressing applied questions of the type which dominate research on human factors, since it maintains levels of objectivity that enable replication by other observers, as well as the validation of its findings through a process of methodological triangulation involving experimental methods" [10,11,64].

Most entities have no physical form; instead Computer Science deals with a large number of virtual concepts (performance, complexity, etc.) that today have imprecise definitions and can often be measured only by secondary or even tertiary proxies [6].

Other disciplines deal with virtual entities as well. Consider a study that collects data on how a virtual learning environment alleviates isolation in long-distance learning and provides a means of building contact and support among geographically disconnected students. Such virtual concepts were indeed measured and done in such a way that repeated studies could add rigor to the conclusions drawn [2, 64].

These are some of the limitations in Computer Science empirical research and how other sciences have gotten around the same barriers to knowledge discovery. Section 2 provides two brief case studies where we attempt to illustrate the limitations to objectification in Computer Science. It is believed that these limitations place significant limitations on what is achievable via empirical exploration in Computer Science.

2. Objectification of Concepts in Computer Science

Let us look at an example of this process as an illustration. Algorithmic Information Theory [10] seems at first glance to be highly precise. Algorithmic Information Theory looks at the relationship between Shannon's Information Theory and Turing Compatibility Theory. Its central concept is to measure the complexity of an abstract entity by the size of the smallest program that can generate it [12]. Most concepts are mathematically defined and completely specified. Everything seems exact and perfect. Within Algorithmic Information Theory, the Kolmogorov Complexity can be thought of as the minimal description of an arbitrary string which can include algorithms [13]. Kolmogorov Complexity [63], can be used to provide a theoretical definition of an objective evaluation of a pseudo-irreducible form of a signal, and hence to provide precise differences or similarities between two arbitrary signals. Signals are not required to have any special properties and can be as general as two arbitrary strings.

While it can be stated that Kolmogorov Complexity is objective, this is clearly a theoretical position, as Kolmogorov Complexity is uncomputable[1] in anything apart from contrived situations. However, recently Cilibrasi and Vitanyi [14] have demonstrated that Kolmogorov Complexity can be successfully approximated by current compression techniques. Kolmogorov Complexity can be viewed as the ultimate compressor—producing for any arbitrary string (or file or image), a minimum description of that string, given some form of description language. Hence, practical compression approaches that compress arbitrary strings or files or images can be viewed as approximations to the optimal, however unattainable, compressor. Kolmogorov Complexity can be viewed as the limiting case for compression technology.

Specifically, Cilibrasi and Vitanyi introduce NID (Normalized information distance) [2], which *approximates* Kolmogorov Complexity *within known limits*. Further, they prove that NID is a valid metric within these limits. They *claim* that NID can "discover all similarities between two arbitrary entities; and represents object similarity according to the dominant shared features between two objects."

NID can be stated as:

Let $K(x|y)$ refer to the Kolmogorov Complexity, that is, the length of the shortest binary program that accepts as input y and outputs x; and let $K(x)$ refer to the

---

[1] In a Turing sense.

Kolmogorov Complexity of x that is the length of the shortest binary program with no inputs that outputs x.

The meaning of $\max\{K(x|y), K(y|x)\}$ [14] can be explained as the length of the shortest binary program (with the reference universal prefix Turing machine) that with input x, computes y, and with input y, computes x. Given these definitions, NID can be defined as:

$$\text{NID}(x, y) = \frac{\max\{K(x|y), K(y|x)\}}{\max\{K(x), K(y)\}}.$$

More details about NID can be found in Li et al. [2]. However, the fact that Kolmogorov Complexity is incomputable implies again that NID cannot be used directly. Fortunately, Cilibrasi and Vitanyi provide an approximation to this metric based upon real-world compressors (C) rather than the ideal compressor (K). Here, a compressor is an entity that uses an encoding algorithm to produce a representation that is smaller than the input [15].

2.1 Normalized Compression Distance

Normalized compression distance (NCD) is a parameter-free similarity distance which is believed to be able to uncover all similarities with a single metric [2] and is a practical metric approximating NID. It is computed from the lengths of compressed data files, images, strings, etc. [14], using real-world compressors. NCD is specifically formulated for real-world compressors (C) rather than the ideal compressor (K). For an arbitrary compressor C, NCD is given by

$$\text{NCD}(x, y) = \frac{C(xy) - \min\{C(x), C(y)\}}{\max\{C(x), C(y)\}}.$$

Clearly, the relationship between the denominators of NID and NCD is straightforward. However, the relationship between the numerators is far from straightforward.

It is shown that the numerator can be rewritten as [2]:

$$\max\{K(x, y) - K(x), K(x, y) - K(y)\},$$

while noting that

$$K(x, y) = K(xy) = K(yx),$$

where xy and yx denote the concatenation of two signals.

It is then argued [2] that this numerator can be effectively approximated by

$$\min\{C(xy), C(yx)\} - \min\{C(x), C(y)\}$$

If we now assume that the symmetry property holds for the real-world compressor,

$$\min\{C(xy), C(yx)\} = C(xy)$$

Clearly, it is important to understand that NCD is an *approximation* of NID *and that the symmetry property of real-world compressors will be invalid for a wide range of compressors.*

In addition, many real-world compressors may invalidate common properties found in theoretical measurement systems, *for example, is monotonicity* $(C(xy) \geq C(x))$ *a guaranteed property of all block-coding compressors?* Hence, these approximations will require empirical verification within any context. That is, while Algorithmic Information Theory is precise when abstract, when it is ported into a real-world setting to allow the actual measurement of real quantities, it must go through a number of transformations which introduce noise (which often does not possess known characteristics), which may be severe in many situations. Let us imagine that our context is to measure the actual difference between two arbitrary images.

2.2   Compressors and Images

At first glance, this looks like a no-brainer—just use image encoding algorithms JPEG [16] or JPEG2000 [17]! However, upon investigation, the situation quickly becomes a series of decisions often without a solid rationale to guide the decision maker, a series of compromises, and a series of approximations. The NCD equation requires that the two sources be concatenated; while this is straightforward, it will lead to a nonrectangular composite image under most circumstances. Hence, we will have to introduce some compromise, some padding, to reconstruct a rectangular image. Constructing the padding again seems relatively straight—add a small image to the composite image, which will make it rectangular, while making sure that the contents of the padding image are noncompressible. Is this really justified? If we add padding that can be compressed, this will affect the NCD value; if we add padding that cannot be compressed, we are penalizing images with incompatible dimensions. Is either position absolutely correct? Let us go with the ''cannot be compressed'' option—perhaps we can add an image to the ''smaller'' image (as ''smaller'' we imply the image with the dimension which needs to be minimally expanded to allow the two concatenated images to form a rectangle) to align the dimensions. This padding image could be constructed from colored (white, pink, . . .) noise resulting in something that is relatively uncompressible—though we have still affected the NCD value. However, we still have to resolve the spatial relationship between the smaller image and the padding image:

- Should they abut? If so, which side (top or bottom; right or left)?; or
- Should the smaller image be centered in a padding image?

Again, we are making choices which impact on the result (NCD values). Next, we need to investigate which 2D compressor to choose. The major characteristic of compressors is being lossy or lossless; a compressor is lossless if there exists a decompressor that can construct the original message from its encoded representation, and lossy otherwise [14]. Which type of compressor is most suitable for use in the NCD estimation is likely to be problem dependent. If lossy compressors are possible, then we need to form an idea of what is a suitable value for reconstructed image quality, perhaps using the mean opinion score or the peak signal to noise ratio as metrics to guide us— but again, we are making decisions and numerical compromises to arrive at a concrete solution. Perhaps, lossless is the more appropriate choice; now we do not require the estimation of any parameters. However, the various compressors still give us considerably different results which vary from image pair to image pair. Again, we are left making decisions, compromises, and numerical approximations.

In conclusion, while algorithm complexity theory and Kolmogorov Complexity are some of the most precise topics in Computer Science, their precision remains as long as the ideas are considered as abstract concepts. Once we start attempting to make the ideas concrete, the precision quickly disappears and the investigator is left to make a large number of decisions, compromises, and approximations in order to achieve a concrete solution. These issues imply that other investigators are unlikely to repeat the numerical observations found by the first investigator. Furthermore, the volume of issues which impact on the numerical results found by the original investigator is significant; and hence, the probability of them reporting or even realizing all them is limited. Please note: the Kolmogorov Complexity situation outlined above is not an extreme case, and in fact, in many ways, represents an extremely simple situation for a Computer Science investigator. Areas in Computer Science where humans as subjects are the norm are in general much more challenging and complex situations for investigators to explore and possess significantly greater numbers of decisions, compromises, and approximations in order to achieve concrete solutions.

2.3 Complexity and Imprecise Definitions Abound

Computer Science differs from many other scientific disciplines because of its limited number of physical components and concepts. Physical components allow us to invoke ideas from the physical sciences to produce (pseudo-depends upon the degree of abstraction required) precise definitions and relationships. This provides a solid basis for many empirical investigations and allows results to be easily reproduced and to have unique interpretations. In contrast, Computer Science often deals with attributes that are more meta-physical than physical, have imprecise definitions which vary over time, domain, and problem statement, and often have no "mechanism" to allow us to either observe or measure them directly.

Consider the "definition" of Trust taken from Beatty et al. [18]. This definition represents a meta-analysis of the literature on the definition of Trust. Points to be noted are

- The definition considers the attribute only within a limited domain (e-commerce). So what do the results imply for the definition in say organizational settings?
- To produce the definition, the researchers considered any on-line activity as a proxy for e-commerce behavior. Using proxies in Computer Science is extremely common because of imprecision of definitions—however, it is not without substantial risk.
- Trust seems to be defined in terms of a large number of attributes (anything with a direct link to trust has potentially a direct relationship. The number on the link indicates the number of studies that "found" this relationship. The number in the node is the number of studies which activity considered this attribute when exploring this question. Some researchers even defined attributes as themselves! See the weights on the self-references to nodes.)
- These defining attributes are highly interrelated with other attributes that define Trust. Forget linearity.

These defining attributes also have complex, imprecise definitions based upon a network of attributes. Each of these attributes within this network of attributes has in turn a definition based upon a network of attributes, and so on.

As can be seen in Fig. 1, most of the variables surrounding trust are ill defined. Clearly one-shot studies or replication is not going to work here. A more open-ended framework is needed, as in triangulation (which is defined more fully in Section 3, below). Triangulation brings many benefits to the table including:

- Consider the large number of judgment calls and small tweaks that have to be made with compression algorithms. Add to that the complexity of the different compression algorithms, lossless versus lossy parameters, and dictionary sizes. All these factors make the problem difficult to deal with in replication settings. Triangulation is the remaining choice in this scenario and as a bonus, the use of multiple methods will help by reducing the bias in any particular research method.

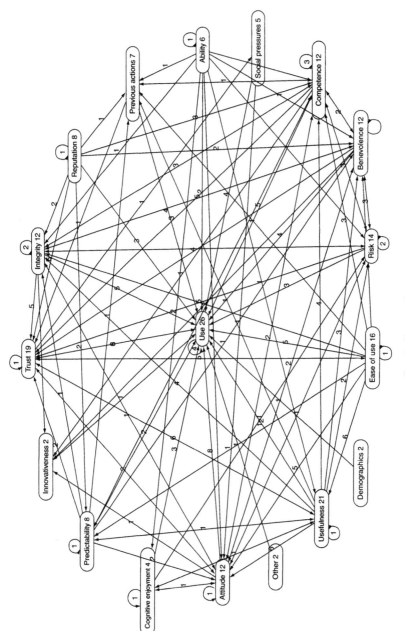

Fig. 1. Trust attributes.

- Multiple methods play the weakness of one method off against the strengths of another. For example, in the study of on-line trust, one could use a combination of browser plug-ins along with structured interviews to establish a framework upon which to study on-line trust.
- Triangulation uses unobtrusive measures that do not necessarily require inter-action with the subject and leave the response pristine. An example of this could be studying how much time a user of an interactive development environment (IDE) spends in critical code.
- Another way of checking the data from diversified data sources is to look for reoccurring patterns in the collected data. In Schadewitz et al. [19], researchers used discipline-specific methods to collect information on design patterns in collaborative learning environments. They then used theoretical triangulation to increase the validity of their findings.
- Gives a framework through which subjects can validate and improve research-ers' work and a way for fellow observers to review the researchers' output [20]. The result of this is lending validity to the academic audience of a study [21]. This has application in the compression problem in attacking difficult issues such as how to concatenate multidimensional images or data types (e.g., video with jpeg). The entire compression problem is a messy problem and triangula-tion provides a framework for its complexities compared to one-shot studies or replication frameworks.
- A way of dealing with the situation where people say one thing and do something different.
- A way of including researcher acumen with results. Triangulation is often looked upon as a convergence strategy. In reality, the data converge only occasionally and inconsistency and divergence are more the norm. In such situations, the onus is on the researcher to combine the empirical information at hand with a comprehensive understanding of the phenomena being studied and a general grasp of the context surrounding the problem.
- Removing the effects of a confounding variable [22] in a case study by amassing collusive data.
- Can discover facts through a lack of information. For example, in one study researchers discovered a lack of quality assurance (QA) procedures in a project mainly through their own acumen. For example, in Bratthal and Jorgensen [23] researchers discovered a lack of QA procedures by personally observing that they did not exist.
- Provides results with a higher validity than those from a single study.

- In Bratthal and Jorgensen [23], the researchers suggest that by building on several sources of confirmative data, they can produce results that have higher validity than those built form a single source.
- Its value does not lie as a methodological way of amassing and processing data. It is simply a way of providing more and better information to the investigator to offer poignant views about the common world we all share. An example here is in defining trust. As can be seen in the diagram, trust is a massive interconnection of terms that themselves are highly connected, highly imprecise, and highly qualitative.
- It can help in goal setting in that it is a progressive technique with a clear framework for advancing ideas. As an example, part of goal setting is having a reliable way to measure outcomes. Relying on any single measure can be misguiding. Using several measures with triangulation can provide a more total picture than any individual measure alone.

3. Triangulation: Introduction

Triangulation refers to a multiple method research approach originating in the social sciences that adds rigor to studies. Webb et al. [24] sought to overcome a "stagnating" dependence on single working definitions of theoretical concepts. They also sought to supplement the classic research techniques of the interview and questionnaire with inconspicuous measures that do not require interaction with the respondent and that themselves do not bias the outcome. In maintaining that all research methods are biased, Webb et al. [24] state the case for the use of a collection of methods (mixed methods). They believed that the use of multiple methods would reduce the effect of bias of any one of them. They further argued that if a hypothesis can withstand a barrage of balanced test methods, then it contains the validity of a degree unreachable by one verified using the limited framework of a solitary method [24].

In 1970, Denzin also argued for the use of mixed methods on the same empirical events. Denzin's views would go on to be very influential in encouraging social researchers, from a variety of schools of thought, to use a mixture of methods and observers to reduce bias and improve validity within the context of empirical research methods. Specifically, he argues that no individual method can always be considered the best one. Every method has its good points and bad points. He calls on sociologists to realize this and adopt a stance that mobilizes them to tackle problems with all timely and suitable methods (i.e., multimethod triangulation) [25].

So triangulation comes down to playing the weaknesses of one research method against the strengths of another. There are several definitions for triangulation, the one that comes closest to this idea can be found in this passage:

"While a survey study tends to test research assumptions, classroom observation is an exploratory process of learning, which helps to shape the research design and refine the observation scheme. This type of multiple method approach provides cross-examination mechanisms, often referred to as triangulation." [26,27]

The point here is that triangulation is not a complex methodology and that triangulation data collection techniques are not complex either. The table below lists a number of triangulation data collection techniques, all of which are familiar.

Data collection techniques suitable for triangulation
Round tables and interest groups
Dialogs
Surveys
Work Journals
Analysis of usage patterns within an IDE
Documentation Studies

3.1 Triangulation: The State of the Art

If one conscientiously collects and second checks data, using a multitude of sources and modes of confirming data, corroboration mechanisms will, for the most part, be built into the finding–gathering procedure. There is not much else to do other than to state the processes used. In this way triangulation can be thought of as a state of mind [28].

That triangulation is a state of mind is something that most people would at least partly agree on. As for triangulation actually having a state of the art, fewer people would agree on this. In the literature reviewed so far, no one has defined a state of the art so for all practical purposes, it is best to drop the idea. Regarding this "state of mind," let us ask instead: What do I need to know about triangulation to be practical?

One of the first things you will come across are Denzin's [29] four types of triangulation. Here it is presented in the context of software engineering:

1. Data triangulation is about gathering data, using multiple sampling methods, with the aim of varying times and scenarios. It is important to alter subjects,

though this is difficult in Software Engineering situations because the cross-sectioning frame is poorly understood.

2. Researcher triangulation is about using more than one researcher to work on findings. Note that as triangulation gains further acceptance in Computer Science, this definition is open to broader interpretation.

3. Using more than one theory to interpret the finding is called theoretical triangulation.

4. Methodological triangulation uses more than one procedure for collecting findings. The author refers to [65] for a description of a general approach and [30,70] for application to software engineering problem. One further note: like researcher triangulation, the definition of methodological triangulation is becoming broader also [6].

It is now good time to review some of the advantages of triangulation. One advantage states that without triangulation lacking cross-checking by multiple observers or subjects to enhance and strengthen the researcher's findings, some researchers have problems having their work recognized by the academic world [31,32]. Another reason to use mixed methods is to deal with the situation where what people do and what they say are entirely different, as in Jorgenson [23] where project staff were asked how much of their efforts were spent on fault correction in their software. It was discovered that their estimates were around twice as high as the amount of time actually spent correcting faults.

Opposition to triangulation falls into the school of thought that it is hard to compare different evidence. This is a common theme in the literature criticizing triangulation. Now open this up to further examination. First of all, are people expecting too much from triangulation? Consider the following: "Triangulation is not magic. The researcher ought not to expect that the use of multiple methods will produce findings that will inevitably come together to form a nice clear picture" [33].

It is important that practitioners of triangulation make their views heard in order to vanquish the belief that everything in triangulation is cut and dry.

So what is the next logical step? It is to simplify Denzin's four categories of triangulation while at the same time silencing his critics. Denzin actually suggests only three types of triangulation. The fourth, theoretical triangulation, is troublesome at the best of times, and in a real-world scenario, probably unachievable [34–36].

Denzin is the first to question the plausibility of this idea. Note that it can just as easily apply to Computer Scientists:

"My use of theoretical triangulation must in no way be construed as a defence of eclecticism. Indeed, sociologists committed to a given perspective will probably not employ theoretical triangulation. The great value of this strategy, as I see it, however, is its assurance that no study will be conducted in the absence of some theoretical perspective. In this sense it is most appropriate for the theoretically uncommitted, as well as for analysis of areas characterized by high theoretical incoherence.'' [29,36]

Now consider this critique on triangulation:

Methodological triangulation does not always increase validity and theoretical triangulation does not always do away with bias. In general, theories are the products of varied schools of thought and combined together can show a bigger picture but not an unbiased one. Likewise, different procedures have come from different theory schools so putting them together can provide greater dimension but not greater correctness. To put it another way, there is an argument for triangulation although not the one Denzin puts forward [37].

While the critics above do make some points, it is not clear whether they really understand the value of theoretical triangulation.

3.2   Convergence and Researcher Acumen

Many texts talk of triangulation as a convergence strategy. What few of them mention is that it can lead to inconsistent data and contradictory data. Consider the following passage:

Practicing researchers and evaluators know that the image of data converging upon a single proposition about a social phenomenon is a phantom image. More realistically, we end up with data that occasionally converge, but are often inconsistent and even contradictory. And we do not throw our hands up in despair because we cannot say anything about the phenomenon we have been studying. Rather, we attempt to make sense of what we find and that often requires embedding the empirical data at hand with a holistic understanding of a specific situation and general background knowledge about this class of social phenomena. This conception shifts the focus on triangulation away from a technological solution for ensuring validity and places the responsibility with the researcher for the construction of plausible explanations about the phenomena being studied [36].

So we see that it takes a certain amount of acumen on the part of the researcher to make sense of the findings. In the face of inconsistent, contradictory, and suspiciously collusive converging data the researcher is by no means at wits end.

A close examination of the explanations offered here suggests that several levels of evidence are required for the researcher to construct plausible explanations. There are obviously data on hand. There is also a holistic understanding of the project itself, its history, the intentions of the developers, the ongoing relationships within the project, and so on. This understanding about a project or program is frequently unarticulated, a part of that vast body of tacit knowledge that we all have. And lastly, the researcher/evaluator has a store of knowledge and understandings about the social world which allows such projects and their evaluations to exist [36].

Researcher acumen again comes into play in the area of software engineering. Here, we first focus on a few reasons why software engineering is so different from the social sciences and then focus on the commonalities that make triangulation usable.

Some of the key differences between Software Engineering and the Social Sciences are that Software Engineering seems to have more in common with Simon's [5] "sciences of the artificial" than with "sciences of the natural." Another crucial difference is that real Software Engineering problems are wicked problems [38]! Also consider that because of the complexity of the problems, practitioners seek "good enough" solutions rather than optimal solutions, or *satisfying* to utilize Simon's term from economics [5], or *bounded rationality* from a behaviorist perspective [39]. And finally, Software Engineering is in many ways all about people, be it users, customers, developers, or managers; it is impossible to consider any aspect of Software Engineering without understanding the humans involved. Unfortunately, understanding humans, their behavior, motivations, etc., is extremely difficult and extremely poorly understood. This limitation again places significant limitations on all Software Engineering empirical approaches. As Gomory [40] put it in his famous essay, "embedded within our increasingly artificial world will be large numbers of complex and thoroughly idiosyncratic humans" [6].

It is the last point that is of interest. It is the human element that binds all aspects of software. Software is written by humans to be maintained by humans who will eventually evolve the software. So, in order to visualize a true picture of what Software Engineering is about, one must investigate the actual human-software worker working on real-world problems in real-world settings [41]. There is a clear human element to software engineering.

So what about using triangulation in software engineering? There is a growing need for an alternative to "one-shot studies." The expression "one-shot studies" comes up in software engineering literature and, for our purposes, can be explained as a single study based on experiments that cannot show anything convincible to others [42].

In contrast, triangulation brings to the table a plethora of methods with weaknesses that do not have a single soft spot and with strengths that augment each other [65]. The point here is that triangulation is an established research technique in software engineering, despite not appearing "conventional" on the surface.

3.3 Triangulation: An Actual Study

Returning to researcher acumen, in the article "Can you Trust a Single Data Source Exploratory Software Engineering Case Study?" [23], the researchers on several occasions used their acumen to bring the data to convergence. Case studies as a research strategy can be challenging [43] for both the researcher doing the study and the reader in locating particular researcher biases. In a case study, not all of the variables can be controlled, and so it is difficult to claim that the relationships found contain validity as it can be said that the variables rely on a per chance complicating element. There are two ways to deal with this:

1. Do a number of case studies, or use numerous cases inside a single study
2. Perform triangulation inside a solitary study to collect collaborative data [44]

The first approach is not desirable because among other things, it can cause the researcher to raise the level of abstraction, thus making the case less interesting to practitioners. However, triangulation with researcher acumen was the more beckoning choice as it does not require multiple cases and it compresses the lead time needed to study a phenomenon.

Now on to the nuts and bolts of the study. The study analyzes a case study of a project performed in an organization. This can be seen in Fig. 2 [23].

A list of the individual data sources used is given as follows: Project documents, information from the time-reporting system, notes from meeting observations, focused interviews, open-ended interviews, and trouble reports [23].

Basically, triangulation using sources of data within the case study is studied. The interaction of the data sources is shown in Fig. 3.

And finally, the raw data from Bratthal and Jorgensen [23] are given below: They can be broken down into three categories:

T1: Factors that decrease project lead time
T2: Factors that add to project lead time
T3: Factors that have repercussions on future projects

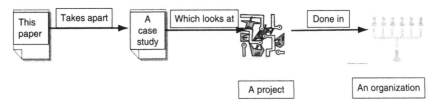

Fig. 2. Case study. (See color insert at the back of the book.)

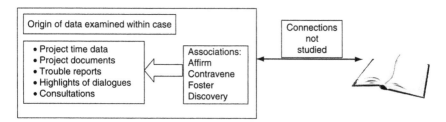

Fɪɢ. 3. Data sources.

There are a number of findings in this study. Our objective is to focus on those that involve researcher acumen to illustrate that triangulation is not a deterministic process.

(T1) Project units located jointly together: Researcher acumen brought this finding to light. Without colocation, the communications links observed would have taken longer to set up.

(T1) Generally, the project can get hold of seasoned staff as well as experts. Here the researchers stayed out of the picture. The only way for them to establish that the project staff was experienced would be interviews, since there was a low correlation between years of experience and actual results.

(T1) The project manager was well seasoned. Again the researchers did not become involved since they realized that it would be difficult to prove that this is of lead-time benefit without extended researcher involvement.

(T1) The project phases are concurrent: A contradiction appears; the time-reporting system and project documentation report contradictory findings. The final decision lies in the researcher's experience in what can be performed concurrently and what cannot.

(T2) Project is without inspections or reviews: An interesting situation, since it was discovered through lack of information. This is a strong case for triangulation since it is unlikely that any single data source could confirm this lack of information with a high degree of reliability. In this finding, the value of inspections/reviews in respect of lead time was suggested by researcher's experience.

(T3) The project is missing external QA: Since no QA procedures were in place, the researchers concluded that the lack of QA was a source of lead time increase.

(T3) Time data could not be used for subsequent projects: Time records for the project did not follow the structure of the activities of the project. In the researcher's experience, this caused a loss to lead time. If it cannot be observed, then it cannot be benchmarked. If it cannot be benchmarked, it cannot be managed.

In summary, this study suggests that a case study built on multiple sources of confirmation can have a higher validity than studies that rely on a single data source. For example, the finding that the project phases are concurrent could not have been brought to light unless multiple data sources were used. This finding and the finding that the project units are jointly located together would not have been made at all unless multiple methods had been used. In the situation where the project phases are concurrent, contradictory data decreased the reliability of the case study. The authors also note that no single data source could have been used to make all the findings made in the exploratory case study.

So the case study brings to the table hard evidence as to the value of triangulation. Also we can see for the first time the concrete use of mixed methods and how they play off each other. Researcher bias is also an issue, if the researchers had known less than they did, then the results of the case study could have been different. The project the researchers studied lasted 39 weeks and involved 29 people. Yet only two researchers were able to produce so many findings.

3.4 Lack of Triangulation Examples in the Literature

At this point the reader may be left with a sentiment echoed in the following passage:

> "Yet those who most strongly advocate triangulation (e.g., Ref. [24,29,69]) fail to indicate how this prescribed triangulation is actually performed and accomplished. Graduate training usually prepares us to use one method or another as appropriate and preferred, but not to combine methods effectively. And even those who use multiple methods do not generally explain their "technique" in sufficient detail to indicate exactly how convergent data are collected and interpreted." [45]

The literature review conducted so far indicates that Jick's sentiment holds as true now as it did in 1979. None of the literature reviewed thus far provides a convincing step-by-step play of accounts to explain exactly how triangulation brings out a desired outcome. By this point we can ask some informed questions about triangulation. For example, from a researcher point of view, how much do we need to know? From a data collector's point of view, how many data sources do we need to get if we just want a good enough result? We talk a lot about mixed methods, but how much do we really know about quantitative and qualitative methods?

A literature review to date has provided no answers to these questions. The best one can expect from the literature is that it provides enough information to ask the right questions to the right people. What has been discovered in the literature review is a central group of concepts that keep coming up different places [46]. What no one has done is to put all these concepts in one place, until now. For the remainder of this section we focus on some core concepts around triangulation so that the reader has them available in one place as a starting point.

3.5   Convergence, Inconsistency, and Divergence

Convergence, inconsistency, and divergence: These are the three possible outcomes for triangulation. We want convergence but what if we do not get it? Consider the following passage: Because of the researcher's inexperience with triangulation and the positive image it has, people automatically expect that it will lead to convergence of findings into a single conclusion. In fact there are three possible outcomes. The first is convergence and due to inexperience with triangulation, it is a widely held belief that it will lead to convergence. The concept is fairly simple; findings from different forms to triangulation, including other types not listed in this paper, will produce a solitary conclusion about a studied happening [36].

The second outcome of triangulation is inconsistency. This is more often the situation than convergence. When we use a multitude of data suppliers and procedures, we can be left with multiple viewpoints or findings that do not converge to a single conclusion. Instead we are left with half-baked ideas containing contradictions and vagueness. We are left in a position where we cannot credibly make any claims about the findings we have collected [36].

It is true that inconsistency can solely be the circumstance of the data collected. It is also noteworthy that it can be caused by human factors. For example, a researcher often has to wear many hats and if they try to be an expert on several types of methods for methodological triangulation, they may be stretching themselves too thin. Another example was noted in an interview with a researcher using triangulation; part of the success in his use of researcher triangulation was that the other researchers were located in the same room.

The last outcome is divergence. Worse than the data being inconsistent, it can be contradictory. What that means is that we are left with a collection of findings that supports conflicting points of view of the concept under study [36].

Should one accept that convergence is the sole aim of triangulation, then it follows that the second and third outcomes are useless. Of course, we are all aware that this is not the case. What it comes down to is triangulation providing additional and excelling confirmation data to the concept under study. The real value of triangulation is providing confirming data to the scientist so that they can provide meaningful clarifications about the concept under study [36].

3.6 Triangulation: Data Collection

Let us examine an actual working document. It is clear that even the mixed method researcher does not have all the answers offhand. It also brings to mind some thoughtful questions for the reader:

A Checklist of Questions for Designing a Mixed Methods Procedure [47]
Is a basic definition of mixed methods research provided?
Does the read have the sense for the potential use of a mixed methods strategy?
Are the criteria identified for choosing a mixed methods strategy?
Is the strategy identified, and are its criteria for selection given?
Is a visual model presented that illustrates the research strategy?
Are the procedures of data collection and analysis mentioned as they relate to the model?
Are the sampling strategies for both quantitative and qualitative data collection mentioned? Do they relate to the strategy?
Are specific data analysis procedures indicated? Do they relate to the strategy?
Are the procedures for validating both the quantitative and qualitative data discussed?
Is the narrative structure mentioned, and does it relate to the type of mixed methods strategy being used?

It is important to remember that a study does not have to be a mix of qualitative and quantitative methods. A mixed method study, for example, could contain a mix of qualitative methods.

Here is another passage that brings data collection more down to earth: Treat all methods, simple and complex, with consideration and diligence. Plan all your undertakings to ensure that your findings are clear and concise. It is a case of garbage in-garbage out, that is, a poorly worded question will solicit a similar quality answer that cannot be evaluated. Treat people like people, humans in a societal setting. Also be wary that a researcher can be interruptive simply by being there. The authors cite [48] as a starting point for research ethics in software engineering studies [41].

Creswell also includes some tips on how to include mixed methods in a proposal. His suggestions are as follows:

1. Give a brief background of its evolution. Start with its history in [66] and proceed to ideas about convergence or triangulating different data source types that can be found in Jick [45].

2. Come up with a definition for mixed methods research, using the definition in Chapter 1 of Creswell [47] as a base. This definition focuses on collecting qualitative and quantitative data concurrently.
3. Provide a concise passage about the increasing attention given to mixed methods, using academic publications, books, etc. as evidence.
4. Make mention of the type of questions likely to confront a researcher.

Priority is another consideration in mixed method studies. Is priority given to qualitative or quantitative methods? Is equal priority given? A leaning toward the qualitative or quantitative is based on the investigator's interests, his onlookers (e.g., his academic peers), and what is to be stressed in the research. Realistically, prioritization occurs through a variety of means. Examples include which data set is stressed initially, how much processing each data set has been given, and how theory is used in the research's framework [47].

3.7 An Example of Triangulation in Computer Science: Software Engineering

So how is triangulation normally found in sociology, psychology, and education finding its way into Computer Science? Let us look at software engineering. In the near past years, there have been some top level requests for further research based on experience and experiments [46,49,67]. In particular, the International Software Engineering Research Network (ISERN) has been organized to encourage empirical work to be done as a group effort [70].

Now consider the difficulty of obtaining empirical evidence in software engineering [50–52]:

The human side of Software Engineering along with the requirements of empirical validity leads one to believe that the chances of obtaining conclusive findings from empirical works are quite low [53,54]. This is especially true for one-shot studies as mentioned previously [55]. Replication goes further than one-shot studies but who is to say that the faults in the original study are not repeated in the replications? [56]. Triangulation or a multimethod modus operandi uses varied but affirming methods in research. It can be said that the a multimethod approach deals with the shortcoming of one-shot studies by assaulting problems with an armory of methods without any fixed weaknesses and strengths that are self reinforcing [65,70].

Now lest the reader be led into a sense that triangulation will save the day, consider this almost anecdotal passage that highlights the lack of software engineering research skills to be found in the field:

"It is essential to know which empirical research paradigm is most suitable to cover all of the many facets of Software Engineering empirical studies. The paradigm defines what empirical researchers must aim for in an attempt to demonstrate a rigorous approach within their study." [6,49]

Which empirical research paradigm covers all dimensions of software engineering is fundamental to investigations. This paradigm tells investigators what to strive for so that they can demonstrate rigor in their work. The problem is that most empirical investigators have no idea what paradigm they are using or do not even know that they exist. In addition, most Software Engineer empirical investigators are comfortable with mixing investigative styles (quantitative, qualitative, etc.) inside a study. Of course, the different styles coincide with different paradigms; it appears that investigators are devoting more of their energy toward providing insights than trying to stick with any particular paradigm. So, if Software Engineering is embracing an "anything goes" empirical approach, how does one include this approach, or "reality," within a framework of knowledge advancement? [6,57].

Miller goes on to say "we are fortunate that other domains embrace our approximate needs, and they have developed frameworks for exploration. It is these frameworks that give us a useful starting place. Specifically, these domains use triangulation" [6].

So in the case of software engineering, it seems that we are lucky that triangulation fits part of the bill. Really, the exercise to the reader is to think about other fields and circumstances where triangulation can be used. One example, recently iterated to the author, is a local nongovernmental organization that uses triangulation in their funding proposals as a mechanism to measure how the nongovernmental organization will "change the world" should their proposal be approved.

3.8   Validity and Goal Setting

There are many different definitions [58] for validity, but there are two types of validity that are of interest in triangulation. Internal validity is "the extent to which causal conclusions can be made from the study" [70]. External validity is "the extent to which results may be generalized to the population under study and other settings" [70]. In fact, in the research on triangulation, several different types of validity come up.

Some would argue that construct validity and conclusional validity are also important. Construct validity has meaning when what we see in the real world agrees with our conceptual model of that world. There are a number of blurry concepts that we theorize from the real world, and when they match those real-world blurry concepts, we can claim construct validity [59]. An example would be programmer maturity. Regarding conclusional validity, since it is one of the least understood validities, we will quote the definition directly. "Conclusion validity is the degree to which conclusions we reach about relationships in our data are reasonable" [59]. Conclusional validity comes into play toward the end of the study, often when there is pressure to draw a conclusion and a favorable one at that. It is here where researcher triangulation can lower the odds of a false conclusion being drawn: something it seems that has not been researched fully.

All research studies begin with establishing a set of clear, thoughtful goals, since many subsequent design decisions will depend on them. The goals should explain the purpose of the study and the phenomenon being researched. The study goals drive the formulation of research questions; these in turn drive research design [50,60], which in turn influences the selection of data collection techniques [41,61]. As a general reality, research studies are rarely this organized and the term "all over the map" has been used to describe some social scientists and their research approaches. Still, one has to start somewhere. Table I presents a summary of data collection techniques.

One is not left without options if one's goal setting efforts come to no avail. In mixed methods, two primary perspectives are available that among other things can help a researcher focus on a goal. They are the evolutionary perspective or the complementary perspective.

An evolutionary perspective is used when little research has been conducted on a phenomenon or where the research hypotheses require increased focus. Focusing on a research hypothesis will aid in goal setting if not setting it altogether as a side effect. The first step is an initial exploratory study gathering qualitative data. At this

TABLE I
DATA COLLECTION TECHNIQUES

Data quantity	Technique	Description
Small	Round Table and product survey groups	An open discussion about "modus operandi" and software product, useful for gathering ideas and emotional responses
Small	Modeling ideas	Making ideas about operations and output explicit
Medium	Become a team member	As a passive team member, you gain a deeper understanding by learning why things are done the way they are done
Large	Data mining project work repositories	Unfolding of product development, growth of slip-ups
Large	Software Gauging	Implementing code into the tools of the software engineer to monitor habits

stage, the initial study is designed to study a wide variety of topics in the area of interest. The data are collected, analyzed, and the important findings of the initial study are refined and used as hypotheses for a following study. Then the process is repeated, usually using a research method different from the initial study. The process iterates until a single hypothesis is rigorously investigated. Primary research methods should have high potential for theory generation; later methods should have high potential for theory confirmation [70].

In contrast, the complementary perspective's objective is to enhance the validity of research findings. This can also help with goal setting as it is an active process with an articulated framework to push thinking forward. In this perspective, a phenomenon is studied independently using two or more research methods. These independent studies do not have to be conducted by the same group; they can be coordinated as a series of studies by different groups within the discipline. When results agree, the empirical methods employed are said to have confirmatory power. In addition, the researchers can have greater confidence that their findings are not the result of individual methods employed. When results disagree, new hypotheses should be investigated which take into account the differences in research methods [70].

3.9 Conclusion

As a field of study, Computer Science has yet to set commonsensical norms due to its youth. In the areas of objectification or quantification, it is common for Computer Science to borrow concepts without thought to their limits or not being explicit about what they are trying to achieve. We saw the limitations that sprung up when humans were involved. Therefore, this leads us to a search for frameworks that cover the same limitations. One limitation that was covered was that Computer Science has more in common with sciences of the artificial than with those of the natural. In this situation, we looked to Cognitive Science for frameworks. Likewise, we look to cognitive ethnography and virtual learning environments for frameworks. To overcome these limitations, we looked to Cognitive Science, Cognitive Ethnography, and virtual learning environments for frameworks [62, 64].

Next, we looked at two practical examples of Computer Science problems in need of workable frameworks. First, we turned to Algorithmic Information Theory and in particular the Kolmogorov Complexity. While the Kolmogorov Complexity appears precise and uncomplicated, it is impractical and suited only for contrived examples. Luckily, an approximation to the Kolmogorov Complexity exists. In transforming the Kolmogorov Complexity into an approximation, noise is introduced by a number of changes. Also, since it is an approximation, a wide range of real-world compressors will not conform to the symmetry property.

Looking closer at the approximation, we realize that we must make a number of decisions about its use without any guiding rationale. We realize that when we try to make solid decisions, we start to become aware of our choices, trade-offs, and educated guesses that we have made so far. Furthermore, the bulk of issues that affect the findings are often extensive making the chances of them being noted or even fully thought through questionable. In closing this section, we saw that although the Kolmogorov Complexity and algorithm complexity theory are among some of the most exact topics in Computer Science, they stay exact only in a world of abstraction.

In the second example, we looked at the complexities around the definition of trust. A quick look at Fig. 1 will confirm the complexity. As we look closer at the figure, we see that each attribute itself is based on a network of attributes. These points and others make it clear that a suitable framework for trust has yet to be found.

Alas, all is not lost. Triangulation is recommended as a solution framework and its benefits are listed in point form. The next section on triangulation opened with an introduction and a discussion of the state of the art. Triangulation we see is more than a convergence strategy; it is a way for a researcher to include their acumen into the triangulation results. We then examined an actual study where the researchers on several occasions used their acumen to bring about convergence and add rigor to the study. Mention was made of the lack of triangulation examples in the literature. Moving on, we see that convergence, inconsistency, and divergence are the three possible outcomes of triangulation with convergence as the expected outcome but hardly the norm. We then looked at an example of triangulation in Software Engineering and how important it is to have an empirical paradigm when conducting investigations. Lastly, we examined how triangulation can help in goal setting.

As we saw earlier, single shot studies on their own can produce nothing conclusive. Consequently, we can be judgmental about the time and effort spent on them. Triangulation, on the other hand, brings rigor to studies and obtains more genuine results. It is necessary to foster community efforts to produce groups who use triangulation to explore common empirical questions concurrently.

Notes: There are many definitions of "validity." In this study, validity is defined according to [68]: "An account is valid or true if it represents accurately those features of the phenomena, that it is intended to describe, explain otherwise."

REFERENCES

[1] P.J. Denning, D.E. Comer, D. Gries, M.C. Mulder, A.B. Tucker, A.J. Turner, et al., Computing as a discipline, Commun. ACM 32 (1) 1989 January.
[2] M. Li, X. Li, B. Ma, P. Vitanyi, The similarity metric, IEEE Trans. Inf. Theory 50 (2004) 3250–3264, December.

[3] F. Brooks, No silver bullet: Essence and accidents of software engineering, IEEE Comput. 20 (4) (1987) 10–19, April.

[4] F. Brooks, Three great challenges for half-century-old computer science, J. ACM 50 (1) (2003) 25–26.

[5] H.A. Simon, Sciences of the Artificial, third ed., MIT, Cambridge, 1996.

[6] J. Miller, Triangulation as a basis for knowledge discovery in software engineering, Empir. Softw. Eng. J. 13 (2) (2008) 224.

[7] H.A. Simon, Cognitive science: The newest science of the artificial, Cogn. Sci. 4 (1) (1980) 33–46.

[8] A.M. Hines, Linking qualitative and quantitative methods in cross-cultural survey research: Techniques from cognitive science, Am. J. Community Psychol. 21 (6) (1993) 729–746.

[9] R. Guindon, Designing the design process: Exploiting opportunistic thoughts, Hum. Comput. Interact. 5 (1990) 305–344.

[10] G. Chaitin, Algorithmic Information Theory, Cambridge University Press, Cambridge, 1987.

[11] I. Sommerville, T. Rodden, P. Sawyer, R. Bentley, M. Twidale, Integrating ethnography into the requirements engineering process, in: Proceedings of the IEEE Requirements Engineering Conference, San Diego, 1993.

[12] G. Chaitin, Algorithmic information theory, IBM J. Res. Dev. 21 (1977) 350, (Toward a mathematical theory of life, in: The Maximum Entropy Formalism (R.D. Levine and M. Tribus, Ed.), MIT press, Cambridge, MA, 1979).

[13] P. Vitányi, M. Li, Minimum description length induction, Bayesianism, and Kolmogorov complexity, 1999. arxiv.org cs.LG/9901014.

[14] R. Cilibrasi, P. Vitanyi, in: Clustering by compression, IEEE International Symposium on Information Theory Yokohama, Japan, 2003.

[15] G. Blelloch, Introduction to data compression, 2000. (Course notes for: Algorithms for the real world).

[16] G.K. Wallace, The JPEG Still Picture Compression Standard, Commun. ACM 34 (1991) 30–44, April.

[17] M.D. Adams, The JPEG-2000 Still Image Compression Standard, ISO/IEC JTC 1/SC 29/WG 1N 2412, Int. Org. for Stand./Org. Int. de Normal, Paris, France, 2001.

[18] P. Beatty, I. Reay, S. Dick, J. Miller, Consumer Trust in E-Commerce Websites: A Meta-Study. ACM Computing Surveys, 2008 (in print).

[19] N. Schadewitz, A.V. Nguyen-Ngoc, E. Law, Identifying design patterns in international collaborative learning—Two contrasting case studies, 2009.

[20] V. Basili, R. Selby, D. Hutchens, Experimentation in software engineering, IEEE Trans. Softw. Eng. 1986.

[21] R. Glass, I. Vessey, V. Ramesh, Research in Software Engineering: An Analysis of the Literature, J. Inf. Softw. Technol. 44 (8) (2002) 491–506, June.

[22] V. Basili, F. Shull, F. Lanubile, Building knowledge through families of experiments, IEEE Trans. Softw. Eng. 25 (4) (1999) 456–473.

[23] L. Bratthall, M. Jørgensen, Can you trust a single data source exploratory software engineering case study? Empir. Softw. Eng. 7 (1) (2002) 9–26.

[24] E. Webb, D. Campbell, R. Schwartz, L. Sechrest, Unobtrusive Measures: Nonreactive Research in the Social Sciences, Rand McNally, Chicago, IL, 1966.

[25] N.K. Denzin, The Research Act in Sociology, Butterworth, London, 1970.

[26] L. Cheng, Changing Language Teaching Through Language Testing: A Wash Back Study, Cambridge University Press, Cambridge, 2005, p. 72.

[27] M. Hammersley, P. Atkinson, Ethnography: Principles in practice, Tavistock, London, 1983.

[28] M.B. Miles, A.M. Huberman, Qualitative Data Analysis, Sage, Beverly Hills, 1984, p. 235.

[29] N.K. Denzin, The Research Act: A Theoretical Introduction to Sociological Methods, McGraw-Hill, New York, NY, 1978.

[30] J. Daly, Replication and a Multi-Method Approach to Empirical Software Engineering Research, 1996. (Ph.D. Thesis. Department of Computer Science, University of Strathclyde, Glasgow, UK).

[31] N.K. Denzin, Y. Lincoln (Eds.), Collecting and Interpreting Qualitative Materials, Sage Publications, Thousand Oaks, CA, 1988.

[32] B. Kaplan, D. Duchon, Combining qualitative and quantitative methods in information systems research: A case study, MIS Q. 1988.

[33] M.Q. Patton, Qualitative Evaluation Methods, Sage, Beverly Hills, CA, 1980.

[34] P. Downward, A. Mearman, Methodological triangulation at the Bank of England: An investigation, 2005. (Discussion Paper 505. University of the West of England press, Bristol School of Economics).

[35] J. Kimchi, B. Polivka, J.S. Stevenson, Triangulation: Operational definitions, Nurs. Res. 40 (6) (1991) 364–366.

[36] S. Mathison, Why triangulate? Educ. Res. 77 (2) (1988) 13–17.

[37] N.G. Fielding, J.L. Fielding, Linking Data: Qualitative and Quantitative Methods in Social Research, Sage, Beverley Hills, CA, 1986.

[38] H. Rittel, M. Webber, Dilemmas in a general theory of planning, Policy Sci. 4 (1973) 155–169.

[39] G. Gigerenzer, R. Selten, Bounded Rationality, MIT, Cambridge, MA, 2002.

[40] R.E. Gomory, An essay on the known, the unknown and the unknowable, Sci. Am. 272 (1995) 120.

[41] T.C. Lethbridge, S.E. Sim, J. Singer, Studying software engineers: Data collection techniques for software field studies, Empir. Softw. Eng. 10 (3) (2005) 311–341.

[42] G. Dickson, A programmatic approach to information systems research: An experimentalist's view, in: The Information Systems Research Challenge: Experimental Research Methods, I. Benbasat (Ed.), Harvard Business School, 1989.

[43] B. Kitchenham, L. Pickard, S.-L. Pfeeger, Case studies for method and tool evaluation, IEEE Softw. (1995) 52–62.

[44] R.K. Yin, Case Study Research: Design and Methods, second ed., Sage Publications, USA, 1984.

[45] T. Jick, Mixing qualitative and quantitative methods: Triangulation in action, Admin. Sci. Quart. 24, 1979.

[46] R. Glass, The software research crisis, IEEE Softw. 11 (6) 1994.

[47] J. Creswell, Research Design: Qualitative, Quantitative and Mixed Methods Approaches, second ed., Sage publications, 2003.

[48] J. Singer, N.G. Vinson, Ethical issues in empirical studies of software engineering, IEEE Trans. Softw. Eng. 28 (12) (2002) 1171–1180, December.

[49] V. Basili, The role of experimentation in software engineering: Past, current, and future, in: 18th International Conference on Software Engineering, IEEE, Berlin, Germany, 1996, pp. 442–449.

[50] J. Miller, J. Daly, M. Wood, M. Roper, A. Brooks, Statistical power and its subcomponents—Missing and misunderstood concepts in empirical software engineering research, Inf. Softw. Technol. 4 (39) (1997) 285–295.

[51] J. Miller, Statistical significance testing—A panacea for software technology experiments? J. Syst. Softw. 2 (73) (2004) 183–192.

[52] M. Zelkowitz, D. Wallance, Experimental validation in software engineering, Inf. Softw. Technol. 11 (39) (1997) 735–743.

[53] T. Dyba, V. Kampenes, D. Sjøberg, A systematic review of statistical power in software engineering experiments, Inf. Softw. Technol. 8 (48) (2006) 745–755.

[54] B. Kitchenham, S. Pfleeger, L. Pickard, P. Jones, D. Hoaglin, K. El Emam, et al., Preliminary guidelines for empirical research in software engineering, IEEE Trans. Softw. Eng. 8 (28) (2002) 721–734.

[55] J. Miller, Replicating software engineering experiments: A poisoned chalice or the Holy Grail, Inf. Softw. Technol. 47 (4) (2005) 233–244.

[56] A. Brooks, J. Daly, J. Miller, M. Roper, W. Wood, Replication's role in experimental computer science, 1994. (Technical Report EFoCS-5-941 [RR/94/172], Department of Computer Science, University of Strathclyde, Glasgow, Scotland, UK).

[57] M. Oivo, New opportunities for empirical research, in: V.R. Basili, H.D. Rombach, K. Schneider, B. Kitchenham, D. Pfahl, R.W. Selby (Eds.), Empirical Software Engineering Issues. LNCS, vol. 4336, Springer, Heidelberg, Germany, 2007, p. 22.

[58] B. Curtis, Measurement and experimentation in software engineering, in: Proceedings of IEEE, Los Alamitos, CA, 1980, pp. 1144–1157.

[59] W.M.K. Trochim, Research Methods: The Concise Knowledge Base, Atomic Dog Publishing, 2006.

[60] V. Mandic, J. Markkula, M. Oivo, Towards Multi-Method Research Approach in Empirical Software Engineering, 2009. (University of Oulu, Department of Information Processing Science, Rakentajantie 3, 90014 University of Oulu, Finland).

[61] M. Shaw, What makes good research in software engineering? Int. J. Softw. Tools Technol. Transf. 4 (1) (2002) 1–7.

[62] A. Hramiak, Initial evaluation and analysis of post graduate trainees' use of a virtual learning environment in initial teacher training, Electron. J. e-Learn. 5 (2) (2007) 103–112.

[63] M. Li, P. Vitanyi, An Introduction to Kolmogorov Complexity and its Applications, second ed., Springer, New York, NY, 1997.

[64] L. Ball, T. Ormerod, Putting ethnography to work: The case for a cognitive ethnography of design, Int. J. Hum. Comput. Stud. 53 (1) (2000) 147–168.

[65] J. Brewer, A. Hunter, Multimethod Research: A Synthesis of Styles, Sage, Thousand Oaks, 1989.

[66] D.T. Campbell, D.W. Fiske, Convergent and discriminant validation by the multitrait-multimethod matrix, Psychol. Bull. 56 (1959) 81–105.

[67] N. Fenton, S. Peeger, R. Glass, Science and substance: A challenge to software engineers, IEEE Software 11 (4) (1994) 86–95.

[68] M. Hammersley, What's wrong with ethnography? London, Routledge, 1992.

[69] H.W. Smith, Strategies of Social Research: The Methodological Imagination, Prentice Hall, Englewood Cliffs, NJ, 1975.

[70] M. Wood, J. Daly, J. Miller, M. Roper, Multi-Method Research: An Empirical Investigation of Object-Oriented Technology, Syst. Softw. 48 (1) (1999) 13–26.

StarLight: Next-Generation Communication Services, Exchanges, and Global Facilities

JOE MAMBRETTI

Northwestern University, Illinois, USA

TOM DEFANTI

University of California, San Diego, USA

MAXINE D. BROWN

University of Illinois at Chicago, USA

Abstract

Communication services, architecture, and technologies are rapidly evolving in response to application demand and research innovation. These changes are motivating a fundamentally new approach to the design and provisioning of services, facilities, and infrastructure. Traditionally, such resources have been designed and implemented as centralized fixed utility services, with almost no options for specialization and customization, especially by processes at the network edge. Supporting infrastructure has been created and deployed much like buildings are constructed, using a set of highly defined plans, resulting in hardened structures intended to exist basically unchanged for many years. However, this approach leads to severe restrictions on the creation, deployment, enhancement, and customization of services. Furthermore, this approach does not recognize the inherent potential of digital resources for affecting ongoing improvements through rapid continual change and for specialization and customization. Consequently, a new communication design model is being created, implemented in prototype, and placed into production at select sites around the world. This new model is based on multiple emerging trends in advanced network research. This model supports a much broader range of communication services than traditional systems and highly versatile functionality by providing

ADVANCES IN COMPUTERS, VOL. 80
ISSN: 0065-2458/DOI: 10.1016/S0065-2458(10)80005-1

191

a structural programmable framework. This structure encapsulates network resources as addressable modules that can be discovered, integrated, and customized to create many different types of communication services in advance or dynamically, in direct response to changing requirements.

1. Introduction

Communication services, architecture, and technologies are rapidly evolving to take advantage of major potentials for improvements at all levels. This chapter presents an overview of these major changes, which are motivated by both responses to new application demands and to a desire to take advantage of research innovation. These topics are important for anyone involved in developing, operating, or using digital communication services. These changes are motivating a fundamentally new approach to the design and provisioning of services, facilities, and infrastructure. Traditionally, communication systems have been designed and implemented as centralized fixed utility services, with almost no options for specialization and customization, especially by processes at the network edge. Supporting infrastructure has been created and deployed much like buildings are constructed, using a set of highly defined plans, resulting in hardened structures intended to exist basically unchanged for many years. However, this approach is highly limiting in a world that requires rapid responses to ongoing changes in service requirements. Traditional inflexible designs lead to severe restrictions in the creation, deployment, enhancement, and customization of services. Furthermore, this approach does not recognize the inherent potential of digital resources for affecting ongoing improvements through rapid continual change and for specialization and customization.

Consequently, a new communication design model is being created, implemented in prototype, and placed into production at select sites around the world. This new model is based on multiple emerging trends in advanced network research [1,2]. This model supports a much broader range of communication services than traditional systems and highly versatile functionality by providing a structural, programmable framework. This structure encapsulates network resources as addressable modules that can be discovered, integrated, and customized to create many different types of communication services in advance or dynamically, in direct response to changing requirements.

A major attribute of this design model is a high level of abstraction that separates functional capabilities from underlying physical infrastructure and configurations. In part, this objective is achieved by using a service-oriented architecture (SOA) along with sophisticated intermediate network middleware—intermediate software components that allow for high degrees of flexibility, adjustability, and customization. This model also supports techniques to take advantage of new innovative technologies that provide for much more flexibility than traditional network resources. It also supports innovative operational processes to allow for the support of more sophisticated and distributed processes, and new methods for optimal resource utilization. These new models of communication services are being implemented at advanced facilities, including the StarLight international communications exchange in Chicago, which is part of the Global Lambda Integrated Facility (GLIF).

1.1 Traditional Communication Services Architecture

For many decades, the traditional communication services architecture was oriented to optimize support for analog-based services. Given the massive installed base of this architecture and its technology infrastructure, the development and deployment of alternative digital-based communication services has been a fairly gradual process. These digital services and technologies were initially designed for communications among computers, which required an alternative approach to existing analog-based communications. This alternative was developed initially through the ARPAnet program and later through the National Science Foundation's (NSF) NSFnet. During the early years of their development, digital communications comprised only a very small part of all communication systems. In the early 1990s, when the NSFnet was evolving from a private research network to the commercial Internet, the majority of the installed base consisted of multiple analog-oriented communication systems. As a result, the Internet was implemented as an overlay network on widely deployed mid-level bearer systems, such as ATM (Asynchronous Transfer Mode), supported by core wide-area transport used on analog-oriented technologies, such as SONET/SDH (Synchronous Optical Networking/Synchronous Digital Hierarchy), which are multiplexing protocols for sending digital bits over optical networks. Each of these layers operated fairly independently with minimal interactivity among layers. One consequence of this approach is that traditional network architecture has provided support for only a restricted, small range of communication services, each with only a minimal number of attributes. These services have been closely integrated with specific underlying physical hardware deployed with rigid configurations. As a result, enhancing existing services, deploying new services, and customizing services have been difficult and costly projects. Also, many advanced new services could not be deployed on existing infrastructure, especially those that required autonomous intradomain signaling for resource utilization.

Although the Internet has been the most successful communication service in history, its full potential has not yet been realized. Even today, wide-area implementations are still being designed to accommodate the restrictions of underlying legacy communications systems. The current Internet is operated as an overlay with common, undifferentiated, centrally managed communication services, supported by a highly restrictive underlying infrastructure. Because of the inherent design and implementation restrictions of this infrastructure, traditional architectural models have become barriers to future applications and services developments.

However, over the last two decades, much progress has been made in creating a new architectural model, driven in large part by several macro trends, including advanced driver applications, powerful new innovations in core technologies, and new communications services architectural models that enable high levels of functional abstraction. Unlike the restricted legacy approaches, these new models provide for a significant degree of programmability and they can be designed to support an almost unlimited range of services and capabilities, including those that are based on highly distributed implementations [3].

1.2 Driver Applications

The Internet was originally developed during a time when bandwidth was highly limited. It was designed to support extremely large numbers of small, short-duration content streams. Also, current Internet service quality parameters are minimal, supporting primarily undifferentiated best-effort capabilities. However, increasingly applications require capabilities that support high-volume, long-duration streams with guaranteed assurances of high-quality communication services. Increased capacity is a requirement not only for overall aggregate traffic but also for individual data streams.

Data-intensive science applications have always been major drivers of technology because they encounter technical barriers long before these limitations are experienced within other application domains. Currently, multiple science domains are motivating the creation of new advanced communication services to meet the requirements of the most data-intensive applications in the world, including those in high-energy physics, astronomy, computational astrophysics, genomics, computational chemistry, and others. Also, the current Internet does not provide adequate quality support for digital media, although digital media applications are one of the fastest growing segments of communications. Many of current network capabilities support digital media as a highly special, not common, service. New services are required to support large-volume, high-quality digital media, 3D digital media, and ultra-high-definition digital media. Digital media must be supported as a common, ubiquitous service, not as a highly specialized capability.

Another driver consists of data-intensive analytic applications, such as those employing advanced data-mining techniques. Increasingly, important data is hosted in large-scale repositories around the globe. The value of that data is often not realized by its use at any single location, but through combined use with other data from other distributed locations. These globally distributed yet highly integrated data streams are becoming the basis of the digital economy.

Cloud computing is another driver for next-generation communications. Advanced cloud-computing applications are being deployed in commercial and consumer environments. Cloud computing allows large-scale generic information technology resources to be accessed and utilized by tens of thousands of distributed applications, on computers, mobile devices, and smart objects, using high-performance communications. Because cloud computing is network dependent, its full benefits can only be realized by utilizing a more sophisticated model of communication.

Multiple medical applications are being developed that require multiple advanced capabilities that are not provided by commodity Internet services. These applications must be implemented in highly distributed environments, with high quality and exceptional security. They integrate distributed databases with multiple devices ranging from instruments, to monitoring equipment, to specialized sensors.

1.3   Emerging Network Services Architecture

1.3.1   An Overview

To address the requirements of next-generation applications, it is essential to create an architecture that allows for the design of communications environments that can support not only a small range of static communication services but a very wide range of services that can be continually expanded and enhanced. This goal is only possible by providing a communications environment that has multiple, extremely flexible, programmable capabilities. Such an architecture can be designed to provide for high levels of abstraction and virtualization, attributes which elevate functionality above the particular characteristics of individual physical resources, software implementations, and configurations. This approach is a major departure from traditional communications systems, which are essentially designed and implemented for specific highly defined capabilities, with a limited number of services that are tightly integrated with underlying defined sets of physical resources. Consequently, any change is complex and cost prohibitive.

The alternative approach provides for a highly distributed, multidomain programmable communications environment that can be used to create an unlimited number of services. Essentially, this environment is comprised of multiple resource components that can be discovered, assembled, configured, reconfigured, and discarded after use. The characteristics of the environment can change dynamically and continually in response to altered conditions and requirements. In this environment, all physical components are encapsulated as software objects with APIs. These components can be programmed to create many different types of services, including highly specialized custom services. This environment allows services to be created and controlled directly and deterministically not only by the organization that manages the environment but also by second parties, edge sites, end users, and individual applications. This approach frees service creation and control from the constraints of communication services provided as a centralized utility. This model provides major opportunities for creating multiple types of decentralized, peer-to-peer, *ad hoc*, and mobile implementations.

1.3.2   Network Services Architecture: Architectural Structure

The development of this architecture is proceeding within the larger context of information technology activities related to both R&D and standards development, especially those oriented toward distributed systems. Multiple communities are developing general frameworks for a SOA based on emerging industry standards and on methods being developed in research laboratories. These architectural frameworks are being developed for many service-oriented designs based on functionality supported by multiple modular processes that can be gathered and implemented into high-level capabilities [3,4].

These frameworks provide an environment in which a high level of service abstraction of capabilities and functions can be made known to processes through advertisements transmitted as standard, open communication messages. These high-level services interact with intermediate software components positioned between those services and core facilities and resources encapsulated as addressable software objects. This intermediate software can support specialized workflow languages related to communication services. Increasingly, advanced services require maintaining state, and workflow languages can assist in maintaining state and providing state information to processes, including support for context-aware automated response capabilities. Using this approach for communication services fundamentally improves advanced capabilities at all levels. This approach provides a potential for supporting many different types of communication services, and allows for precise selection of specific service attributes for a high degree of customization.

1.4   Multiservices Architecture

The standard network architecture model is described, in part, as a series of seven layers, with different sets of functions placed at each layer. Traditionally, these layers have been kept fairly separate, supporting services at a single layer with minimal interoperability among layers. This traditional hierarchical architectural model limits signaling among layers [5]. New architectural models provide methods for transitioning away from this traditional model to less rigid approaches [6]. Other initiatives are developing advanced concepts of "hybrid networking," or "multiservice networking," which allows for coordinated services at all levels [3]. These hybrid techniques can support new types of extremely high-performance, high-quality services.

For example, the exceptional success of the Internet is based on its support for a reliable, highly scalable, common Layer 3 (L3) service for many types of applications. However, even though the capabilities of this service have been well demonstrated, it does not meet all of the requirements of all applications. Currently, the most widely deployed and used Internet services are implemented and supported as best-effort, nondeterministic, packet-routed services, with almost no ability to adjust those services at the edge of the network. Using traditional architectural models, specialized services usually can be implemented only within a single domain, and they are almost always limited in scalability, difficult to manage, and costly to operate. As a result, deterministic, differentiated services have rarely been implemented.

An increasingly wide range of L3 services exist, including those based on TCP, UDP, SCTP, and their variants, composites, and alternatives, supported by IPv4 and IPv6, unicast, multicast, with or without DiffServ capabilities, and various types of tunneling and packet-switching protocols. In addition, multiservice techniques make possible providing L3 services that are complemented by those at L2 and L1, and provide options for substituting L3 paths with L1 and L2 paths. However, "multiservice" should not imply an environment that merely supports multiple services, but one in which applications and processes can individually discover, select, and use those services, even blending different streams supported by different integrated services within a single application. Also, basic services should be able to adjust dynamically by *ad hoc* integrations with other types of services; for example, L3 streams enhanced by L2/L1 streams.

A multiservices environment should enable options to accept a predefined default service, to select and blend different services, to ensure specific levels of determinism, and to highly customize individualized network services (e.g., setting precise levels of latency, jitter, security, redundancy, and path direction). The environment should also provide options for discovering, integrating, utilizing, and reconnecting individual core components, including specialized L3 services with customized attributes, specific L2 channels and crossconnections, and addressable lightpaths. Options would include those for national- and global-scale point-to-point L2 services, and L1 wavelength-based transport, such as end-to-end lightpaths, and options for assigning single dedicated wavelengths, multiple wavelengths, and sublambdas and specific physical network elements, such as ports. The environment should enable these communications capabilities to be extended directly into and integrated with edge devices, such as instruments, sensors, computers, clusters, storage devices, and individual applications.

1.5   Architecture: Communication Services Signaling

Currently, no standard signaling mechanism exists for discovering, obtaining, and integrating network resources by external processes, which is required for provisioning distributed services within and across domains. Although a SOA approach provides for a high level of process abstraction and eliminates many requirements for specialized signaling, it does not completely address all requirements. A particular challenge is developing an interdomain signaling method.

The required architecture must allow for edge-initiated signaling and must be integrated with processes that optimize matches between application requirements and available network resources. This signaling should be accomplished using specialized communications, either in-band or out-of-band. This architecture should enable both link state and stateless protocol implementations, and provide for information propagation channels among core network elements.

To address these issues, multiple network architecture research projects have been established, using in-band and out-of-band IP communications and signaling as a foundation, to undertake functions previously provided only by management and control processes, through traditional management and control planes. These functions include those dealing with access policy, scheduling, resource discovery, reservations, allocations, and overall resource management, traffic engineering, physical configurations, addressing, routing at L1, L2, and L3 (including topology discovery), protection, fault detection, and restoration.

Currently, the majority of these research activities are basing these capabilities on emerging SOA standards. For example, the World Wide Web Consortium has created the Web Services Definition Language (WSDL) and the Web Services Resource Framework (WSRF) [7]. Implementations have been developed that use a SOA based on WSRF to provision multiservice network environments, enabling network services and related core resources to be exposed as Web Services; for example, employing web tags to describe those services. With this approach, a Web Services "wrapper" encapsulates a resource, which is advertised as a module that can be used by other services. The Open Grid Services Architecture, created by the Open Grid Forum [8], is leveraging the work of the OASIS (Organization for the Advancement of Structured Information Standards) group to create standardized software tools to be used for encapsulation so that processes can be abstracted and integrated with other processes, including network services [9]. Multiple international networking research organizations have established activities to examine optimal designs for WSDL schema that can implement supersets of Network Service Interface functionality, including those using WSRF stateful elements. Also, the OASIS organization is creating the UDDI (Universal Description, Discovery, and Integration) protocol, which can be integrated into a Web Services stack as a standard method for publishing and for discovering the network-based software components of a SOA. The Web Services-Inspection Language (WSIL) is a related standard that specifies an XML format, or "grammar," which examines a location for available services as well as rules that indicate how the information discovered through that process can be made available. Keyword searching for service descriptions and Uniform Resource Identifiers can be effective tools for building UDDI or WSIL interconnections. Another project is leveraging these efforts as part of an effort to create a Network Description Language.

Integrating these high-level processes with mid-level intermediate network processes and techniques for distributed resources programming and partitioning provides communication environments that are significantly more powerful and flexible than traditional centralized systems.

2. Future Network Services and Facility Prototypes

2.1   Network Facilities

Multiple advanced network research communities have been investigating and experimenting with more flexible communication environments described in the previous sections for many years. More importantly, they have also been implementing them as prototypes and operating them as production facilities, beginning in the early 1990s with the implementation of facilities designed to support scientific research. The next few sections describe several of these facilities.

2.2   Network Access Point and MREN

In 1993, when the NSF began transitioning the NSFnet to the commercial sector, the research community in the Chicago metro area established one of the nation's first Internet exchange points, the Network Access Point (NAP). This NAP was one of three originally planned, although four eventually were established initially. Unlike other early exchange points, the Chicago NAP was based on ATM technology, which allowed participating networks to avoid, as an option, multiple intermediate routers. Consequently, the Chicago research community created the Metropolitan Research and Education Network (MREN) with a core facility at the NAP and L2 circuits to multiple universities and national research labs. Each participating organization could stream L3 traffic over the L2 circuits to any of the other organizations with only one intermediate node. By eliminating multiple core routers and basing transport on L2 paths, this approach provided a unique high-performance streaming service, required by data-intensive science projects. This approach also allowed for specialized communication channels to be implemented, not shared by commodity Internet traffic, to ensure that all resources could be dedicated to the highest priority traffic. In addition, this model allowed for a higher degree of service customization, as these channels could be implemented with specialized protocols. A few years later, this model was established on a national scale by the NSF through the vBNS (very-high-performance Backbone Network Service) initiative. MREN also assisted in creating the first exchange facility for US federal agency networks, the Next-Generation Internet eXchange (NGIX), at the NAP. This facility was the first instance of a special type of major exchange facility that subsequently became known as a ''Giga-POP,'' because it could support gigabit per second transport. Although these facilities minimized the number of core routers used for transport, like all major exchanges, they were based on routed core nodes. However, these wide-area network facilities demonstrated the changing balance between L2 and L3 transport methods, primarily locating L3 nodes only at the network edge.

2.3 STAR TAP

This approach was expanded on an international scale through the Science, Technology And Research Transit Access Point (STAR TAP), which was initially created at the NAP in 1997 as the world's first persistent infrastructure for the long-term interconnection and interoperability of advanced international networks, supporting applications, performance measuring, and technology evaluations [10]. The STAR TAP facility, by 2000, became a model for international exchanges. STAR TAP was the first facility in the world to demonstrate the potential of minimizing core routers for international traffic. Participating organizations from other countries used this facility to interconnect, using L2 SONET/SDH channels to support long-haul transport channels that were interconnected at STAR TAP. Once again, this time at a global scale, the potential to provide high-quality, high-performance services while minimizing the number of core routers in long-haul networks was demonstrated. For the data-intensive science community, the STAR TAP facility provided the highest performance services in the world; for example, the highest performance paths among countries in Europe was through the STAR TAP exchange. Similarly, it was the highest performance exchange among Asian countries.

2.4 The StarLight International Exchange Facility

By the late 1990s, it became clear that over the next decade, a next-generation exchange based on optical networking would be required to meet the aggressive demands of advanced applications and to take advantage of emerging technologies, especially new optical components. At that time, all data network exchanges were exclusively L3 exchanges, as almost all are today. However, application requirements and new optical technologies motivated the consideration of a multiple service communications exchange. The MREN and STAR TAP facilities demonstrated the potential of minimizing core routers to achieve not only high-performance and high-quality communication services, even for large-scale, high-volume data flows, but also for a much greater degree of service and network programming and customization. The next step was to design and implement a facility that provided options for eliminating all core routers end-to-end internationally.

The StarLight national and international communications exchange was the first such facility in the world. This facility was specifically designed to provide such options and to exchange traffic at all basic layers, including interconnecting and switching lightpaths at 1, 2.5, and 10 Gbps [11]. StarLight was designed as a highly flexible customizable environment to support multiple, programmable, customized networks. The facility was designed primarily to support large-scale, data-intensive global science research [12,13].

2.5   StarLight as a Partitionable Environment

Traditional communication architectural models assume that all aspects of the services and supporting infrastructure are known in advance. The StarLight facility was designed to not only support known communication services but to also support future services not yet conceptualized. The facility allows for the *ad hoc* creation of new services using the repositories of available resources. In addition, this design allows not only basic network resources to be provided to external processes but also capabilities for managing, controlling, and monitoring these resources.

When StarLight was designed, almost all communication exchanges were closed, tightly integrated, monolithic environments. In contrast, the StarLight facility was designed by researchers, for researchers. It was implemented to be an open flexible environment comprised of resources that could be partitioned and devoted to individual networks, communication services, projects, and applications. Furthermore, its design allowed for each partition to have allocated its own core resources as well as all requisite management and control functions. Within this environment, unique sets of specialized communication capabilities could be customized by edge processes, including individual applications. This approach directly addresses the challenge of supporting multiple applications with diverse requirements, including those requirements that vary at different times. This approach enables specialized applications to be supported within their own partitioned environments. A flexible environment can automatically and continually change to adjust to fluctuating demands.

The design of the StarLight facility enabled the development of globally distributed network environments within which it is possible to create customized integrated heterogeneous networks. For example, the StarLight facility enables multiple distributed network resources, including major international- and national-scale services, such as 10 Gbps optical lightpaths, to be partitioned and subpartitioned and integrated into separate domains, each with defined sets of management and engineering functions [14–17]. Such partitioned resources can be allocated to external processes (e.g., networks, organizations, projects, and applications) that interact with and design their own networking environment. Currently, the mechanisms used to provide these partitioning functions are a combination of automated services and manual provisioning methods. However, almost all the partitioned domains are completely managed and controlled by external processes related to discovery, acquisition of resources, provisioning, management, engineering, reconfigurations, and even protection and restoration. As a result of this design approach, the StarLight facility successfully supports dozens of major national and international advanced networks as well as over 20 major experimental network research test beds.

At this time, there is no agreement on the best architectural design approach for the complete set of tools for an exchange facility as a whole or for partitioned segments. However, the StarLight consortium, including its international partners, participates in a number of projects that are developing new, innovative suites of tools to enable dynamic services and infrastructure provisioning at major national and international exchange facilities. These tools support processes that establish continuous interactions among top-level services, intermediate software, and software-encapsulated physical resources. Such tools include direct dynamic path provisioning, such as protocols, edge APIs, external process signaling, physical resource encapsulation, state information capture, and monitoring processes. The StarLight facility uses a larger, more diverse set of tools than at any other communications exchange in the world.

While these tool sets differ in some respects, they have many common attributes. For example, they can communicate messages that allow *ad hoc* services and paths to be created, deleted, and monitored. They transmit defined messages that can be sent to a compatible server process that can establish paths among network elements. They can interrogate the network about current basic state information. They can identify and establish the appropriate paths through a controlled network topology, and configure and reconfigure those paths. They can determine specific paths and topologies and store those topologies for later use, or they can create topologies dynamically. These techniques can be used for L3 tunnels, MPLS paths, vLANs, dynamic lightpath provisioning, and dynamic L2 path provisioning, implemented within environments based on IEEE standards, for example, 802.1p, 802.17, and 802.1q (Virtual Bridged Local Area Networks), which is an architecture that enables traffic from multiple subnets to be supported by a single physical circuit and defines a method of explicit frame tagging. These and related methods are being used to create large-scale highly programmable networks [3].

2.6 Operation Issues

The StarLight facility represents a major departure from traditional communications infrastructure support methods, which are supported by highly centralized, hierarchical, and expensive Network Operation Centers (NOCs), incorporating management planes and control planes designed specifically for that centralized operations model. To move beyond these NOC limitations, StarLight implemented distributed operation processes, which is an important attribute for future advanced networks. This approach allows provisioning and support decisions to be placed at the network edge instead of at a centralized site.

2.7   Global Lambda Integrated Facility

The international advanced networking community is also implementing next-generation multiservice communications infrastructure based on the concepts described here. The StarLight consortium and its international partners are creating and operating a global foundation for next-generation large-scale communication services and infrastructure, based on flexible, international exchange facilities, including StarLight [18,19]. The StarLight community is a founding partner of an international consortium that is creating a large-scale distributed ''facility,'' within which multiple networks and services can be created—the Global Lambda Integrated Facility (GLIF). GLIF participants are National Research and Education Networks, consortia and institutions involved in optical networking and research, and are engaged in creating and exploring prototypes of multiple, innovative communication services and technologies.

3.   Future Directions

3.1   International Global Environment for Network Innovations

The StarLight consortium is participating in the NSF Global Environment for Network Innovations (GENI) initiative. GENI is an open and broadly inclusive research initiative, whose mission is to provide a virtual laboratory for exploring future internets at scale. GENI provides opportunities for academia, industry, and the public to understand, innovate, and transform networks for twenty-first-century communications. GENI is prototyping a major national infrastructure for network research experimentation and early advanced prototypes.

The StarLight consortium is developing the International GENI (iGENI), a unique distributed infrastructure to support worldwide research and development for next-generation network communication services and technologies. To a large degree, this initiative extends much of the existing innovative network research, including experimental activities, supported by the StarLight facility. This infrastructure will be integrated with current and planned GENI resources, and operated for use by GENI researchers conducting experiments that involve multiple aggregations and federations (at multiple sites). iGENI infrastructure will connect distributed network research resources with other GENI national backbone transport resources, with current and planned GENI regional transport resources, and with international research networks and projects.

3.2   NSF IRNC Experimental Networks Program

The StarLight consortium is also participating in the NSF's International Research Network Connections (IRNC) Experimental Networks Program. This initiative encourages the development of data-intensive scientific applications and supporting communication services and technologies. This initiative provides another opportunity to migrate StarLight innovations to advanced networking communities around the world.

3.3   Emerging Architecture, Technologies, and Concepts

Currently, the most advanced concepts in communication services and network design are being driven by data-intensive science projects. Increasingly, these issues are being recognized by the developers of communication services and networks for other application areas, including those focused on organizations, buildings, automobiles, homes, and exterior environments, including those that are sensor based [20]. In all of these areas, there are common issues that must be addressed, such as mechanisms for advertising available network resources, providing network policy authentication and authorization, interconnecting resources, and implementing highly distributed management and control processes. The advanced methods and techniques being developed at StarLight and related facilities have a major potential to be useful to these other areas. The experimental projects noted here may assist in expediting this type of technology transition.

4.   Summary

Traditionally, communication services and networks have been designed and deployed as rigid resources, with minimal options for enhancement, specialization, and customization. Consequently, this approach has not been sufficiently flexible to meet multiple new application demands or to take advantage of many new innovations emerging from research laboratories. In response, a new communication design model is being created, implemented in prototype, and placed into production at selected sites around the world. This approach envisions communications resources not as rigid infrastructure but as a flexible, programmable environment that can be continually changed to meet new requirements.

ACKNOWLEDGMENTS

For supporting the initiatives described here, the authors thank the National Science Foundation, the Department of Energy, Northwestern University, the University of Illinois at Chicago, Argonne National Laboratory, Fermi National Accelerator Laboratory, SURFnet, and CANARIE.

REFERENCES

[1] K. Bergman, J. Mambretti, J. St Sauver, B. Wing, Networking Research Challenges Workshop Report, 2008. Large Scale Networking Coordinating Group, Networking and Information Technology Research and Development Program, (NITRD) (Department of Energy: Office of Science, National Science Foundation Directorate for Computer and Information Science and Engineering).

[2] T. Ndousse, N. Ghani, J. Mambretti, D. Petravick, B. Wing, N. Rao, et al., Workshop Report on Advanced Networking for Distributed Petascale Science: R&D Challenges and Opportunities, 2008.

[3] F. Travostino, J. Mambretti, G. Karmous-Edwards (Eds.), Grid Networks: Enabling Grids with Advanced Communication Technology. John Wiley & Sons, New York, 2006 (July).

[4] J. Mambretti, Infrastructure as Platform: Services-Oriented Architecture, Virtualization, and 21st Century Communications, vol. 59. Annual Review of Communications, International Engineering Consortium, 2006 (Reprinted in "Analysts Corner" IEC Newsletter, May 2006).

[5] H. Zimmerman, OSI reference model—The ISO model of architecture for open systems interconnection, IEEE Trans. Commun. 28 (1980) 425–432.

[6] General Principles and General Reference Model for Next Generation Networks, ITU-T Y. 2011, October, 2004.

[7] Web Services Resource Framework (WSRF) Technical Committee, Organization for the Advancement of Structured Information Standards. www.oasis-open.org.

[8] www.ogf.org.

[9] www.oasis-open.org.

[10] STAR TAP received major funding from NSF awards ANI-9980480 and ANI-9712283 to UIC, and DOE funding to ANL. www.startap.net/starlight.

[11] StarLight received major funding from NSF award ANI-0229642 to UIC and NU, and DOE funding to ANL. www.startap.net/starlight.

[12] M. Brown, Blueprint for the future of high-performance networking, Commun. ACM 46 (11) (2003) 30–77. (Special issue, November).

[13] T. DeFanti, C. De Laat, J. Mambretti, B. St Arnaud, TransLight: A global scale lambda grid for e-science, Commun. ACM 46 (11) (2003) 34–41. (Special issue on "Blueprint for the future of high performance networking, November).

[14] T. DeFanti, M. Brown, J. Leigh, O. Yu, E. He, J. Mambretti, et al., Optical switching middleware for the OptIPuter, IEICE Trans. Commun. E86-B (8) (2003) 2263–2272. (Special issue on photonic IP network technologies for next-generation broadband access, August).

[15] J. Mambretti, D. Lillethun, J. Lange, J. Weinberger, Optical dynamic intelligent network services (ODIN): An experimental control plane architecture for high performance distributed environments based on dynamic Lightpath provisioning, IEEE Commun. Mag. (Special Issue with Feature Topic on Optical Control Planes for Grid Networks: Opportunities, Challenges and the Vision).

[16] ITU G.8080/Y.1304. Architecture for the automatically switched optical network (ASON).

[17] D.B. Hoang, T. Lavian, S. Figueira, J. Mambretti, I. Monga, S. Naiksatam, et al., DWDM-RAM: An architecture for data intensive services enabled by next generation dynamic optical networks, in: Proceedings of the Global Telecommunications Conference Workshops, IEEE, 2004, pp. 400–409. (December).

[18] www.glif.is.

[19] T. DeFanti, M. Brown, J. Mambretti, J. Silvester, R. Johnson, TransLight: A major US component of the GLIF, CTWatch Q. 1 (2) 2005. (May).

[20] P. Vicat-Blanc Primet, T. Kudoh, J. Mambretti (Eds.), in: Networks for Grid Applications, Second International Conference, GridNets 2008, Beijing, China, October 8–10, 2008. Revised Selected Papers in Springervol. XIII, 2009, p. 264. (Lecture Notes of the Institute for Computer Sciences, Social-Informatics and Telecommunications, Engineering, vol. 2).

Parameters Effecting 2D Barcode Scanning Reliability

AMIT GROVER

Identity Theft and Financial Fraud Research and Operations Center, University of Nevada, Las Vegas, Nevada, USA

PAUL BRAECKEL

Identity Theft and Financial Fraud Research and Operations Center, University of Nevada, Las Vegas, Nevada, USA

KEVIN LINDGREN

Identity Theft and Financial Fraud Research and Operations Center, University of Nevada, Las Vegas, Nevada, USA

HAL BERGHEL

Identity Theft and Financial Fraud Research and Operations Center, University of Nevada, Las Vegas, Nevada, USA

DENNIS COBB

Identity Theft and Financial Fraud Research and Operations Center, University of Nevada, Las Vegas, Nevada, USA

ADVANCES IN COMPUTERS, VOL. 80
ISSN: 0065-2458/DOI: 10.1016/S0065-2458(10)80006-3

209

Abstract

This paper describes a case study to identify the various parameters that affect the scanning reliability of 2D barcodes for high content density applications. A review of the numerous options for 2D symbologies showed that, in theory, these symbologies are capable of encoding relatively large amounts of data, but in practice, barcode scan-ability decreases as the encoded content increases. With specific attention to higher content (or capacity) applications, a case study was performed to identify the 2D symbologies with the highest scanning reliability, to be termed ''scan-ability,'' as well as the various parameters that impact this scan-ability. The paper is divided into four logical sections. The introduction section covers the goal and the specific requirements of the project. Section 2 discusses in detail the various parameters that impact the scan reliability of high-capacity 2D barcodes. Section 3 focuses on the testing methodology employed and Section 4 summarizes the conclusions of the detailed testing. Based on our requirements, our findings indicated that the best three scan reliability measurements of 96%–99% were all obtained using the PDF417 symbology with different media types and scanners.

1. Introduction

A barcode is a symbol that contains encoded plaintext data that can be read by standard optical scanners/decoders, thereby automating data representation and retrieval while eliminating potential human error. Common barcode applications include tracking of consumer goods at grocery stores, checkout terminals, document management tools, inventory management, ticketing, mobile tagging, mobile airline boarding passes, etc. The corelation between the barcodes and the corresponding messages is termed as *symbology*. Symbologies are classified as linear and two-dimensional (2D).

The goal of this case study was not only to identify the various parameters that affect the scanning reliability of 2D barcodes but also to identify the most reliable barcode and its appropriate configuration for high content density applications. The need for this study is rooted in a project for developing a secure credentialing system, where there is a need to have data encoded in high-capacity 2D barcodes on viz. Polyvinyl chloride (PVC) and polyester media.

Initial experimentation showed that the scanning reliability of these high-capacity 2D barcodes was not as high as a typical "grocery store checkout" system. Since the average user's typical experience with barcodes is the checkout line at the grocery store, the expectation from using a barcode is quick and reliable scanning. The primary difference between this expected result and a second-generation 2D barcode was in the data content density. The typical "grocery store" items use a very small amount of data in the barcode, mainly a "primary key," which requires referencing a backend database to read the complete information about the scanned item. Our particular application required eliminating this dependency on a backend database, thereby requiring a large amount of data to be encoded directly in the barcode itself. Even though the barcodes that we used were within the theoretical data capacity limits for different barcode symbologies, the less than perfect scan reliability prompted us to explore other potential factors.

These secondary factors included the barcode symbology itself, the encoder which conforms to the relevant barcode symbology, the printer which creates the physical barcode, the media on which the barcode is printed, and the decoder that interprets the encoded content. This case study describes a series of internally designed tests, and interpretation of the test results, to precisely identify the impact of data content density, error correction level, type of encoding, scanner characteristics, type of media, and printer on the scan-reliability of 2D barcodes.

2. Factors that Affect Barcode Scan Ability

As per the Layman's guide to ANSI, CEN, and ISO bar code print quality documents published by the Association for Automatic Identification and Mobility (AIM) [1], *"through the years, bar codes had been printed that met the existing standards, but would not scan. And often bar codes printed out of specified standards did scan."*

Years of extensive testing by different groups from ANSI, Committee for European Normalization (CEN), and ISO, have identified the following critical parameters for bar code scan reliability: Aperture and wavelength of the scanner, reflectance and surface opacity of the media, printer characteristics, scan grade and reflectance profile, and symbol grade and the operative scanning environment. In addition to these factors, our case study considered other parameters such as the type of symbology used, the content density of the encoded data, the error correction level used, and the method of encoding. Each of these factors, as they relate to this particular case study, is examined in detail in the subsequent sections. The symbologies used may be linear or 2D. Error correction techniques are used to increase the scan-ability to handle partial data corruption. The barcode may be printed on different kinds of media such as paper, polyester, and PVC. Each of these media offer different benefits and are typically selected based on the intended usage profile for the barcode. Once the barcode is physically printed on the media, various decoders or scanners may be used to decode it based on the type of barcode used.

2.1   Barcode Symbologies

While linear symbologies, such as Universal Product Code (UPC), Code 39, Code 128, EAN, MSI, Intelligent Mail Barcode, Pharmacode, to name a few, were limited in their data-carrying capacity, the 2D symbologies enable large amounts of data to be encoded and decoded in machine-readable formats [2, 25]. Common examples of 2D symbologies include DataMatrix, PDF417, Aztec Code, Codablock, MaxiCode, QR Code (Quick Response Code), Datastrip 2D, etc. [3]. Some common examples of various barcode symbologies are shown in Table I (the Kaywa website [20] was used to generate the QR Code).

Based on the volume of usage, the symbologies may be classified as:

- 1D or stacked symbologies, such as UPC and Code 128. These barcodes are not the focus of this study and will not be discussed in detail.
- Symbologies having widespread industry usage such as PDF417, QR Code, DataMatrix, and Aztec Code.
- Proprietary and Emerging symbologies such as Datastrip 2D [24] and Microsoft's High Capacity Color Barcode (HCCB).

TABLE I
BARCODE SAMPLES

| UPC-A | Code 128 | PDF417 | QR code |
| DataMatrix | Aztec code | High capacity color barcode (HCCB) | DataStrip 2-D |

2.1.1   Symbologies Having Widespread Presence

One of the most widely known barcode symbologies is the UPC symbology, which is a linear barcode used for tracking retail merchandise and other point-of-sale management functions. UPC implementation has different variations, including UPC-A, UPC-B, UPC-D, UPC-E, and UPC-5, although UPC-A is by far the most widely used symbology [28]. It is able to encode 12 bytes of numeric data wherein 11 digits constitute the data and 1 extra digit is used as a check digit for error correction [4]. Each digit is represented graphically as a combination of two bars and two spaces. While UPC-B does not use a check digit, UPC-D differs from UPC-A in that it uses a variable-length code instead of the standard 12 digits used by UPC-A. UPC-E is optimized for applications that require a smaller barcode and produces a compressed code with only 6 digits as opposed to 12 digits [5]. UPC-5 is a 5-digit extension to standard UPC codes used for encoding retail pricing for books. The printed symbol contains both a machine-readable part as well as a human-readable part. The structural breakdown of a typical UPC barcode is shown in Fig. 1.

The following sections provide a brief overview of the 2D symbologies evaluated for this particular project as well as a comparative summary, which may be referenced for quick interpretation.

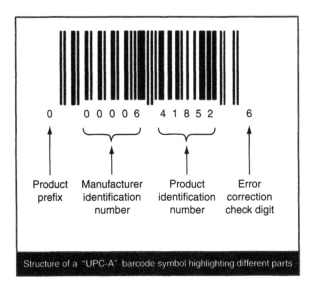

FIG. 1. UPC-A barcode structure.

2.1.1.1 *The PDF417 Symbology.* Portable Data File 417,
though classified as a 2D barcode, is in fact a multirow, variable-length "stacked" symbology developed in 1992 by Symbol Technologies. This unique characteristic allows it to be decoded by many 1D hybrid scanners, apart from regular 2D scanners. The symbol is composed of 3–90 stacked rows. A PDF417 symbol character, or codeword, is the individual building block for the barcode and consists of 17 modules arranged into four bars and four spaces, thereby giving it the name of 417 [17]. The integral sections of the barcode as depicted in Fig. 2 include clearly defined *Start* and *Stop* patterns, the data columns, and the quiet zone.

PDF417 offers encoding a maximum data character capacity of 1850 text ASCII characters, 2710 numerals, or 1108 bytes [2]. This amount of data encoded is a result of the manner in which the algorithm encodes the type of data, for example, numerals require a smaller codeword size to encode than an alphabet letter (Table II).

PDF417 uses Reed Solomon error correction [6]. Error correction levels are user selectable and can be set from 0 (zero) for no error correction to 8 (eight), which is the highest level. This level indicates the amount of redundancy that is added to the encoded barcode. The benefit is the increased scan-ability; however, the downside is that the effective content size is reduced because the error correction takes up content space. Table III illustrates the specifications [2] pertaining to codewords and error correction.

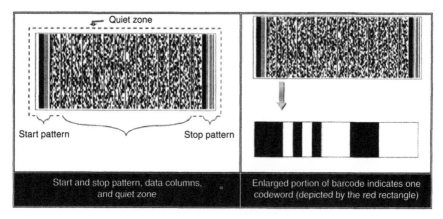

Fig. 2. PDF417 barcode characteristics.

TABLE II
PDF417 CODEWORDS PER CHARACTER TYPE

Character type	Character	Codeword
Alphabetical	1	0.5263
Numeric	1	0.3448
ASCII	1	0.8333

TABLE III
COMMONLY USED ERROR CORRECTION LEVELS FOR PDF417

No. of data codewords	Error correction level	No. of error correction codewords
1–40	2	8
41–160	3	16
161–320	4	32
321–863	5	64

2.1.1.2 *The QR Code Symbology.* QR Code, or Quick Response code, is a 2D matrix code created in 1994 by the Japanese Denso Corporation. As opposed to a stacked barcode, a matrix code is one in which encoding is based on the positioning of the elements or black dots in the matrix. These are among the most popular barcodes being used for mobile tagging (providing information using 2D barcodes on cell phones) applications today. The QR Code data capacity for different encodings is shown in Table IV [7].

TABLE IV

DATA ENCODING CAPACITY FOR QR CODE

Data encoding	Max. number of characters
Numeric	7089
Alphanumeric	4296
Binary	2953
Japanese Kanji characters	1817

TABLE V

QR CODE ERROR CORRECTION LEVELS

Level of error correction	Data retrievable (%) (% CW that can be restored)
Level L	7
Level M	15
Level Q	25
Level H	30

TABLE VI

DATA ENCODING CAPACITY FOR DATAMATRIX

Data encoding	Max. number of characters
Numeric	3116
Alphanumeric	2335

The QR Code uses Reed Solomon error correction and supports four different levels of error correction as detailed in Table V [29].

2.1.1.3 The DataMatrix Symbology.

DataMatrix, shown in Table I, is a highly scalable 2D matrix symbology popularly used for marking small inventory articles and electronic components [18,19]. As shown in Table I, it is characterized by an "L" shaped centering pattern which has solid black lines along the left and bottom sides of each of its square or rectangular data regions [31]. Each data region is composed of a collection of modules arranged in an even number of rows and columns. Based on data content density, a data matrix code can have a symbol from 1 mil to 14 in. per side [26]. The newer version of DataMatrix supports Reed Solomon error correction and reconstructs data by using polynomial—over-sampling [21]. The DataMatrix Code data carrying capacity for different encodings is shown in Table VI [8].

TABLE VII

DATA ENCODING CAPACITY FOR AZTEC CODE

Data encoding	Max. number of characters
Numeric	3832
Alphabetic	3067
Bytes	1914

TABLE VIII

COMPARISON OF THE DATA CAPACITIES OF VARIOUS SYMBOLOGIES

2-Dimensional barcode symbology	Data carrying capacity (max number of characters)			
	Numeric	Alphanumeric/ alphabetical	ASCII/binary/ bytes	Japanese Kanji characters
PDF 417	2710	1850	1108	
QR Code	7089	4296	2953	1817
DataMatrix	3116	2335		
Aztec Code	3832	3067	1914	

2.1.1.4   The Aztec Code Symbology.

The Aztec Code, shown in Table I, is another popular 2D matrix symbology that has been in use since 1995. Based on a square grid, its characteristic "bulls-eye" pattern of concentric square rings facilitates quick centering for the encoder irrespective of the barcode orientation. The grid grows in size around the bulls-eye center with additional square modules as more data are added. Based on the data content density, the symbol size varies from 15×15 to 151×151 modules per square. The Aztec Code supports Reed Solomon error correction and the permissible values are 5–95% [9].The Aztec Code data capacity for different encodings is shown in Table VII.

A quick comparison of the data capacities of these symbologies is shown in Table VIII.

2.1.2   Proprietary and Emerging Symbologies

A number of emerging 2D symbologies are optimized for high content density applications. The following symbologies were considered but not included for actual testing as they include proprietary elements that did not fit our vision of the secure credentialing project.

2.1.2.1   The Datastrip 2D Symbology.   Datastrip 2D is a high-density 2-dimensional matrix symbology optimized to hold high-capacity data including encrypted color photographs and other biometric data used for secure credentialing [3,27]. It was developed by Softstrip Systems and was originally known as Softstrip. It can support a data density of up to 1000 bytes/sq. in. Its biggest advantage is that it can store large amounts of data in a fraction of the space used by other popular 2D barcode symbologies [30]. However, since certain implementation aspects were not in conformance with the project requirements, this symbology was not considered for our testing.

2.1.2.2   The HCCB Symbology.   Announced at CES in 2009, Microsoft's High Capacity Color Barcode (HCCB) is currently one of the newer symbologies that was developed with the intention of enhancing the encoding of higher capacity content. Similar to the matrix barcodes, HCCB uses a grid of colored triangles referred to as symbols to encode data and has an announced capacity of encoding 3500 characters per square inch [10]. The factors that impact on this encoding amount are the grid size, the symbol density, and the number of colors used for the symbols, which is either eight or four. The actual encoding and decoding however is proprietary and must be licensed. Printing may be performed with off-the-shelf inkjet or color printers. Current usages of this symbology is limited because of its proprietary status and include the Microsoft Tag, which is a mobile tagging service that accesses product information, and the ISAN-IA, which is a version method for audio and video products. Somewhat unique to this particular symbology, the HCCB incorporates tamper-proof quality through the use of digital signing based on Elliptic Curve Cryptography. All in all, the HCCB addresses the concern of encoding higher capacities and is also rumored to be more forgiving when it comes to poor barcode image quality.

2.2   Content Density

Testing showed that data content density played an important role in the scanning reliability of 2D barcodes. Barcodes can be classified based on their data content density or capacity. For the purpose of this case study, lower content density is defined as content density, including optimum error correction, that does not exceed 50% of the theoretical data capacity limit of the respective barcode type. On the other hand, higher content density is defined as content density including optimum error correction that exceeds 50% of the theoretical data capacity limit of the respective barcode type.

2.3   Error Correction

Error correction is an important feature supported by most 2D barcode symbologies. This involves encoding additional data in the barcode that helps in reconstructing the data in case of partial damage or defect in the generated barcode. This ability to compensate for partial damage improves the credibility of barcodes as a reliable machine-readable format. There are error corrections settings associated with most symbologies with the intention of increasing the readability. However, there is a fine balance when selecting the desired setting because of an increase in the overall encoded barcode content (and a corresponding decrease in the actual information that can be encoded within the prescribed capacity limits) that results from using the error correction. One must balance this value with the string to be encoded in order to stay in line with the capacities associated with the specific symbology. Error correction levels for PDF417 and QR Code are tabulated in Table III and Table V, respectively.

2.4   Scan Grade and Reflectance Profile

A scan reflectance profile (SRP) is a collection of % reflectance values measured across a barcode by a scan line. As per the American National Standards Institute bar code print quality specification, ANSI X3.182 [11], the SRP considers the following eight parameters to obtain a scan grade:

- Edge determination
- Minimum reflectance
- Minimum edge contrast
- Symbol contrast
- Modulation
- Defects
- Decode-ability (printing accuracy as compared to the algorithm)
- Decode (pass/fail)

The minimum grade achieved by any of the parameters above represents the overall SRP grade.

2.5   Symbol Grade

The average of 10 SRP grades gives what is known as the ''Symbol Grade.'' As per the ISO/IEC 15416 and ANSI X3.182, and EN 1635 standards, these 10 scans should be conducted at different heights [16].

The numeric values and the corresponding symbol grades are defined as given in Table IX.

TABLE IX
SYMBOL GRADE AND NUMERIC VALUE CORRESPONDENCE

Numeric value (x)	Symbol grade
4.0 = x = 3.5	A
3.5> x = 2.5	B
2.5> x = 1.5	C
1.5> x = 0.5	D
0.5 > x	F

2.6   Encoder

For the purpose of this chapter, barcodes were printed using two separate encoders, viz, Bartender Enterprise edition 9.01 from Seagull Scientific and CardFive Vision 8.1 Professional from Number Five Software. While Bartender is an industry-standard software optimized for encoding barcodes, CardFive Vision is primarily an ID card design software that also supports encoding of barcodes. While initial testing suggested 100% positive results for barcodes generated using Bartender, the encoding quality achieved through CardFive was not found to be that encouraging. Hence, for reliability and consistency, all further tests including the preliminary as well as extensive tests detailed below were done using barcodes generated by Bartender. It may be noted here that apart from Bartender, any standard commercial barcode encoder may be suitable as long as the barcodes generated are of a high quality. To eliminate any potential of the encoder adversely impacting the readability, independent external testing using barcode verifiers indicated that our barcodes received a quality grading of ''A.''

2.7   Printer

The scanning reliability of barcodes is impacted significantly by the quality of printing which is determined to a great extent by the printer resolution and the type of print head being used. As per the AIM and GS1 publications [1,12], the following print considerations are important:

- The generated barcodes should always be an even multiple of printer pixels.
- There must be sufficient quiet zones around the bar code as required by the respective barcode specifications

TABLE X
COMPARISON OF PRINTER SPECIFICATIONS

Name and model number	Media type	Resolution (DPI)	Dot shape	Printing technology
Zebra S4M	Label printer	203	Square	Direct thermal
DataCard SP75	Card printer	300	Square	Dye-sublimation/resin thermal transfer
Xerox Phaser 6360 DN	Document printer	600	Round	Laser

- The distortion introduced by general-purpose printers (with round dot shape) should be catered for. The round dot-shape results in printing wider bars and narrower spaces because the printed dot size is bigger than the pixel size.

For the purpose of this case study, the following printers were used for printing the barcodes:

(i) Zebra S4M label printer
(ii) DataCard SP75 card printer
(iii) Xerox Phaser 6360 DN laser printer

A brief comparison of the relevant specifications of these printers is tabulated in Table X [13–15].

When considering the printer as a factor, it must be noted that a direct comparison of resolution alone without taking the printing technology into consideration would be misleading, since a square dot-shape produces a straight edge thus having the ability to print higher density barcodes more accurately as opposed to a printer with a round dot shape of the same DPI value. Since the direct thermal and thermal transfer technologies are optimized for printing high-capacity bar codes and since our target media for the case study was labels and PVC cards, only the first two printers mentioned above were used for most of the tests. The laser document printer was used for testing the effect of glossiness on scan reliability as it allowed a direct comparison between glossy and nonglossy media.

2.8   Media

For the purpose of this case study, we focused on our target media, viz. labels and PVC cards that are both glossy in nature. The absorbance or the optical density of the media affects the quantum of refraction and is thus another important factor that impacts on the scan-ability of the barcodes. There is a marked difference in the optical density of glossy as well as nonglossy media and though glossy media provide a much higher optical density, they also provide a higher level of reflectivity from the printed surface. While reflectivity is the fraction of incident light reflected by the surface in question; the optical density or absorbance, A, is defined as

$$A_\lambda = -\log_{10}(I/I_0)$$

where I is the intensity of the transmitted light at a given wavelength λ and I_0 is the intensity of the incident light.

To cater for the difference in absorbance and reflectivity of different media, a specific test, the "Effect of Glossiness on scan reliability test," was carried out with the following two types of media:

- Normal nonglossy paper
- Glossy paper

2.9   Decoder/Scanner Characteristics

The scan reliability of barcodes is also affected by the type of scanner/decoder, or the actual hardware that will decode the encoded barcode. The scan reliability is greatly affected by the combination of the scanner light-wavelength and aperture size (size of the scanning spot relative to the bar-width) used. The angle at which scanner light is incident on the surface affects the reflectance. Light incident at 45° to the surface will minimize reflection from glossy surfaces, thereby producing optimum scan reliability. As per the Layman's guide [1], variations in these two parameters might drastically alter the overall scan grade quality (Table XI).

As per GS1, a global leader involved in the design and implementation of standards including those of bar codes, depending on scanner technology, there are six functional bands. For optimum scan-reliability, scanners should be chosen on the basis of applications that pertain to these bands [12].

TABLE XI

SCAN GRADE W.R.T. APERTURE DIAMETER AND WAVELENGTH

Aperture diameter (mil)	Aperture diameter (mm)	Wavelength (nm)	Scan grade	Quality
5	0.125	633	1/D	Poor
10	0.25	633	3/B	Good
10	0.25	900	0/F	Fail

TABLE XII
COMPARISON OF SCANNER SPECIFICATIONS

Characteristic	Symbol DS 6707SR	Symbol DS 3478
Light source	650-nm laser diode	650-nm laser diode
Field of view	40° horizontal	30° horizontal
	30° vertical	22.5° vertical
Yaw tolerance	±60° from nominal	±50° from nominal
Pitch tolerance	±65° from nominal	±60° from nominal
Roll tolerance	±360° from nominal	±180° from nominal

Since Motorola (a.k.a. Symbol) scanners possess a majority of the scanner hardware market share; the following two different Symbol scanners were used for testing:

- Symbol DS 6707SR wired scanner with SE6707 scan engine
- Symbol DS 3478 wireless scanner with SE4400 scan engine

The specific difference between these two scanners is the embedded scan engine, which is the heart and soul of the scanner and responsible for the actual decoding process [22, 23]. A brief comparison of the technical specifications that are directly relevant to our tests is given in Table XII.

3. Testing Methodology

Our comprehensive testing involved internal as well as external testing. The internal testing methodology, which is described in Section 3.1, used a series of carefully designed tests to evaluate the impact of various parameters that influence barcode scanning reliability. The internal testing comprised several stages including preliminary sampling followed by more extensive testing with the results of each test leading to the need for the successive tests.

The external testing, which is described in Section 3.2, was used to assess the quality–grade of the barcodes by using an independent and verifiable industry standard process. This external testing augmented the internal testing where resources were not available to actually perform the testing.

3.1 Internal Testing

To provide a point of reference and for the sake of comprehensive testing, 1D as well as 2D barcodes with lower content density were also tested. Since the focus of this paper is higher capacity barcodes, the results of the lower capacity testing are mentioned without going into further details. Testing was performed by performing individual scans, termed iteration, of the sample barcodes and then calculating success rate, which is called the barcodes *scan-ability.*

3.1.1 Barcodes with Lower Content Density

Multiple scan iterations using different types of scanners as well as encoders for all 1D as well as lower content density 2D barcodes tested produced 100% scan reliability.

3.1.2 Barcodes with Higher Content Density

Samples of various barcode symbologies were subjected to preliminary testing involving twenty scan-iterations each and all samples that achieved a scan reliability of 40% or more were then subjected to extensive testing involving fifty scan-iterations each. The testing methodology is explained in detail in the succeeding sections.

3.1.2.1 Preliminary Testing.   In order to narrow the scope of viable barcodes, and based on the specific requirements of our project wherein the physical print size was a limiting factor, the four commonly used 2D barcodes (Table XIII) were encoded for preliminary testing. This test involved twenty scan iterations of each barcode sample and the result was a percentage of successful scan

TABLE XIII
PRELIMINARY TESTING

S. No.	Barcode type	Scanning reliability
1	PDF417 9.8 mil 2x, 13 col EC : 6	95 %
2	QR cvode 14.8 mil error correction M (15%)	90 %
3	Aztec 14.8 mil with error correction 40%	45 %
4	Aztec 14.8 mil with error correction 45%	80 %
5	Aztec 19.7 mil (no image)	90 %
6	DataMatrix 14.8 mil with ECC 200	50 %
7	DataMatrix 9.8 mil	0 %

reliability. This preliminary scan test served as a smoke test to provide a quick initial point of reference, based on a wide range of possible barcodes and the settings associated with each particular barcode. In particular, the suggested settings for each symbology were used to encode the barcode.

Based on the results of this preliminary testing, the low-performing barcode namely *DataMatrix 9.8 mil* (S. No. #7) was eliminated from further testing. On the other hand, for the mediocre-performing *Aztec 14.8 mil with error correction 40%* (S. No. #3), an additional sample with a 50% error correction was added for further testing. Similarly, an additional *QR Code sample with an error correction of 30%* was also included for further testing.

3.1.2.2 Extensive Testing. This involved fifty scan iterations for each sample barcode and enumerating the results as a percentage scan reliability value. The number of scans was suggested by the scanner vendor as being sufficient to successfully sample the success rate. For a better understanding of scan results and to ensure that our testing results were not biased by the use of only one type of scanner, reliability was enumerated separately for different scanners, viz. the Symbol DS 6707SR (SE6707) wired and the Symbol DS 3478 (SE4400) wireless scanners. For the purpose of this testing, a ''good scan'' is defined as a successful scan in less than 2 s, a ''delayed scan'' is a successful scan that takes 2–7 s, and a ''No scan'' is failure to scan even after 7 s. The delayed scan measurement was introduced to account for the fact that while not actually a ''No Scan,'' longer than a 2-s scan time is less than optimal in a deployed situation; however, the tracking of such scans becomes valuable for measurement when longer scan times are acceptable. Delayed scans are acting as a buffer between the two possibilities.

3.1.2.2.1 Reliability testing. The first in a series of specific extensive tests, ''Reliability Testing'' involved extensive scanning of different types of 2D barcodes, viz. the PDF417, DataMatrix, Aztec, and QR Code with both the scan engines. The goal of reliability testing was to identify barcode symbologies along with the corresponding scan engine that produced the highest percentage scan reliability.

These test results, summarized in Table XIV with the relevant rows highlighted with the arrow marking ←, indicate that PDF417 9.8 mil 13 col, error correction: 6 with SE6707 and QR Code 14.9 mil, error correction (30%) with SE4400 emerged as the most reliable scans, which were then subjected to further testing.

3.1.2.2.2 Content density testing. Having shortlisted PDF417 and QR Codes based on the reliability testing results, each of the two barcode symbologies was subjected to rigorous ''content density testing.'' The purpose of this test was to determine the impact of the content density on the scan reliability of the barcodes.

TABLE XIV
RELIABILITY TESTING

Symbology	Scan engine	% Good scan	% Delayed scan	% No scan	
PDF417 9.8 mil 13 col EC:6 (label)	SE6707	94%	6%	0%	←
	SE4400	68%	22%	10%	
QR code 14.8 mil error correction M (15%) (Label)	SE6707	60%	38%	2%	
	SE4400	70%	18%	12%	
QR code 14.8 mil, error correction M (15%) (Card)	SE6707	40%	38%	22%	
	SE4400	82%	16%	2%	
QR code 14.8 mil, error correction (30%) (card)	SE6707	56%	32%	12%	
	SE4400	94%	2%	4%	←
Aztec 14.8 mil with error correction 40% (label)	SE6707	60%	26%	14%	
	SE4400	32%	10%	58%	
Aztec 14.8 mil with error correction 45% (label)	SE6707	70%	22%	8%	
	SE4400	32%	12%	56%	
Aztec 14.8 mil with error correction 50% (label)	SE6707	52%	36%	12%	
	SE4400	22%	8%	70%	
Aztec 19.7 mil (no image) (label)	SE6707	60%	26%	14%	
DataMatrix 14.8 mil with ECC 200 (label)	SE6707	28%	48%	24%	

We designed different capacity barcodes ranging from 162 bytes to 929 bytes. The different byte sizes were selected based on the specific requirements of the project and thus subsequent test samples do not have a uniform data capacity difference.

In Table XV, the rows indicating test results for a data capacity of 844 bytes are highlighted with the arrow marking, ← as that is the preferred data capacity for our project. This test indicated that for PDF417, the scan reliability starts dropping after content density increases more than approx. 60% when the wireless scanner (SE4400) is used. However, the content density has no effect whatsoever on scan reliability with the wired scanner (SE6707).

For the QR Code, the testing indicated a substantial drop in scan reliability as the content density increased to more than 844 bytes with either the SE6707 or SE4400 Scan Engines (Table XVI). This indicates mixed results for the effect of content density on scan reliability of QR Code. There is a trend toward a decrease in the reliability as the content of the barcode increases. The success rate is higher with the

TABLE XV
CONTENT DENSITY TESTING FOR PDF 417

SE 4400	Size in bytes, %capacity	% Good scan	% Delayed scan	% No scan	
PDF4179.8 mil EC = 6	162, 14%	100%	0%	0%	
	224, 20%	100%	0%	0%	
	492, 45%	98%	2%	0%	
	625, 56%	100%	0%	0%	
	694, 63%	96%	2%	2%	
	844, 76%	88%	8%	4%	←
	929, 84%	78%	16%	6%	
SE 6707	Size in bytes, %capacity	% Good scan	% Delayed scan	% No scan	
PDF4179.8 mil EC = 6	162, 14%	100%	0%	0%	
	224, 20%	100%	0%	0%	
	492, 45%	100%	0%	0%	
	625, 56%	100%	0%	0%	
	694, 63%	100%	0%	0%	
	844, 76%	100%	0%	0%	←
	929, 84%	100%	0%	0%	

wired scanner when one takes into account the delayed scans because in essence these are successful scans though just not as ideal.

3.1.2.2.3   Error correction level based testing for QR Code and PDF417.
To fine-tune the results of the previous test and to achieve high scan reliability with high content density barcodes, the required 844 byte samples (of PDF417 and QR Code) were tested with different levels of error correction encoded into them. The purpose of this test was to determine the impact of error correction level on the scan reliability of the 2D barcodes. For QR Code, samples with a content density of 844 bytes with error correction levels of 7%, 15%, 25%, and 30% were tested. The results are tabulated in Table XVII.

The rows highlighted with the arrow marking ← indicate the best scan results for the two different scanners. It was observed that the size of the actual barcode, not just the amount of data, seemed to play a role in the scanning reliability. It was observed that barcodes with a 30% error correction were so big that it seemed to

TABLE XVI
CONTENT DENSITY TESTING FOR QR CODE

QR code 14.8 mil EC = 15%	Size in bytes	% Good scan	% Delayed scan	% No scan	
SE 4400	162	98%	2%	0%	
	224	94%	6%	0%	
	492	66%	22%	12%	
	625	92%	6%	2%	
	694	96%	2%	2%	
	844	76%	12%	12%	←
	929	44%	24%	32%	
SE6707	162	100%	0%	0%	
	224	92%	8%	0%	
	492	88%	12%	0%	
	625	50%	46%	4%	
	694	74%	26%	0%	
	844	82%	18%	0%	←
	929	46%	48%	6%	

adversely affect the scan reliability. Based on data content requirements of the present project, our recommendation is to use 25% error correction to achieve optimum scan reliability.

For PDF417, samples with a content density of 844 bytes with error correction levels of 3, 4, 5, and 6 were tested with both the scan engines. The results are tabulated in Table XVIII.

For PDF417, the results indicate that the higher the error correction, better the scan reliability.

3.1.2.2.4 Effect of Glossiness on scan reliability. After taking into consideration the primary factor of data content density, we shifted our focus to other secondary factors that impact on the scan reliability of barcodes. Since the primary technique used by most 2D scanners is imaging, which involves taking a photo of the barcode before trying to decode it, the difference in absorbance and reflectivity of glossy and nonglossy media impacts on their readability. The purpose behind this

TABLE XVII
IMPACT OF ERROR CORRECTION LEVEL FOR QR CODE

QR Code 844 Bytes	Error correction	% Good scan	% Delayed scan	% No scan	
SE 6707	7%	88%	12%	0%	
	15%	84%	16%	0%	
	25%	98%	2%	0%	↓
	30%	60%	40%	0%	
SE 4400	7%	90%	10%	0%	
	15%	88%	10%	2%	
	25%	92%	6%	2%	↓
	30%	74%	20%	6%	

TABLE XVIII
IMPACT OF ERROR CORRECTION LEVEL FOR PDF 417

PDF417 844 bytes	Error correction	% Good scan	% Delayed scan	% No scan	
SE6707	3	84%	16%	0%	
	4	94%	6%	0%	
	5	98%	2%	0%	
	6	98%	2%	0%	←
SE4400	3	26%	26%	48%	
	4	60%	18%	22%	
	5	78%	14%	8%	
	6	86%	10%	4%	←

test was to determine the potential impact of the finish of the physical media, in particular glossy versus nonglossy, on the scanning reliability. To resolve this concern, the symbologies were scanned separately on a "glossy" as well as a "nonglossy" media. The results are tabulated in Table XIX.

3.1.2.2.4.1 Effect of glossiness testing for QR Code 844 bytes data capacity. The highlighted rows indicate the best scan reliability for glossy as well as nonglossy paper using different scan engines. The results indicate a clear drop in the scan reliability of QR Code barcodes when printed on glossy surface (cards as well as labels) as compared to nonglossy plain surface.

3.1.2.2.4.2 Effect of glossiness testing for PDF417 844 bytes data capacity. The test results indicate a significant degradation in the scan reliability on glossy surface compared to nonglossy surface at lower error correction levels for the SE6707 as shown in rows highlighted by a ⊠ marking. For the SE4400, the corresponding rows highlighted by the arrow marking ← indicate significant degradation in the scan reliability on glossy surface at all levels of error correction (Table XX).

3.1.2.2.5 Comparison of target media (card and label) with optimal scan settings. Since our target media (label or PVC card) are glossy, we decided to do yet another test to determine which of the two target media (card or label) produced a

TABLE XIX
EFFECT OF GLOSSINESS TESTING FOR QR CODE

Non-glossy paper	Error correction	% Good scan	% Delayed scan	% No scan	
SE 6707	7%	88%	12%	0%	
	15%	84%	16%	0%	
	25%	98%	2%	0%	←
	30%	60%	40%	0%	
SE 4400	7%	90%	10%	0%	
	15%	88%	10%	2%	
	25%	92%	6%	2%	←
	30%	74%	20%	6%	
Glossy paper	Error correction	Good scan %	Delayed scan %	No scan	
SE6707	7%	70%	28%	2%	
	15%	70%	30%	0%	←
	25%	66%	34%	0%	
	30%	44%	44%	12%	
SE4400	7%	96%	4%	0%	
	15%	98%	2%	0%	←
	25%	82%	14%	4%	
	30%	44%	20%	36%	

better scan reliability. It may be pertinent to mention here that there is a difference not only in the glossiness of the media (card and label) but also in the printing quality as cards were printed using the DataCard SP75 card printer while the labels were printed using the ZebraS4M label printer having different characteristics (as mentioned in Section 2.7).

These results in Table XXI indicate that PDF417 is the better choice for labels; however, for badges, the wireless scanner produced identical scan reliability results of 76% for both PDF417 and QR Code.

TABLE XX
EFFECT OF GLOSSINESS TESTING FOR PDF 417

Media	Scan engine	Error correction	% Good scan	% Delayed scan	% No scan	
Non glossy	SE6707	3	94%	6%	0%	⟨×⟩
		4	100%	0%	0%	
		5	98%	2%	0%	
	SE4400	6	100%	0%	0%	
		3	50%	30%	20%	
		4	80%	14%	6%	
		5	94%	4%	2%	
		6	94%	4%	2%	←
Glossy	SE6707	3	84%	16%	0%	⟨×⟩
		4	94%	6%	0%	
		5	98%	2%	0%	
		6	98%	2%	0%	
	SE4400	3	26%	26%	48%	
		4	60%	18%	22%	
		5	78%	14%	8%	
		6	86%	10%	4%	←

3.2 External Testing

In order to address the potential for the encoder or the printers to influence the performed testing, it is necessary to set a baseline for the quality of created barcodes. This took the form of grading the test samples that was performed independently and externally by Motorola Technical and Engineering Services using barcode verifiers and they confirmed the quality of the internally encoded barcodes as "Grade A." This eliminates the potential of encoder and printer errors on the scan reliability of the barcodes.

TABLE XXI
COMPARISON OF TARGET MEDIA

Symbology	Scan engine	Media printed on	Good scan %	Delayed scan %	No scan %
PDF 417 844 EC 6	SE 6707	Label	99%	0%	1%
		Card	96%	4%	0%
	SE 4400	Label	98%	2%	0%
		Card	76%	12%	12%
QR code 844 14.8 25%	SE 6707	Label	52%	40%	8%
		Card	52%	36%	12%
	SE 4400	Label	64%	10%	26%
		Card	76%	14%	10%

4. Conclusion

For our target material (card or label, which are both glossy), and with a data content capacity of 844 bytes,

- The best case scenario is a 96–99% scan reliability for cards and labels, respectively, using PDF417 Barcodes with the SE6707 scan engine.
- The scanning reliability of PDF417 with the SE4400 scan engine varied from 76% for cards to 98% for labels.
- For QR Code with 844 bytes and 25% error correction, the SE4400 scan engine produced a success rate of 76% for cards and 64% for labels, whereas the SE6707 Scan engine produced a success rate of 52% for both labels and cards.

These results are summarized in Table XXII.

Comparing these results to the standards for each of the tested symbologies, theoretically they are capable of encoding high content-data; however, testing showed that the content for readable symbols was greatly impacted by many factors. The results thus indicate that for our specific application, the scan reliability of PDF417 barcodes was much better than that of QR Code barcodes with high-capacity data encoding (more than 800 bytes) printed on glossy media and read using either SE6707 scan engine or SE4400 scan engine.

TABLE XXII
SUMMARY OF RESULTS

Rank	Scan-reliability	Symbology	Scanner	Media
Best	99%	PDF 417	SE 6707	Label
2nd	98%	PDF 417	SE 4400	Label
3rd	96%	PDF 417	SE 6707	Card
4th	76%	QR Code	SE 4400	Card
5th	76%	PDF 417	SE 4400	Card
6th	64%	QR Code	SE 4400	Label
Worst	52%	QR Code	SE 6707	Card & Label

REFERENCES

[1] Layman's Guide to ANSI, CEN, and ISO Bar Code Print Quality Documents, Association for Automatic Identification and Data Capture Technologies (AIM), Pittsburg, PA, 2002 (November).

[2] Sizing Applications for 2D Barcode Symbols, 2007. http://www.intermec.com/learning/content_library/white_papers/index.aspx (Intermec Technologies Corporation, Available from: accessed 07.12.09).

[3] http://www.aimglobal.org/technologies/barcode/2d_symbologies_matrix.asp (accessed 07.12.09).

[4] http://www.morovia.com/education/symbology/upc-a.asp (accessed 07.12.09).

[5] http://www.computalabel.com/aboutupc.htm (accessed 07.12.09).

[6] http://www.morovia.com/education/symbology/pdf417.asp (accessed 07.12.09).

[7] http://www.denso-wave.com/qrcode/qrfeature-e.html (accessed 07.12.09).

[8] http://www.idautomation.com/fonts/datamatrix/faq.html#Data_Matrix_Specifications (accessed 07. 12.09).

[9] http://www.barcode.ro/tutorials/barcodes/aztec.html (accessed 07.12.09).

[10] http://research.microsoft.com/en-us/projects/hccb/about.aspx (accessed 07.12.09).

[11] American National Standards Institute, Bar Code Print Quality Specification, ANSI X3.182, 1990.

[12] GS1 General Specification, v 7.0, v 7.0, Jan 2006: Bar Code Production and Quality Assessment, 2006.

[13] http://www.zebra.com/id/zebra/na/en/index/products/printers/industrial_commercial/s4m.1.tabs.html (accessed 07.12.09).

[14] http://www.cdatacard.com/id-card-printers/sp75-plus-id-card-printer?contentId=null (accessed 07. 12.09).

[15] http://www.office.xerox.com/printers/color-printers/phaser-6360/enus.html (accessed 07.12.09).

[16] GS1 Systems, GS1 Bar Code Verification for Linear Symbols, v 4.3, 2009. (May).

[17] ISO/IEC 15438:2001, Information Technology—Automatic Identification and Data Capture Techniques—Bar Code Symbology Specifications—PDF417.

[18] Laser Marking: Matrix Codes on PCBS, 2005. (Rick Stevenson, Printed Circuit Design & Manufacture, December).

[19] http://www.spec2000.com/50.html (accessed 07.12.09).

[20] http://qrcode.kaywa.com/ (accessed 07.12.09).

[21] http://www.idautomation.com/datamatrixfaq.html#Data_Matrix_Overview (accessed 07.12.09).

[22] Symbol DS 6707SR Manual. Available from: http://support.symbol.com/support/product/manuals.do (accessed 07.12.09).

[23] Symbol DS 3478 Manual. Available from: http://support.symbol.com/support/product/manuals.do (accessed 07.12.09).

[24] http://www.adams1.com/stack.html (accessed 07.12.09).

[25] http://www.barcodeman.com/faq/2d.php (accessed 07.12.09).

[26] http://www.mecsw.com/specs/datamatx.html (accessed 07.12.09).

[27] http://www.aimglobal.org/members/news/templates/template.aspx?articleid=3312&zoneid=26 (accessed 07.12.09).

[28] http://www.taltech.com/TALtech_web/resources/intro_to_bc/bcsymbol.htm (accessed 07.12.09).

[29] http://mdn.morovia.com/manuals/qrcode-fontware/ch02s01.php#id4817307 (accessed 07.12.09).

[30] http://www.datastrip.com/index.html (accessed 07.12.09).

[31] http://barcodes.gs1us.org/dnn_bcec/Standards/Barcodes/GS1DataMatrix/tabid/452/Default.aspx (accessed 07.12.09).

Advances in Video-Based Human Activity Analysis: Challenges and Approaches

PAVAN TURAGA

Department of Electrical and Computer Engineering, Center for Automation Research, UMIACS University of Maryland, College Park, Maryland, USA

RAMA CHELLAPPA

Department of Electrical and Computer Engineering, Center for Automation Research, UMIACS University of Maryland, College Park, Maryland, USA

ASHOK VEERARAGHAVAN

Mitsubishi Electric Research Labs, Cambridge, Massachusetts, USA

Abstract

Videos play an ever increasing role in our everyday lives with applications ranging from news, entertainment, scientific research, security, and surveillance. Coupled with the fact that cameras and storage media are becoming less expensive, it has resulted in people producing more video content than ever before. Analysis of human activities in video is important for several important applications. Interpretation and identification of human activities requires approaches that address the following questions (a) what are the appropriate atomic primitives for human activities, (b) how to combine primitives to produce complex activities, (c) what are the required invariances for inference algorithms, and (d) how to build computational models for each of these. In this chapter, we provide a broad overview and discussion of these issues. We shall review state-of-the-art computer vision algorithms that address these issues and then provide a unified perspective from which specific algorithms can be derived. We will then present supporting experimental results.

1. Introduction

Recent years have seen a tremendous explosion of video content fueled by inexpensive video cameras and the growth of the Internet. Video installations are found in airports, stores, offices, and hospitals. Home video content has witnessed a large growth due to the rising popularity of several video-sharing websites. Automatic recognition of human activities from video in these varied domains is one of the most promising applications of computer vision. In recent years, this problem has caught the attention of researchers from industry, academia, security agencies, consumer agencies, and the general populace. One of the earliest investigations into the nature of human motion was conducted by the contemporary photographers Etienne Jules Marey and Eadweard Muybridge in the 1850s who photographed moving subjects and revealed several interesting and artistic aspects involved in human and animal locomotion. The classic Moving Light Display experiment of Johansson [1] provided a great impetus to the study and analysis of human motion perception in the field of neuroscience. This then paved the way for mathematical modeling and recognition of human actions, which naturally fall into the purview of computer vision and pattern recognition.

To state the problem in simple terms, given a sequence of images with one or more persons performing an activity, can a system be designed that can automatically recognize what activity is being or was performed? As simple as the question seems, the solution has been that much harder to find. In this chapter, we review the major approaches that have been pursued over the last 20 years to address this problem, and provide a unifying perspective.

The rest of the chapter is organized as follows. In Section 2, we discuss the challenges in automatic analysis of human activities. Potential applications that illustrate the impact of the activity recognition technology are presented in Section 3. In Section 4, we discuss low-level feature extraction methods which form the lower level of any activity recognition method. Midlevel models for representing simple human actions are discussed in Section 5. In Section 6, we discuss models for higher level complex activities. A unified perspective of these approaches based on features, primitives, and conjunctions of primitives is presented in Section 7. In Section 8, we present a detailed understanding of the primitive space constructed from linear dynamical systems (LDSs). In Section 9, we show how complex activities can be represented using a cascade of dynamical systems. A generalization of this approach by incorporating time-varying models is discussed in Section 10. Finally, in Section 11, we present a discussion pertaining to invariances within the framework of dynamical systems.

2. Challenges

Several factors contribute toward the complexity of understanding human activities. Firstly, human actions vary widely in their temporal and spatial extents. The term "action" typically refers to simple motion patterns usually executed by a single person and lasting for short duration. Examples of actions include bending, walking, swimming, etc. (e.g., Fig. 1). "Activities" refer to the complex sequence of actions performed by humans who could be interacting with each other in a constrained

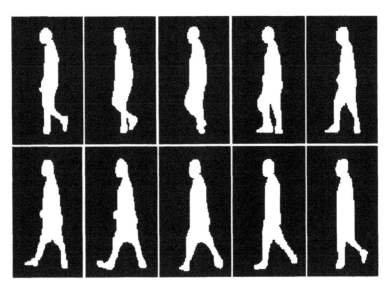

FIG. 1. Near-field video: Example of walking action. Figure taken from Veeraraghavan et al. [54].

manner. They are typically characterized by much longer temporal durations, for example, two persons shaking hands, a football team scoring a goal, or multiple robbers attacking a bank (Fig. 2). However, the gestures of a music conductor or the constrained dynamics of a group of humans (Fig. 3) are neither as simple as an "action" nor as complex as an "activity." Real-life activity recognition systems typically follow a hierarchical approach. At the lower levels are feature extraction modules such as background–foreground segmentation, tracking, and object detection. At the midlevel are action-recognition modules. At the high level are the reasoning engines which encode the activity semantics/structure based on the lower level action primitives.

Next, it is preferable if activity recognition systems are invariant to a variety of transformations including (a) viewpoint, (b) execution rate, and (c) anthropometry. Camera deployments vary significantly in their physical locations and viewing angles. Surveillance cameras in airports are typically ceiling mounted, whereas consumer webcams are near frontal. One needs to devise representations not just for a single view, but generalize them to other views. The wide variation in motion-based features

FIG. 2. Medium-field video: Example video sequence of a simulated bank attack. (A) Person enters the bank, (B) robber is identified to be an outsider. Robber is entering the bank safe, (C) a customer escapes, (D) robber makes an exit.

FIG. 3. Far-field video: Modeling dynamics of groups of humans as a deforming shape. Figure taken from Vaswani et al. [9].

induced by camera perspective effects and occlusions will otherwise make any reasoning engine brittle in performance. The second major source of observed variability in features arises from the individual differences in execution styles or rates while performing the same action. Variations in execution style exist both in interperson and intraperson settings. The same action may be different at different times of the day, or can be influenced by external factors such as shoes, carrying a load, etc., or internal factors such as health, mental states, and so forth. Needless to say, variations across different individuals are even more pronounced. Finally, anthropometric variations such as those induced by the body size, body shape, gender, etc. are other important variables that require careful attention. Unlike viewpoint and execution-rate variabilities which have received significant attention, a systematic study of anthropometric variations has been undertaken only in recent years.

Analysis of videos containing human activities typically proceeds from a sequence of images to a higher level interpretation in a series of steps. The major steps involved are the following:

1. Extraction of robust low-level features
2. Midlevel action descriptions from low-level features
3. High-level semantic interpretations from primitive actions

These issues have received significant attention in computer vision literature [2–6]. It is not possible to discuss the entire breadth of efforts in this area. In the remainder of this chapter, we shall provide an overview of each of these stages of processing and discuss how they contribute toward holistic activity recognition. First, we discuss some applications that highlight the potential impact of this research agenda.

3. Applications

In this section, we present a few applications that highlight the potential impact of vision-based activity recognition systems.

3.1 Behavioral Biometrics

Biometrics involves the study of approaches and algorithms for uniquely recognizing humans based on physical or behavioral cues. Traditional approaches are based on fingerprint, face, iris, and can be classified as physiological biometrics, that is, they rely on physical attributes for recognition. These methods require cooperation from the subject for collection of the biometric. Recently, "behavioral biometrics" have been gaining popularity, where the premise is that behavior is as useful a cue to recognize humans as their physical attributes. The advantage of this approach is that subject cooperation is not necessary and it can proceed without interrupting or interfering with the subject's activity. Since observing behavior implies longer term observation of the subject, approaches for action recognition extend naturally to this task. Currently, the most promising example of vision-based behavioral biometric is human gait [7].

3.2   Activity-Based Indexing of Video

Video has become a part of our everyday life. With video-sharing websites experiencing relentless growth, it has become necessary to develop efficient indexing and storage schemes to improve user experience. This requires learning of patterns from raw video and summarizing a video based on its content. One of the significant sources of information in most videos is human activities. Human activities can be used as keys to index videos, which will then enable searching according to the activity of interest. This is particularly useful for content such as sports videos, home videos, and news.

3.3   Security and Surveillance

Security and surveillance systems have traditionally relied on a network of video cameras monitored by a human operator who needs to be aware of the activity in the camera's field of view. With recent growth in the number of cameras and deployments, the workload of human operators has been stretched. Hence, security agencies are seeking vision-based solutions to these tasks which can replace or assist a human operator. Automatic recognition of anomalies in a camera's field of view is one such problem that has attracted attention from vision researchers (cf. Refs. [8,9]). A related application involves searching for an activity of interest in a large database by learning patterns of activity from long videos [10,11].

3.4   Interactive Applications and Environments

Understanding the interaction between a computer and a human remains one of the enduring challenges in designing human–computer interfaces. Visual cues are the most important mode of nonverbal communication. Effective utilization of gestures and activities holds the promise of helping in creating computers that can better interact with humans. Similarly, interactive environments such as smart rooms [12] that can react to a user's activities can benefit from vision-based methods. However, such technologies are still not mature enough to stand the "Turing test" and thus continue to attract research interest.

3.5   Animation and Synthesis

The gaming and animation industry relies on synthesizing realistic humans and human motion, where the requirement is to produce a large variety of motions with some compromise on the quality. The movie industry, on the other hand, has traditionally relied more on human animators to provide high-quality animation. However, this trend is changing [13]. With improvements in algorithms and hardware, much more realistic motion synthesis is now possible. A related application is learning in simulated environments. Examples of this include training of military soldiers, firefighters, and other rescue personnel in hazardous situations with simulated subjects.

4.   Feature Extraction

In this section, we will briefly discuss some relevant aspects of low-level feature extraction. Videos consist of massive amounts of raw information in the form of spatiotemporal pixel intensity variations. But most of this information is not directly relevant to the task of understanding and identifying the activity occurring in the video. A classic experiment by Johansson [1] demonstrated that humans can perceive gait patterns from point light sources placed at a few limb joints with no additional information. Extraneous factors such as the color of the clothes, illumination conditions, background clutter do not aid in the recognition task. We briefly describe a few popular low-level features and refer the readers to other sources for a more in-depth treatment as we progress.

4.1   Optical Flow

Optical flow is defined as the apparent motion of individual pixels on the image plane. It often serves as a good approximation of the true physical motion projected onto the image plane. Most methods that compute optical flow assume that the color/intensity of a pixel is invariant under the displacement from one video frame to the next. We refer the reader to Beauchemin and Barron [14] for a comprehensive survey and comparison of optical flow computation techniques. Optical flow provides a concise description of both the regions of the image undergoing motion and the velocity of motion. In practice, computation of optical flow is susceptible to noise and illumination changes. Applications include [15] which used optical flow to detect and track vehicles in an automated traffic surveillance application.

4.2   Point Trajectories

Trajectories of moving objects have been used as features to infer the activity of an object (see Fig. 4). The image-plane trajectory itself is not very useful as it is sensitive to translations, rotations, and scale changes. Alternative representations such as trajectory velocities, trajectory speeds, spatiotemporal curvature, relative-motion, etc. that are invariant to some of these variabilities have been proposed. A good survey of these approaches can be found in Cedras and Shah [3]. Extracting unambiguous point trajectories from video is complicated by several factors such as occlusions, noise, and background clutter. Accurate tracking algorithms need to be employed for obtaining motion trajectories [6].

4.3   Background Subtracted Blobs and Shape

Background subtraction is a popular method for isolating the moving parts of a scene by segmenting it into background and foreground (cf. Ref. [16]). As an example, from the sequence of background subtracted images shown in Fig. 1, the human's walking action can be easily perceived. The shape of the human silhouette plays a very important role in recognizing human actions, and it can be extracted from background subtracted blobs (see Fig. 5). Several methods based on global, boundary,

Fɪɢ. 4. Trajectories of a passenger and luggage-cart. The wide difference in the trajectories is indicative of the difference in activities. Figure taken from Roy-Chowdhury and Chellappa [120].

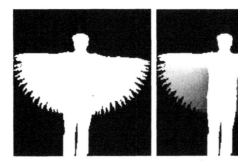

Fɪɢ. 5. Silhouettes extracted from the walking sequence shown in Fig. 1. Silhouettes encode sufficient information to recognize actions. Figure taken from Veeraraghavan et al. [54].

and skeletal descriptors have been proposed to quantify the shape of the silhouette. Global methods such as moments [17] consider the entire shape region to compute the shape descriptor. Boundary methods, on the other hand, consider only the shape contour as the defining characteristic of the shape. Such methods include chain codes [18] and landmark-based shape descriptors [19]. Skeletal methods represent a complex shape as a set of 1D skeletal curves, for example, the medial axis transform [20]. These methods have found applications in shape-based modeling of the human silhouette as in Bissacco et al. [21] for modeling human gait. Bobick and Davis [22,23] proposed "temporal templates" for action recognition. In their approach, the first step involved is background subtraction, followed by an aggregation of a sequence of background subtracted blobs into a single static image. They propose two methods of aggregation—the first method gives equal weight to all images in the sequence, which gives rise to a representation called the "Motion Energy Image". The second method gives decaying weights to the images in the sequence with higher weight given to new frames and low weight to older frames. This leads to a representation called the "Motion History Image" (MHI) (e.g., see Fig. 6). Blank et al. [24,25] proposed using background subtracted blobs stacked together to create an (x, y, t) binary space-time (ST) volume (e.g., see Fig. 7). From this ST volume, 3D shape descriptors are extracted by solving a Poisson equation [24,25].

4.4   Filter Responses

These approaches are based on filtering a video volume using a large filter bank. The responses of the filter bank are further processed to derive action-specific features. These approaches are inspired by the success of filter-based methods on other still image recognition tasks such as texture segmentation [26]. Chomat and

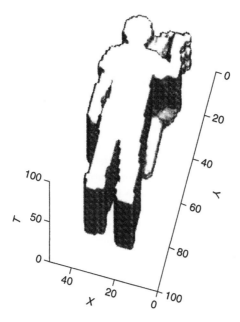

FIG. 6. 3D space-time object, similar to Blank et al. [24], obtained by stacking together binary background subtracted images of a person waving his hand.

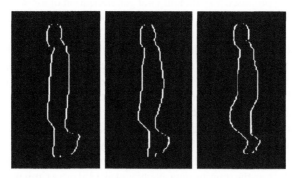

FIG. 7. Temporal templates similar to Davis and Bobick [22]. Left: Motion energy of a sequence of a person raising both hands, right: Motion history of the same action.

Crowley [27] model a segment of video as a (x, y, t) spatiotemporal volume and compute local appearance models at each pixel using a Gabor filter bank at various orientation and spatial scales and a single temporal scale. A given action is recognized using a spatial average of the probabilities of individual pixels in a frame. Since actions are analyzed at a single temporal scale, this method is not applicable to variations in execution rate. As an extension to this approach, local histograms of normalized ST gradients at several temporal scales are extracted by Zelnik-Manor and Irani [28]. The sum of the chi-square metric between histograms is used to match an input video with a stored exemplar. Filtering with the Gaussian kernel in space and the derivative of the Gaussian on the temporal axis followed by thresholding of the responses and accumulation into spatial-histograms was found to be a simple yet effective feature for actions in a far field settings [8]. Spatiotemporal filter structures such as oriented Gaussian kernels and their derivatives [29] and oriented Gabor filter banks [30] have been suggested for describing the spatiotemporal properties of cells in the visual cortex. Filtering approaches are fast and easy to implement due to efficient algorithms for convolution. In most applications, the appropriate bandwidth of the filters is not known *a priori*, thus a large filter bank at several spatial and temporal scales is required for effectively capturing the action dynamics. Moreover, the response generated by each filter has the same dimensions as the input volume, hence using large filter banks at several spatial and temporal scales is prohibitive.

4.5   Part-Based Approaches

Several approaches have been proposed that model a video volume as a collection of local parts, where each part consists of some distinctive motion pattern. Laptev and Lindeberg [31,32] proposed a spatiotemporal generalization of the well-known Harris interest point detector [33], which is widely used in object recognition applications and applied it to modeling and recognizing actions in ST. This method is based on a 3D generalization of scale-space representations. A given video is convolved with a 3D Gaussian kernel at various spatial and temporal scales. Then, spatiotemporal gradients are computed at each level of the scale-space representation which are then combined within a neighborhood of each point to yield stable estimates of the spatiotemporal second-moment matrix. Local features are then derived from these smoothed estimates of gradient moment matrices. In a similar approach, Dollar et al. [34] model a video sequence by the distribution of ST feature prototypes. The feature prototypes are obtained by k-means clustering of a large set of features—ST gradients—extracted at ST interest points from the training data. Neibles et al. [35] use a similar approach where they use a bag-of-words model to represent actions. The bag-of-words model is learnt by extracting spatiotemporal interest points and clustering of the features. These interest points can be used in conjunction with machine learning approaches such as SVMs [36] and graphical models [35]. Since the interest points are local in nature, longer term temporal correlations are ignored in these approaches. To address this issue, a method based on correlograms of prototype labels was presented in Savarese et al. [37].

In a slightly different approach Nowozin et al. [38] consider a video as a sequence of sets—where each set consists of the parts found in a small temporally sliding window. These approaches do not directly model the global geometry of local parts, instead considering them as a bag-of-features. Different actions may be composed of similar ST parts but may differ in their geometric relationships. Integrating global geometry into the part-based video representation was investigated by Boiman and Irani [39] and Wong et al. [40]. This approach may be termed as a constellation-of-parts as opposed to the simpler bag-of-parts model. Computational complexity can be large for constellation models with a large number of parts which is typically the case for human actions. Song et al. [41] addressed this issue by approximating the connections in the constellation via triangulation. Niebles and Fei-Fei [42] proposed a hierarchical model where the higher level is a constellation-of-parts much smaller than the actual number of features. Each of the parts in the constellation consists of a bag-of-features at the lower level. This approach combines the advantages of both the bag-of-features and the constellation model and preserves computational efficiency at the same time.

In most of these approaches the detection of the parts is usually based on linear operations such as filtering and spatiotemporal gradients, hence the descriptors are sensitive to changes in appearance, noise, occlusions, etc. It has also been noted that interest points are extremely sparse in smooth human actions and certain types of actions do not give rise to distinctive features [34,35]. However, due to their local nature they are more robust to nonstationary background.

5.   Models for Actions

Once features have been extracted from videos, concise descriptions that encode how the features evolve with time are needed. A powerful class of approaches imposes parametric models for this variation. Parameters of the model are estimated from the training data. Examples of such parametric methods are hidden Markov models (HMMs) and LDSs. These are also referred to as state-space approaches, where the temporal evolution of features is modeled as a trajectory in some configuration space, and each point on the trajectory corresponds to a particular "configuration" or "state"—for instance, a particular pose or stance of the human.

5.1   Hidden Markov Models

One of the most popular state-space models is the HMM. In the discrete HMM formalism, the state space is considered to be a finite set of discrete points. The temporal evolution is modeled as a sequence of probabilistic jumps from one discrete state to the other (Fig. 8). HMMs have found wide applications in speech recognition since the early 1980s. An excellent source for a detailed description of HMMs and its associated three problems—inference, decoding, and learning—can be found in Rabiner [43]. Beginning in the early 1990s, HMMs began to find wide applicability in computer vision systems. One of the earliest approaches to recognize human actions via HMMs was proposed by Yamato et al. [44] where they recognized tennis shots such as backhand stroke, backhand volley, forehand stroke, forehand volley, smash, etc. by modeling a sequence of background subtracted images as outputs of class-specific HMMs. Several successful gesture recognition systems such as those reported in Schlenzig et al. [45,46] make extensive use of HMMs by modeling a sequence of tracked features such as hand blobs as HMM outputs.

HMMs have also found applications in modeling the temporal evolution of human gait patterns both for action recognition and biometrics (cf. Refs. [47, 48]). All these approaches are based on the assumption that the feature sequence being modeled is a result of a single person performing an action. Hence, they are not effective in applications where there are multiple agents performing an action or interacting with each other. To address this issue, Brand et al. [49] proposed a coupled HMM to represent the dynamics of interacting targets. They demonstrated the superiority of their approach over conventional HMMs in recognizing two-handed gestures. Incorporating domain knowledge into the HMM formalism has also been investigated by several researchers. Moore et al. [50] used HMMs in conjunction with object detection modules to exploit the relationship between actions and objects. Hongeng and Nevatia [51] incorporate *a priori* beliefs of state duration into the HMM framework and the resultant model is called Hidden semi-Markov Model (semi-HMMs). Cuntoor and Chellappa [52] have proposed a mixed-state HMM formalism to model nonstationary activities, where the state space is augmented with a discrete label for higher level behavior modeling.

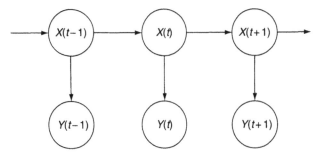

FIG. 8. Graphical illustration of a hidden Markov model.

5.2   Linear Dynamical Systems

LDSs are a more general form of HMMs where the state space is not constrained to be a finite set of symbols but can take on continuous values in $\mathbb{R}^k$, where k is the dimensionality of the state space. The simplest form of LDS is the first-order time-invariant Gauss–Markov processes which is described by Equations (1) and (2)

$$x(t) = Ax(t-1) + w(t), \quad w \sim N(0, Q) \tag{1}$$

$$y(t) = Cx(t) + v(t), \quad v \sim N(0, R) \tag{2}$$

where $x \in \mathbb{R}^d$ is the d-dimensional state vector and $y \in \mathbb{R}^n$ is the n-dimensional observation vector with $d \ll n$. w and v are the process and observation noise, respectively, which are Gaussian distributed with zero-means and covariance matrices Q and R, respectively. The LDS can be interpreted as a continuous state-space generalization of HMMs with a Gaussian observation model. Several applications such as recognition of humans and actions based on gait [53–55], activity recognition [56], and dynamic texture modeling and recognition [57,58] have been proposed using LDSs. First-order LDSs were used by Vaswani et al. [9] to model the configuration of groups of people in an airport tarmac setting by considering a collection of moving points (humans) as a deforming shape. Advances in system identification theory for learning LDS model parameters from data [57,59–62] and distance metrics on the LDS space [63–65] have made LDSs popular for learning and recognition of high-dimensional time-series data. More recently, an in-depth study of the LDS space has enabled the application of machine learning tools on that space such as dynamic boosting [66], kernel methods [67,68], and statistical modeling [69]. Newer methods to learn the model parameters [57] have made learning much more efficient than in the case of HMMs. Like HMMs, LDSs are also based on assumptions of Markovian dynamics and conditionally independent observations. Thus, as in the case of HMMs, the time-invariant model is not applicable to nonstationary actions.

6.   Complex Activities

While time-invariant HMMs and LDSs are efficient modeling and learning tools, they are restricted to linear and stationary dynamics. Consider the following activity— a person bends down to pick up an object, then he walks to a nearby table and places the object on the table and finally rests on a chair. This activity is composed of a sequence of short segments each of which is governed by a simple model. The entire activity can be seen as switching between simpler models. This forms the basic approach toward modeling more complex, temporally extended activities.

6.1 Time-Varying Dynamical Systems

The most general form of the time-varying LDS is given by Equations (3) and (4)

$$x(t) = A(t)x(t-1) + w(t), \quad w \sim N(0, Q) \tag{3}$$

$$y(t) = C(t)x(t) + v(t), \quad v \sim N(0, R) \tag{4}$$

which looks similar to the LDS in Equations (1) and (2), except that the model parameters A and C are allowed to vary with time. To tackle such complex dynamics, a popular approach is to model the process using switching linear dynamical systems (SLDSs) or jump linear systems. An SLDS consists of a set of LDSs with a switching function that causes model parameters to change by switching between models. Bregler [70] presented a multilayered approach to recognize complex movements consisting of several levels of abstraction. The lowest level is a sequence of input images. The next level consists of "blob" hypotheses where each blob is a region of coherent motion. At the third level, blob tracks are grouped temporally. The final level consists of a HMM for representing the complex behavior. North et al. [71] augment the continuous state vector with a discrete state component to form a "mixed" state. The discrete component represents a mode of motion or more generally a "switch" state. Corresponding to each switch state, a Gaussian autoregressive model is used to represent the dynamics. A maximum likelihood (ML) approach is used to learn the model parameters for each motion class. Pavlovic and Rehg [72,73] model the nonlinearity in human motion in a similar framework, where the dynamics are modeled using LDS and the switching process is modeled using a probabilistic finite-state machine. Other applications of this framework include the work of Del Vecchio et al. [74] who used this framework for classifying drawing tasks. Though the SLDS framework has greater modeling and descriptive power than that of HMMs and LDSs, learning and inference in SLDS is much more complicated, often requiring approximate methods [75]. In practice, determining the appropriate number of switching states is challenging and often requires large amounts of training data or extensive hand tuning. Apart from ML approaches, algebraic approaches that can simultaneously estimate the number of switching states, the switching instants, and also the parameters of the model for each state have been proposed by Vidal et al. [76]. However, algebraic approaches are often not robust to noise and outliers in the data.

6.2 Semantic Models

Most activities of interest in applications such as surveillance and content-based indexing involve several actors, who interact not only with each other, but also with contextual entities. The approaches discussed so far are mostly concerned with modeling and recognizing actions of a single actor. Modeling a complex scene, its relation with the objects in the scene, and the semantics of complex activities require higher level representation and reasoning methods. The previously discussed approaches are not suited to deal with the complexities of spatiotemporal constraints on actors and actions, temporal relations such as sequencing and synchronization, and the presence of multiple execution threads. Thus, structural and syntactic approaches such as dynamic belief networks (DBNs), grammars, Petri-nets, etc. are well suited to tackle these problems. Moreover, some amount of domain knowledge can be exploited to design concise and intuitive structural descriptions of activities.

6.2.1 Graphical Models

Graphical models such as Bayesian networks (BN) [77] encode complex conditional dependencies between a set of random variables which are encoded as local conditional probability densities. DBNs are a generalization of the simpler BN by incorporating temporal dependencies between random variables. DBNs encode more complex conditional dependence relations among several random variables as opposed to just one hidden variable as in a traditional HMM. Huang et al. [15] used DBNs for vision-based traffic monitoring. Buxton and Gong [78] used BN to capture the dependencies between scene layout and low-level image measurements for a traffic surveillance application. Modeling two-person interactions such as pointing, punching, pushing, hugging, etc. was proposed by Park and Aggarwal [79] in a two-stage DBN framework.

Petri-nets were defined by Petri [80] as a mathematical tool for describing relations between conditions and events. Petri-nets are particularly useful to model and visualize behaviors such as sequencing, concurrency, synchronization, and resource sharing. Petri-nets are bipartite graphs consisting of two types of nodes—places and transitions. Places refer to the state of an entity and transitions refer to changes in the state of the entity. Petri-nets were used by Castel et al. [81] to develop a system for high-level interpretation of image sequences. In their approach, the structure of the Petri-net was specified *a priori*. This can be tedious for large networks representing complex activities. Albanese et al. [82] proposed a probabilistic Petri-net, where the transitions are associated with a weight which encodes the probability with which that transition fires. By using skip transitions and penalizing them with a low probability, robustness to missing observations in the input stream is achieved. Further, the uncertainty in the identity of an object or the uncertainty in the unfolding of an activity can be efficiently incorporated into the tokens of the Petri-net.

6.2.2 Grammars

Grammars express the structure of a process using a set of production rules. To draw a parallel to grammars in language modeling, production rules specify how sentences (activities) can be constructed from words (activity primitives), and how to recognize if a sentence (video) conforms to the rules of a given grammar (activity model). One of the earliest use of grammars for visual activity recognition was proposed by Brand [83], who used a context-free grammar (CFG) to recognize hand manipulations in sequences containing disassembly tasks. They made use of simple grammars with no probabilistic modeling. Algorithms for detection of low-level primitives are frequently probabilistic in nature. Thus, stochastic context-free grammars (SCFGs) which are a probabilistic extension of CFGs were found to be suitable for integration with real-life vision modules. SCFGs were used by Ivanov and Bobick [84] to model the semantics of activities whose structure was assumed to be known. They used HMMs for low-level primitive detection. The grammar production rules were augmented with probabilities and a "skip" transition was introduced. This resulted in increased robustness to insertion errors in the input stream and also to errors in low-level modules. Moore and Essa [85] used SCFGs to model multitasked activities—activities that have several independent threads of execution with intermittent dependent interactions with each other as demonstrated in a Blackjack game with several participants. In syntactic approaches, one only needs to enumerate the list of primitive events that need to be detected and the set of production rules that define higher level activities of interest. Once the rules of a CFG have been formulated, efficient algorithms to parse them exist [86,87] which have made them popular in real-time applications.

In many cases, it is desirable to associate additional attributes or features to the primitive events. For example, the exact location in which the primitive event occurs may be significant for describing an event, but this may not be effectively encoded in the (finite) primitive event set. Thus, attribute grammars achieve greater expressive power than traditional grammars. Probabilistic attribute grammars have been used by Joo and Chellappa [88] for multiagent activities in surveillance settings.

6.2.3 Logic and Linguistic Models

Logic-based methods rely on formal logical rules to describe commonsense domain knowledge to describe activities. Logical rules are useful to express domain knowledge as input by a user or to present the results of high-level reasoning in an intuitive and human-readable format. Declarative models [89] describe all expected activities in terms of scene structure, events, etc. The model for an activity consists of the interactions between the objects of the scene. Medioni et al. [90] propose a hierarchical representation to recognize a series of actions performed by a single agent. Symbolic descriptors of actions are extracted from low-level features through several midlevel layers. Next, a rule-based method is used to approximate the probability of occurrence of a specific activity by matching the properties of the agent with the expected distributions (represented by a mean and a variance) for a particular action. In a later work, Hongeng et al. [91] extended this representation by considering an activity to be composed of several action threads. Each action thread is modeled as a stochastic finite-state automation. Constraints between the various threads are propagated in a temporal logic network. Shet et al. [92] propose a system that relies on logic programming to represent and recognize high-level activities. Low-level modules are used to detect primitive events. The high-level reasoning engine is based on Prolog and recognizes activities which are represented by logical rules between primitives. These approaches do not explicitly address the problem of uncertainty in the observation input stream. To address this issue, a combination of logical and probabilistic models was presented in Tran and Davis [93] where each logical rule is represented as first-order logic formula. Each rule is further provided with a weight, where the weight indicates a belief in the accuracy of the rule. Inference is performed using a Markov-logic network.

While logic-based methods are a natural way of incorporating domain knowledge, they often involve expensive constraint satisfaction checks. Further, it is not clear how much domain knowledge should be incorporated in a given setting—incorporating more knowledge can potentially make the model rigid and nongeneralizable to other settings. Further, the logic rules require extensive enumeration by a domain expert for every deployment.

In most practical deployments that use any of the aforementioned approaches, symbolic activity definitions are constructed in an empirical manner, for example, the rules of a grammar or a set of logical rules are specified manually. Though empirical constructs are fast to design and even work very well in most cases, they are limited in their utility to specific deployments for which they have been designed. Hence, there is a need for a centralized representation of activity definitions or ontologies for activities which are independent of algorithmic choices. Ontologies standardize activity definitions, allow for easy portability to specific deployments, enable interoperability of different systems, and allow easy replication and comparison of system performance. Though ontologies provide concise high-level definitions of activities, they do not necessarily suggest the right "hardware" to "parse" the ontologies for recognition tasks. We refer the reader to Akdemir et al. [94] for a more detailed discussion of issues related to design and evaluation of ontologies.

We also refer the reader to Turaga et al. [95] for a more detailed review of action and activity recognition methods.

7. A Unified Approach for Recognizing Simple Actions and Complex Activities

In this section, we propose a general framework for activity perception and recognition, from which specific algorithms can be derived. The perception of activities can be seen as proceeding from a sequence of 2D images to a semantic description of the activity. Activity perception can be naturally decomposed into the following three stages:

1. Dynamic sketch
2. Action sketch
3. Semantic sketch

Dynamic sketch: The purpose of early stages of vision is to construct primitive descriptions of the action contents in the frame. These primitive descriptions must be rich enough to allow for inference and recognition of activities [96]. A significant portion of information that is available in videos is actually uninteresting for the purpose of activity-based video indexing and only serves to confound the latter stages of the algorithms. One very important characteristic of this stage is to weed out all the unnecessary sensory information and retain just those elements that are relevant for activity-based video indexing. Visual encoding mechanisms present in the human brain mimic this phenomenon and this is called predictive coding. Barlow [97] and Srinivasan et al. [98] contend that predictive coding is not just a mechanism for compression but actually goes much further and enables animals to process information in a timely manner. We refer the interested reader to early works of Marr and Freeman [96], Barlow [97], and Srinivasan et al. [98] on the importance of this stage of visual processing in order to enable vision systems to react and process information in a timely manner.

Action sketch: Studies into human behavior show that human actions can be temporally segmented into elementary units, where each unit consists of functionally related movement [99]. For example, a car parking activity may be considered to be formed of the following primitives—"Car enters a parking lot," "Car stops in the parking slot," "Person walks away from the car." Such a description requires the ability to segment an activity into its constituents and then develop a description for each of the constituent actions. Each constituent action is like a word describing a short, consistent motion fragment. Hence, this stage can be interpreted as providing a "vocabulary" with which to create sentences (activities).

Representing activities using such linguistic models has been in existence in various other fields and disciplines. Several dance notation schemes are used in practice to interpret complex dance moves. Though not extremely detailed, they are easy to interpret and reproduce in actual steps. It has also been found that the most commonly observed human activities in surveillance settings such as reaching, striking, etc. are characterized by distinctive velocity profiles of the limbs that can be conveniently modeled as a specific sequence of individual segments—constant acceleration followed by constant velocity followed by constant deceleration [100]. This lends credence to the fact that human actions can be modeled as a sequence of primitive actions, where each action is governed by a simple model.

Semantic sketch: Semantic descriptions perform the same function as grammatical rules that characterize a language. They detail how several constituent action primitives may be combined together in order to construct or recover complex activities. The most common rules for creating complex activities from constituent actions are sequencing, co-occurrence, and synchronization. For example, a single-threaded activity can be said to consist of a linear sequence of a few primitives. An example of a single-threaded activity is "Person approaches a door" → "Person swipes the access card" → "Person enters a building." Similarly, a complex multithreaded activity can be seen as a collection of several single-threaded activities with some constraints such as concurrence and synchronization among them. Thus, this stage can be seen as providing the rules for combining the primitives—similar to a set of grammatical rules needed to construct meaningful sentences from individual words.

Based on the above discussions, we assume that a complex activity can be broken down into its simpler action elements. During each action element, the motion of the human remains consistent. Each action element is modeled using a LDS. More complex activities can then be constructed using the primitives using a variety of conjunction operations on the primitives. In our approach, we will discuss a discrete-time switching model, and a time-varying model built from the simpler primitives. First, we give an overview of modeling primitives using LDSs.

8. Understanding the Space of Primitives

Let us consider the LDS model discussed in Section 5.2. Let $f(t)$ be a sequence of features extracted from a video indexed by time t, the LDS model parameterizes the evolution of the features $f(t)$ using the following equations:

$$f(t) = Cz(t) + w(t) \quad w(t) \sim N(0, R) \tag{5}$$

$$z(t+1) = Az(t) + v(t) \quad v(t) \sim N(0, Q) \tag{6}$$

where, $z \in \mathbb{R}^d$ is the hidden state vector, $A \in \mathbb{R}^{d \times d}$ the transition matrix, and $C \in \mathbb{R}^{p \times d}$ the measurement matrix. $f \in \mathbb{R}^p$ represents the observed features while w and v are noise components modeled as normal with 0 mean and covariances $R \in \mathbb{R}^{p \times p}$ and $Q \in \mathbb{R}^{d \times d}$, respectively. For high-dimensional time-series data (dynamic textures, etc.), the most common approach is to first learn a lower dimensional embedding of the observations via PCA, and learn temporal dynamics in the lower dimensional space. Closed form solutions for learning the model parameters (A, C) from the feature sequence $(f_{1:T})$ have been proposed by Doretto et al. [57,60] and are widely used in the computer vision community. Let observations $f(1), f(2), \ldots, f(\tau)$, represent the features for the time indices $1, 2, \ldots, \tau$. Let $[f(1), f(2), \ldots, f(\tau)] = U\Sigma V^T$ be the singular value decomposition of the data. Then $\hat{C} = U$, $\hat{A} = \Sigma V^T D_1 V (V^T D_2 V)^{-1} \Sigma^{-1}$, where $D_1 = [0\,0; I_{\tau-1}\,0]$ and $D_2 = [I_{\tau-1}\,0; 0\,0]$.

For the model of Equation (6), starting from an initial condition $z(0)$, it can be shown that the *expected* observation sequence is given by

$$
E \begin{bmatrix} f(0) \\ f(1) \\ f(2) \\ \cdot \\ \cdot \end{bmatrix} = \begin{bmatrix} C \\ CA \\ CA^2 \\ \cdot \\ \cdot \end{bmatrix} z(0) = O_\infty(M)z(0) \tag{7}
$$

Thus, the expected observation sequence generated by a time-invariant model $M = (A, C)$ lies in the column space of the extended *observability* matrix given by

$$
O_\infty^T = [C^T, (CA)^T, (CA^2)^T, \ldots, (CA^n)^T, \ldots] \tag{8}
$$

Several distance metrics exist to measure the distance between linear dynamic models. The simplest method to measure distance is the $L-2$ norm between model parameters. Martin [65] proposed a more principled method to measure the distance between ARMA models based on cepstral coefficients. A unifying framework based on subspace angles of observability matrices was presented in Cock and Moor [63] to measure the distance between ARMA models. Specific metrics such as the Frobenius norm and the Martin metric [65] can be derived as special cases based on the subspace angles. Recently, Vishwanathan et al. [67] presented a framework to extend the Cauchy–Binet kernels to the space of dynamical systems and incorporated the dependence on initial conditions of the dynamical systems as well. Subspace angles $(\theta_i, i = 1, 2, \ldots, n)$ between two ARMA models are defined in Cock and Moor [63] as the principal angles $(\theta, i = 1, 2, \ldots, n)$ between the column spaces generated by the observability spaces of the two models extended with the observability matrices of the inverse models [63]. The subspace angles $(\theta_1, \theta_2, \ldots)$ between the range spaces of two matrices A and B is recursively defined as follows [63],

$$
\cos \theta_1 = \max_{x,y} \frac{|x^T A^T By|}{||Ax||_2||By||_2} = \frac{|x_1^T A^T By_1|}{||Ax_1||_2||By_1||_2} \tag{9}
$$

$$\cos \theta_k = \max_{x,y} \frac{|x^T A^T B y|}{||Ax||_2 ||By||_2} = \frac{|x_k^T A^T B y_k|}{||Ax_k||_2 ||By_k||_2} \quad \text{for } k = 2, 3, \dots \quad (10)$$

subject to the constraints $x_i^T A^T A x_k = 0$ and $y_i^T B^T B y_k = 0$ for $i = 1, 2, \dots, k-1$. The subspace angles between two ARMA models $[A_1, C_1, K_1]$ and $[A_2, C_2, K_2]$ can be computed by the method described in Cock and Moor [63]. Using these subspace angles θ_i, $i = 1, 2, \dots, n$, three distances, Martin distance (d_M), gap distance (d_g), and Frobenius distance (d_F) between the ARMA models are defined as follows:

$$d_M^2 = \ln \prod_{i=1}^{n} \frac{1}{\cos^2(\theta_i)}, \quad d_g = \sin \theta_{max}, \quad d_F^2 = 2 \sum_{i=1}^{n} \sin^2 \theta_i \quad (11)$$

In experimental implementations, we approximate the extended observability matrix by the finite observability matrix as is commonly done [64].

$$O_m^T = \left[C^T, (CA)^T, (CA^2)^T, \dots, (CA^{m-1})^T \right] \quad (12)$$

The size of this matrix is $mp \times d$. The column space of this matrix is a d-dimensional subspace of $\mathbb{R}^{mp}$, where d is the dimension of the state-space z in Equation (6). d is typically of the order of 5–10. To numerically represent the subspace spanned by the columns of this matrix, we store an orthonormal basis computed by Gram–Schmidt orthonormalization.

The set of all d-dimensional linear subspaces of $\mathbb{R}^n$ is called the *Grassmann manifold* which will be denoted as $\mathcal{G}_{n,d}$. The set of all $n \times d$ orthonormal matrices is called the Stiefel manifold and shall be denoted as $\mathcal{S}_{n,d}$. Since, a subspace is a point on a Grassmann manifold—an LDS can be alternately identified as a point on the Grassmann manifold corresponding to the column space of the observability matrix. Now, the goal is to devise methods for classification and recognition using these model parameters. This implies that we are interested in computing statistical, linguistic, and semantic statistical models over the primitive space—the Grassmann manifold. To do this, we need a deeper understanding of the geometry of this space. We discuss this in the next section.

8.1   The Manifold Structure of Subspaces

On a computer, a subspace is stored as an orthonormal matrix which forms a basis for the subspace. As mentioned earlier, orthonormal matrices are points on the Stiefel manifold. However, since the choice of basis for a subspace is not unique, any notion of distance and statistics should be invariant to this choice. This requires us to interpret each point on the Grassmann manifold as an equivalence of points on the Stiefel manifold, where all orthonormal matrices that span the same subspace are considered equivalent. This interpretation is more formally described as a *quotient* interpretation, that is, the Grassmann manifold is considered a quotient space of the Stiefel manifold. Quotient interpretations allow us to extend the results of the base manifold such as tangent spaces, geodesics, etc. to the new quotient manifold. In our case, it turns out that the Stiefel manifold itself can be interpreted as a quotient of a more basic manifold—the special orthogonal group SO(n). A quotient of Stiefel is thus a quotient of SO(n) as well. Thus, we shall study the Grassmann as a quotient of SO(n). In what follows, first we review relevant results of SO(n), then present the required concepts from differential geometry that enables us to derive distances and statistical models on the special manifolds.

Let GL(n) be the set of $n \times n$ nonsingular matrices; this set is called the *generalized linear group* because it is also a group with the group operation given by matrix multiplication. The set GL(n) possesses an additional structure that makes it a differentiable manifold. One of its properties is that although it is not a vector space, it can be locally approximated by subsets of a vector space. The dual properties of being a group and a differentiable manifold make it a *Lie group*. If we consider the subset of all orthogonal matrices, and further restrict to the ones with determinant $+1$, we obtain a subgroup SO(n), called the *special orthogonal group*. It can be shown that this is a submanifold of GL(n) and, therefore, also possesses the Lie group structure. Since it has n^2 elements and $n + n(n-1)/2$ constraints (unit length columns $\rightarrow n$ constraints and perpendicular columns $\rightarrow n(n-1)/2$ constraints), it is an $n(n-1)/2$D Lie group.

The *Grassmann* manifold is the set of all d-dimensional subspace of $\mathbb{R}^n$. Here, we are interested in d-dimensional subspaces and not in a particular basis. In order to obtain a quotient space structure for $\mathcal{G}_{n,d}$, let SO(d) $\times$ SO($n-d$) be a subgroup of SO(n) using the embedding ϕ_b: (SO(d) $\times$ SO($n-d$)) $\rightarrow$ SO(n):

$$\phi_b(V_1, V_2) = \begin{bmatrix} V_1 & 0 \\ 0 & V_2 \end{bmatrix} \in \text{SO}(n). \tag{13}$$

A point U on $\mathcal{S}_{n,d}$ is represented as a tall–thin $n \times d$ orthonormal matrix. The corresponding equivalence class of $n \times d$ matrices $[U] = UR$, for $R \in$ GL(d) is called the Procrustes representation of the Stiefel manifold. Thus, to compare two points in $\mathcal{G}_{n,d}$, we simply compare the smallest squared distance between the corresponding equivalence classes on the Stiefel manifold according to the Procrustes representation. Given matrices U_1 and U_2 on $\mathcal{S}_{n,d}$, the smallest squared Euclidean distance between the corresponding equivalence classes is given by

$$d^2_{\text{Procrust}}([U_1], [U_2]) = \min_R \text{tr}(U_1 - U_2R)^T(U_1 - U_2R) \tag{14}$$

$$= \min_R \text{tr}(R^TR - 2U_1^TU_2R + I_k) \tag{15}$$

When R varies over the orthogonal group $O(d)$, the minimum is attained at $R = H_1H_2^T = A(A^TA)^{-1/2}$, where $A = H_1DH_2^T$ is the singular value decomposition of A. We refer the reader to Chikuse [101] for proofs and alternate cases.

8.2 Supervised and Unsupervised Learning of Activities from Videos

Many of the video-based analysis tasks of interest involve one of two tasks (a) recognition of an input video as one of several classes or (b) finding underlying structural similarities in a large collection of videos. Given videos of activities, the LDS model parameters $M = (A, C)$ are estimated using the methods described in Section 8. Subsequently, the finite observability matrix $O_m(M)$ is computed. Then for each observability matrix, an orthonormal basis is computed using standard SVD-based algorithms. So, we now have a set of subspaces, or in other words a point cloud on the Grassmann manifold. In recognition problems, we also have corresponding activity class labels provided with each point. In this section, we shall provide methods that follow from the theory described above to solve the supervised and unsupervised learning problems. Toward this task, one can use the Riemannian geometry of the Grassmann manifold to perform calculus. This leads to principled methods for computation of mean of a set of points, estimating class-conditional probability density function (pdfs), clustering, etc. We refer the reader to Turaga [102] for an overview of these approaches. For brevity, here we shall discuss a simpler extrinsic way of statistical modeling.

Given several examples from a class $(U_1, U_2, \ldots, U_n)$ on the manifold, the class conditional density can be estimated using an appropriate kernel function. We first assume that an appropriate choice of a divergence on the manifold has been made such as the one above. For the Procrustes measure, the density estimate is given by Chikuse [101] as

$$\hat{f}(U; M) = \frac{1}{n}C(M)\sum_{i=1}^{n} K[M^{-1/2}(I_k - U_i^TUU^TU_i)M^{-1/2}] \tag{16}$$

where $K(T)$ is the kernel function, M is a $d \times d$ positive definite matrix which plays the role of the kernel width or a smoothing parameter. $C(M)$ is a normalizing factor chosen so that the estimated density integrates to unity. The matrix valued kernel function $K(T)$ can be chosen in several ways. We have used $K(T) = \exp(-\text{tr}(T))$ in all the experiments reported in this chapter. In this nonparametric method for density estimation, the choice of kernel width M becomes important. Thus, though this is a noniterative procedure, the optimal choice of the kernel width can have a large impact on the final results. In general, there is no standard way to choose this parameter except for cross-validation.

8.3   Activity Recognition Experiments

We performed a recognition experiment on the publicly available INRIA dataset [103]. The dataset consists of 10 individuals performing 11 actions, each action executed three times at varying rates while freely changing orientation. We used the view-invariant representation and features as proposed in Weinland et al. [103]. Specifically, we used the $16 \times 16 \times 16$ circular FFT features proposed by Weinland et al. [103]. Each activity was modeled as a LDS. Testing was performed using a round-robin experiment, where activity models were learnt using nine actors and tested on one actor. For the kernel method, all available training instances per class were used to learn a class-conditional kernel density as described in Section 8.2. In Table I, we show the recognition results obtained using four methods. The first column shows the results obtained using dimensionality reduction approaches of Weinland et al. [103] on

TABLE I

COMPARISON OF VIEW INVARIANT RECOGNITION OF ACTIVITIES IN THE INRIA DATASET USING (A) BEST DIM. RED. [103] ON $16 \times 16 \times 16$ FEATURES, (B) BEST DIM. RED. [103] ON $64 \times 64 \times 64$ FEATURES, (C) NEAREST NEIGHBOR USING ARMA MODEL DISTANCE ($16 \times 16 \times 16$ FEATURES), (D) NEAREST NEIGHBOR USING PROCRUSTES DISTANCE ($16 \times 16 \times 16$ FEATURES), AND (E) EXTRINSIC KERNEL METHOD $M = I$

Activity	Best Dim. Red. [103] 16^3 volume	Best Dim. Red. [103] 64^3 volume	Subspace angles 16^3 volume	Procrustes metric 16^3 volume	Extrinsic kernel
Check watch	76.67	86.66	93.33	90	100
Cross arms	100	100	100	96.67	100
Scratch head	80	93.33	76.67	90	96.67
Sit down	96.67	93.33	93.33	93.33	93.33
Get up	93.33	93.33	86.67	80	96.67
Turn around	96.67	96.67	100	100	100
Walk	100	100	100	100	100
Wave hand	73.33	80	93.33	90	100
Punch	83.33	96.66	93.33	83.33	100
Kick	90	96.66	100	100	100
Pick up	86.67	90	96.67	96.67	100
Average	88.78	93.33	93.93	92.72	98.78

These results were first presented in Turaga et al. [69].

$16 \times 16 \times 16$ features. Weinland et al.[103] reports recognition results using a variety of dimensionality reduction techniques (PCA, LDA, Mahalanobis) and here we choose the row-wise best performance from their experiments (denoted "Best Dim. Red.") which were obtained using $64 \times 64 \times 64$ circular FFT features. The third column corresponds to the method of using subspace angles-based distance between dynamical models [63]. Column 4 shows the nearest-neighbor classifier performance using Procrustes distance measure ($16 \times 16 \times 16$ features). We see that the manifold Procrustes distance performs as well as ARMA model distance [63]. Statistical modeling using the extrinsic kernel method outperforms all other methods.

9. Complex Activity Models: Cascade of Dynamical Systems

Most activities involving a single human in surveillance settings consist of the human executing a series of action elements in order to achieve a certain goal. For example, a man driving a car into a parking lot, parking the car, alighting from it, and walking out of the parking lot (series of action elements) contributes to a typical activity. Moreover, several multihuman activities may also be adequately represented by a sequence of actions. Thus, the cascade of LDS (CLDS) model [104] is an appropriate model for representing a wide variety of common activities.

The model for an activity must be able to represent each of the action elements separately while simultaneously being able to detect the boundaries between them. As mentioned earlier, we use the consistency of features within each action element as a cue to discover the boundaries between them. The specific way the action elements interact with each other is used to discover the activities themselves. The overall system overview is shown in Fig. 9. Each of the components will be described in detail in the ensuing discussion.

9.1   Modeling Action Elements

As already discussed, the dynamics of each action element can be modeled using a time-invariant dynamical system. In several scenarios (such as far-field surveillance, objects moving on a plane, etc.), it is reasonable to model constant motion in the real world, using a LDS on the image plane. Given the boundaries between action elements, we model each of these segments using a LDS. An activity is composed of a series of action elements. The activity model is now composed of a cascade or a sequence of such dynamical systems. In reality, most activities have a very specific temporal order for the execution of action elements. For example, if our goal is to get

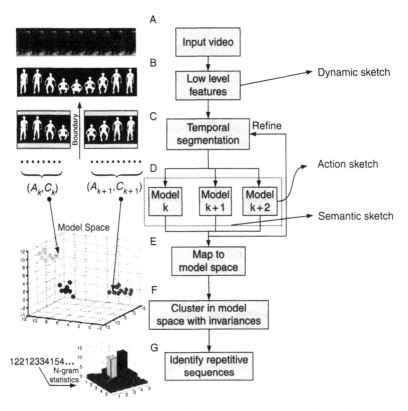

FIG. 9. System overview: (A) Input video, (B) feature extraction (dynamic sketch), (C) temporal segmentation, (D) build and learn dynamical models, (E, F) cluster in model space taking into account invariances on the data, and (G) identify repetitive activities. Figure courtesy Turaga et al. [104]. (See color insert at the back of the book.)

to an office building, then the sequence of actions executed might be—drive into parking lot, park car, alight from car, and walk away from the parking lot. Therefore, we model an activity as a cascade of action elements, with each action element modeled as an LDS. Figure 10 illustrates the complete model for such an activity.

9.2 Learning Model Parameters

Now, we have modeled an activity as a cascade of dynamical systems. But given a video sequence, we first need to segment the video into action elements and discover the relationship among them. The challenge is to accomplish all of this in a

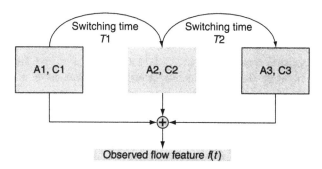

Fɪɢ. 10. Illustration of a cascade of three linear dynamical systems. The temporal order of the execution of these dynamical models and their switching times are shown with arrows. Figure courtesy Turaga et al. [104].

completely unsupervised manner while being invariant to variabilities in an activity like execution rate, resolution of video, rotation and translation, etc. We will now describe an algorithm to automatically segment the video and learn the model parameters in an unsupervised manner.

As mentioned earlier, we use "consistency" of features within each action element as a cue to discover boundaries between them. Naturally, the exact measure of "consistency" is tied to the specific feature at hand. For example, ST curvature [105] is a widely used metric to discover boundaries for point trajectories. Measures for shape deformation such as Yezzi and Soatto [106] are suited for discovering segment boundaries in shape sequences. In this section, we describe a simple method for discovering action boundaries that works well for background subtracted silhouettes and optical flow.

For each time-instant t, we predict the current observation $\hat{f}_t$ using a set of K past observations $\{f_{t-1}, \ldots, f_{t-K}\}$. If the observation f_t deviates significantly from the predicted value by a threshold, that is, if $\left| f_t - \hat{f}_t \right| >$ thresh, then a boundary is detected at the time-instant t. In our case, the prediction $\hat{f}_t$ is derived from the past observations as follows. For the first few (about 5) set of frames after the beginning of a new segment, we cumulatively learn a single set of affine parameters for the change in the feature. For every incoming new frame, we predict the new feature using the estimated set of affine parameters. Learning the affine parameters for each segment can be achieved in closed form using the properties of the Fourier transform [107].

This segmentation scheme is suboptimal due to the assumption of affine motion. To overcome this, we iterate back and forth between learning the LDS model for each segment and tweaking the segment boundaries till convergence is reached.

Taking the output of this initial segmentation as a starting point, we learn the LDS model for each segment. Without loss of generality, let $S_1 = (A_1, C_1)$ and $S_2 = (A_2, C_2)$ be two adjacent segments and their corresponding LDS models. Suppose the temporal span of S_1 is $[t_1, t_b]$ and that of S_2 is $[t_b, t_2]$. Here t_b denotes the boundary between the segments. As described in Section 8, columns of C_k correspond to the top d principal components (PCs) of the observations in segment k. To *evaluate* the boundary according to the learnt models, we compute the reconstruction error of all the observations according to the PCs in the corresponding segments. We move the boundary by an amount τ in forward and backward directions and choose the one that minimizes this error. Thus, we search for the minima of the following cost functional:

$$\Delta(\tau) = \sum_{t=t_1}^{t_b+\tau} \left\| C_1(C_1^T f_t) - f_t \right\|^2 + \sum_{t=t_b+\tau}^{t_2} \left\| C_2(C_2^T f_t) - f_t \right\|^2 \qquad (17)$$

where f_t is the observation at time t and $\tau \in [-T, T]$. In our experiments, we typically chose T to be 10. The new boundary is found as $t_b^{new} = t_b^{old} + \arg\min_\tau \Delta(\tau)$. With the new boundary the models are learnt again, and the process is repeated till convergence, that is, the boundary does not change anymore $\arg\min_\tau \Delta(\tau) = 0$.

Once a long video of activities has been segmented into its primitives, we can estimate a vocabulary of prototypes that will be used to learn linguistic models of human activities. Since, the atomic actions are represented as LDSs, we need a clustering algorithm on this space to provide us with the action prototypes. Here, we used the normalized cuts clustering algorithm with the Procrustes measure on the Grassmann manifold to obtain the clusters. After clustering the action elements each segment is assigned a label. Suppose we have the following sequence of labels $(L_1, L_3, L_2, L_6, L_7, L_8, L_1, L_3, L_5, L_2, L_6, L_1, L_7, L_8)$. Persistent activities in the video would appear as a repetitive sequence of these labels. From this sequence, we need to find the *approximately* repeating patterns. We say *approximate* because oversegmentation may cause the patterns to be not exactly repetitive. We can say that (L_1, L_3, L_2) and (L_6, L_7, L_8) are the repeating patterns, up to one insertion error. To discover the repeating patterns, we build the n-gram statistics of the segment labels as shown in Fig. 9G. We start by building a bigram, trigram, and tetragram models. In our experience, oversegmentation of the video is more common than undersegmentation. Thus, we allow for up to one insertion error while building the n-gram statistics. We prune the bigrams which appear as a subsequence of a trigram. We prune the trigrams in a similar fashion. Finally, we declare the n-grams with a count above a threshold (depending on the length of the video) as the repeating patterns in the video. The cascade structure of individual activities is the exact sequence of the prototypes in the n-grams.

9.3 Experiments: Video Summarization Using Cascade Models

Most video-sharing websites feature user-supplied tags. It is assumed that the tags describe what is going on in a video. This has several drawbacks, since tags are subjective and the same meaning may be conveyed by a multitude of tags. Further, it is not uncommon to encounter tags whose meaning is not known to a user and are sometimes irrelevant to the video. The idea of user-generated tags would also not scale with the increasing size of the dataset. Instead of providing such textual descriptions, we propose to analyze the patterns of motion in a video and automatically extract "clusters" which when visually presented to a user can convey maximum information about the contents of the video. For example, given a tennis video, short segments depicting elements such as forehand, backhand, smash, etc. when visually presented to a user would convey more information than a set of textual descriptions.

We show some clustering results on a near-field video sequence of a human performing five different complex activities—throw, bend, squat, bat, and pick phone. We were able to learn the cascade of dynamical systems model in a completely unsupervised manner. We manually validated the segment boundaries and the corresponding discovered activities. We call each discovered repetitive pattern a *motif*. The classification of the activities into motifs is tabulated in Table II. We see that the table has a strong diagonal structure, indicating that each of the discovered motifs corresponds to one of the activities in the dataset. Motifs 1–5 correspond to "bending," "squatting," "throwing," "pick up phone," and "batting," respectively. This demonstrates that the algorithm does indeed discover semantically meaningful boundaries and also is able to distinguish between various activities by learning the right cascade structure of the action prototypes.

TABLE II
COMPOSITION OF THE DISCOVERED CLUSTERS IN THE UMD DATABASE

Activity type	Motif 1	Motif 2	Motif 3	Motif 4	Motif 5
Bending	10	1	0	2	1
Squatting	2	8	2	0	0
Throwing	0	0	7	0	1
Pick phone	3	0	0	9	0
Batting	0	0	0	1	9

Results first presented in Turaga et al. [104].

A

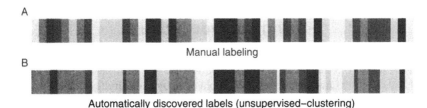

Manual labeling

B

Automatically discovered labels (unsupervised–clustering)

FIG. 11. Color coded activity labeling for a 4000 frame video sequence of the UMD database: (A) Manual labeling and (B) unsupervised clustering result. Image best viewed in color. Figure courtesy Turaga et al. [104]. (See color insert at the back of the book.)

Figure 11 shows activity labels for the entire video sequence extracted manually and automatically. Matching of the colors in the figure indicates that the algorithm is able to discover and identify activities in an unsupervised manner. We found that the errors in labeling are typically near the transition between two activities, where the actual labeling of those frames is itself subject to confusion. To visualize the clusters and to see the *trajectories* of each activity, we embedded each segment into a 6D Laplacian eigenspace. Dimensions 1–3 are shown in Fig. 12A and dimensions 4–6 in Fig. 12B. We see that the trajectories of the same activity are closely clustered together in the Laplacian space.

9.3.1   INRIA: Free-Viewpoint Database [103]

As described earlier, the INRIA multiple-camera multiple video database of the PERCEPTION group consists of 11 daily-live motions performed each 3 times by 10 individuals. The actors freely change position and orientation. Every execution of the activity is done at a different rate. For this dataset, we extract $16 \times 16 \times 16$ circular FFT features as described in Weinland et al. [103]. Instead of modeling each segment of activity as a single motion history volume as in Weinland et al. [103], we build a time series of motion history volumes using small sliding windows. This allows us to build a dynamic model for each segment. We use the segmentation method proposed in Weinland et al. [108]. Using these features, we first performed a recognition experiment on the provided data. Next, we performed a clustering experiment on all 30 sequences (10 actors $\times$ 3 sequences per actor). Segmentation was performed using the method described in Weinland et al. [108]. The clustering results are shown in Table III. The strong diagonal structure of the table indicates that meaningful clusters are found. We also see that some activities such as "Check Watch" and "Cross Arms" are confused. Similarly, "Scratch Head" is most often confused with "Wave Hand" and "Cross Arms."

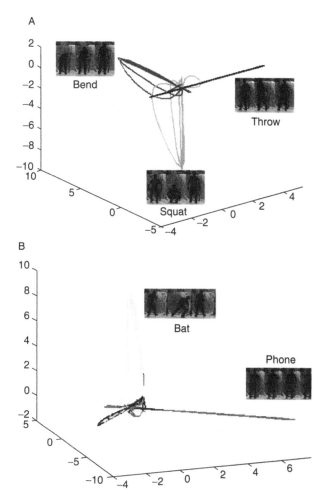

FIG. 12. (A) Visualization of the Clusters in Laplacian space dimensions 1–3. (B) Visualization of Clusters in Laplacian space dimensions 4–6. Best viewed in color. Figure courtesy Turaga et al. [104]. (See color insert at the back of the book.)

Such a confusion may be attributed to the similar and also sparse motion patterns that are generated by those activities.

We also show the actual summarization results obtained on two of the actors— "Florian" and "Alba" in Figs. 13 and 14.

TABLE III
CONFUSION MATRIX SHOWING VIEW-INVARIANT CLUSTERING USING THE PROPOSED
ALGORITHM ON THE INRIA DATASET

Motifs	1	2	3	4	5	6	7	8	9	10	11
Sit down	28	3	0	0	0	1	0	0	0	0	0
Get up	0	31	0	0	0	0	0	0	0	0	0
Turn around	0	0	28	0	0	0	1	0	0	0	0
Check watch	0	0	0	17	5	2	0	6	4	0	0
Cross arms	0	0	0	0	16	3	0	10	1	0	1
Scratch head	1	0	0	3	9	3	0	7	4	0	1
Walk	0	0	0	0	0	0	30	0	0	0	0
Wave hand	0	0	0	6	0	4	0	10	1	0	0
Punch	0	0	0	0	0	4	0	7	9	5	0
Kick	0	0	0	1	0	1	0	0	2	26	0
Pick up	2	2	0	1	0	1	0	0	4	0	23

Results first presented in Turaga et al. [104].

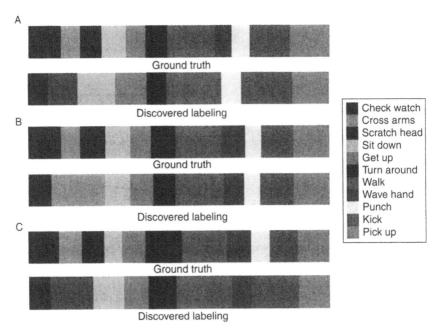

FIG. 13. Color coded activity labeling for three sequences by actor "Florian". First row in each is the ground truth, second row is the discovered labeling. Image best viewed in color. Figure courtesy Turaga et al. [104]. (See color insert at the back of the book.)

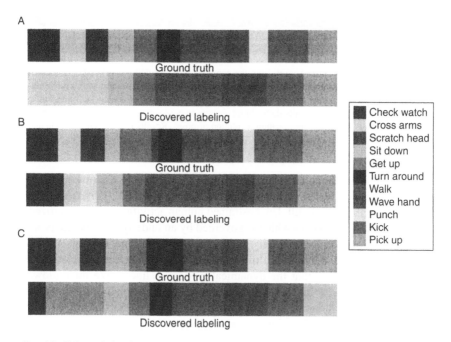

FIG. 14. Color coded activity labeling for three sequences by actor "Alba". First row in each is the ground truth, second row is the discovered labeling. Image best viewed in color. Figure courtesy Turaga et al. [104]. (See color insert at the back of the book.)

10. More General Activity Models: Time-Varying Models

Complex human activities have frequently been modeled as a composition of simpler events. In several domains, it has been observed that human activities are better described as a continuum of actions where the individual boundaries between actions are often blurry [109]. To draw a parallel to language processing, it has been long known in the speech community that words spoken in isolation sound quite different when spoken in continuous speech. This is commonly attributed to "coarticulation" and "assimilation" effects. Similarly, when actions appear in a connected form, it is hard to identify precisely where an action ends and where another begins. Consider the action shown in Fig. 15A and a synthesized version which relies on finding segment boundaries and fitting models to each segment in Fig. 15B. As can be seen, segmentation followed by modeling causes abrupt changes

Fig. 15. (A) Original sequence taken from the common activities dataset [119], (B) synthesis by a sequence of linear dynamic models with boundaries shown by vertical yellow lines, and (C) synthesis by a continuous time-varying model. It can be seen that when actions are segmented and modeled using switching models, the synthesis results show abrupt changes in pose across boundaries whereas the time-varying model results in a much more natural evolution of poses. Results first presented in Turaga and Chellappa [110].

to appear at segment boundaries during synthesis. This effect is also observed in sign language where gestures are influenced by adjacent gestures [109], making segmentation and recognition difficult. Unconstrained human activities are characterized by a complex evolution of poses which is governed by an underlying dynamic process. The underlying process is potentially highly nonlinear and time varying. We model complex activities as outputs of a time-varying linear dynamical process. At each time instant, we assume that the dynamical process is linear. We then allow the parameters of the LDS to vary at each time instant. Let $f(t) \in \mathbb{R}^m$ denote the observations (flow/silhouette, etc.) at time-instant t. Then, the time-varying dynamical model is represented as Turaga and Chellappa [110]

$$f(t) = C(t)z(t) + w(t), \quad w(t) \sim N(0, R(t)) \tag{18}$$

$$z(t + 1) = A(t)z(t) + v(t), \quad v(t) \sim N(0, Q(t)) \tag{19}$$

where $z(t) \in \mathbb{R}^d$ is the hidden state vector of dimension d, $A(t)$ is the time-varying transition matrix and $C(t)$ is the time-varying measurement matrix. $w(t)$ and $v(t)$ are noise components modeled as normal with 0 mean and covariance $R(t)$ and $Q(t)$, respectively. When the model parameters A, C, Q, R are constant, the model reduces to the well-known time-invariant LDS which has been successfully applied in several vision tasks [57]. In summary, the model consists of a sequence of parameters: the measurement matrix $C(t)$ and the transition matrix $A(t)$ and the noise covariances $R(t)$, $Q(t)$.

10.1   Estimating the Time-Varying Parameters

For the time-invariant case, it is easily shown that there are infinitely many choices of parameters that give rise to the same sample path $f(t)$. Resolving this ambiguity requires one to impose further constraints and choose a canonical model. The conditions as proposed in Doretto et al. [57] are that $m \gg d$, rank(C) = d and $C^T C = I$. The number of unknowns that need to be solved for are: $md - (d(d + 1)/2)$

for C, d^2 for A, $d(d + 1)/2$ for Q: resulting in $md + d^2$ unknowns (we have ignored the observation noise covariance as of now). For each observed frame we get m equations. Hence, $d + 1$ linearly independent observations are sufficient to solve for the required parameters ($m(d + 1) > md + d^2$ since $m \gg d$). As seen before, the parameter estimates can be obtained in closed form using prediction error methods.

Estimation of time-varying models for time-series have been studied in various domains such as speech processing, econometric data, and communication channels. A commonly used assumption in these domains is that the time-varying AR (autoregressive) and ARMA (autoregressive moving average) parameters can be expressed as linear combinations of known deterministic functions of time such as the Fourier basis or the exponential basis [111]. Other approaches include Taylor-series expansions of the model parameters such as in Rao [112] for econometric applications. Estimation of time-varying single-input single-output (SISO) AR models have been proposed by estimating an equivalent time-invariant single-input multiple-output (SIMO) process [113] and was applied for channel estimation in communication networks. These approaches are restricted to single-dimensional time-series data. Multidimensional time-varying dynamical models traditionally arise as a result of linearizing a non-LDS. In such cases, the time-varying parameters can be solved for analytically using Taylor-series expansions around a "nominal trajectory" [62]. However, in most practical applications including activity modeling, one does not know what the underlying nonlinear equations are nor does one have the knowledge of a nominal trajectory. Recently, linear parameter varying (LPV) systems have been proposed to model time-varying processes. In these approaches, the time-varying model parameters are considered to be linear combinations of a small set of time-invariant parameters. The linear combination weights, also called the scheduling weights, change with time [114,115]. However, identification of LPV systems is computationally very expensive [115]. In the following, we propose a computationally efficient and conceptually simple method to estimate the time-varying parameters of a dynamical system without making strong assumptions on the nature of the time-varying process.

To begin with, it is easily seen that even in the time-varying case there are infinitely many choices of the model parameters that can give rise to the same sample path $f(t)$. So, we impose the same set of conditions as in the time-invariant case, that is, $m \gg d$, $\text{rank}(C(t)) = d$ and $C(t)^T C(t) = I$. Based on the analysis given above, there are $md + d^2$ unknowns for *each* time instant and m equations per time instant. Obviously this is an ill-posed problem since there are far more unknowns than there are equations. Hence, we impose another condition that the model parameters stay constant in local temporal neighborhoods. The temporal neighborhood in which the parameters are assumed to stay constant should also ensure that $d + 1$ linearly independent observations can be obtained within the neighborhood. In general, it cannot be guaranteed that a fixed $d + 1$ sized neighborhood will satisfy this condition. However, in our experience we found that a neighborhood of size 1.5d–2d was sufficient to meet this condition in most real-world human activities. Typically, d is of the order of 5–10 and complex human activities extend to several hundred frames. It is reasonable to assume that in short windows of about 15–20 frames the dynamics can be easily modeled by simple time-invariant dynamical processes. We now have a sequence of dynamical systems which defines a trajectory on the space of LDS. Before we discuss how we model this trajectory, we first discuss the Grassmann manifold formulation of the LDS space.

Given a video of a long activity, first the time-varying model parameters $M_t = (A_t, C_t)$ are estimated using small temporal sliding windows and the method described in Section 10.1. Subsequently, for each window the observability matrix $O_n(M_t)$ is computed. Then for each observability matrix, an orthonormal basis is computed using standard SVD-based algorithms. So, we now have a sequence of subspaces, or in other words a trajectory on the Grassmann manifold. To compactly parameterize the subspace trajectories, we propose the following approach.

10.1.1   Grassmann Switching Model

Corresponding to an activity class C, suppose we are given M subspace sequences $\{S_i^C(t)\}_{i=1}^M$. We consider the dynamics to be described by a set of K hidden states $L^{(1)}, \ldots, L^{(K)}$. The state at time t is denoted by $Q(t)$ and the observation at time t is denoted by $S(t)$. The overall model for the activity consists of the K hidden states, the intracluster pdfs $f(S(t)|Q(t)=L^{(i)})$, the transition probability matrix, and the prior probability. In general, the Baum–Welch algorithm provides solutions for the above problems in a ML sense. This requires one to have analytical expressions for the intracluster pdfs and the gradient of the likelihood of a sequence in terms of these parameters. In our case, we solve these problems in a much simpler, although suboptimal way, as follows. Given a sequence of subspaces $\{S_i^C(t)\}_{i=1}^M$, the following procedure is adopted to estimate the switching model.

1. Cluster the points into K clusters or hidden-states $L^{(1)}, \ldots, L^{(K)}$.
2. Estimate a pdf within each cluster $f(S(t)|Q(t)=L^{(i)})$.
3. Estimate the transition probabilities $p(Q(t)=L^{(i)}|Q(t-1)=L^{(j)})$ between the clusters.
4. Estimate the prior probability $p(Q(0))$.

As before, we can use any standard clustering algorithm such as normalized cuts. Within each cluster, we can use parametric or nonparametric density estimates as described in Section 8.2 to estimate the intracluster pdf. Once the clusters are found, we form the sequence of cluster labels corresponding to the sequence of subspaces.

The sequence of labels is used to estimate the transition probabilities by bigram counts. Thus, we have now learnt a switching model on the Grassmann manifold for each activity class. Given a new subspace sequence, we need a method to classify it into one of the action classes. In the case of standard HMMs, this problem is solved by the forward–backward algorithm and its variants. We use a simpler version that works much faster and using fewer computations. Given a sequence $S(t)$ and an activity model, we first assign each $S(t)$ into one of the clusters of the model. Let us denote by $Q(t)$ the sequence of cluster labels thus obtained. Then, we compute the likelihood of the sequence as $p(Q(0)) \, \Pi_k f(S(k)|Q(k))p(Q(k)|Q(k-1))$. Though this is suboptimal than the forward–backward algorithm, we found that we obtain significant computational advantages using these approximations. We refer to Turaga and Chellappa [110] for more details of this approach.

10.2   Experiments: Video Summarization and Clustering

We performed a clustering experiment on the figure skating dataset reported in Ref. [116]. This data is very challenging since it is unconstrained and involves rapid motion of both the skater and real-world motion of the camera, including pan, tilt, and zoom. Some representative frames from the raw video are shown in Fig. 16. It should be noted that the authors of Ref. [116] consider discovering action classes from static images. Since, they do not use temporal information, the results of our method based on dynamic models cannot be directly compared with those of Wang et al. [116].

10.2.1   Low-Level Processing

We built color models of the foreground and background using normalized color histograms. The color histograms are used to segment the background and foreground pixels. Median filtering followed by connected component analysis is

Fig. 16.   Sample images from the skating video from Wang et al. [116].

performed to reject small isolated blobs. From the segmented results, we fit a bounding box to the foreground pixels by estimating the 2D mean and second-order moments along x and y directions. We perform temporal smoothing of the bounding box parameters to remove jitter effects. The final feature is a rescaled binary image of the pixels inside the bounding box.

10.2.2 Clustering Experiment

Most figure skating videos consist of a few established elements or moves such as jumps, spins, lifts, and turns. A typical performance by skater or pair of skaters includes several of these elements each performed several times. Due to the complex body postures involved, it is a challenge even for humans to identify clear boundaries between atomic actions. It is difficult to semantically define temporal boundaries of an activity and define a metric for temporal segmentation, making it very difficult to break the video into temporally consistent segments. Instead of performing explicit segmentation, we build models for fixed length subsequences using sliding windows. The results of a temporal segmentation algorithm that can split, such a complex video into meaningful segments, can be easily plugged in. We use 20 frame long overlapping windows for building models of the video. For each segment, we store an orthonormal matrix corresponding to the observability matrix of the model parameters. Then, we performed k-means clustering on the Grassmann manifold using normalized cuts. Also, most of the "interesting" activities such as sitting spins, standing spins, leaps, etc. are usually few and far between. Further, due to the subsequence approach, there will necessarily be several segments that do not contain any meaningful action. As a simple example, a subsequence that contains the transition from a spin to a jump will not fit into either of these action clusters. To discover the "interesting" activities, we first need to remove these outlier segments. First, we cluster all the available subsequences into a fixed number of clusters (say 10). Then, from each cluster we remove the outliers using a simple criterion of average distance to the cluster. Then, we recluster the remaining segments. We show the obtained clusters in Figs. 17–21. We observe that Clusters 1–4 correspond dominantly to "Sitting Spins", "Standing Spins," "Camel Spins," and "Spirals," respectively, (in a spiral the skater glides on one foot while raising the free leg above hip level). Cluster 5 on the other hand seems to capture the rest of the "uninteresting" actions.

Next, we present experiments demonstrating the strength of the model for summarizing and recognizing complex activities. We show the results of summarizing a long video containing a complex activity—the game of Blackjack. For this, we used the dataset reported in Zhong et al. [8]. The game of Blackjack consists of a few elements such as dealing cards, waiting for bids, shuffling the cards, etc. The goal is to estimate a Grassmann switching model for the entire video of Blackjack. The

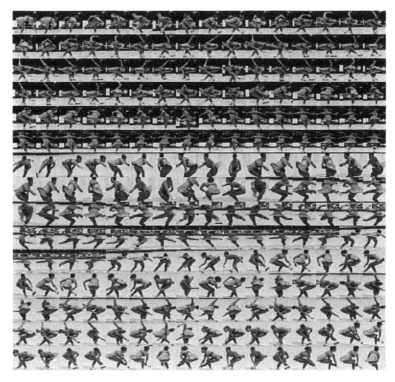

FIG. 17. Shown above are a few sequences from Cluster 1. Each row shows contiguous frames of a sequence. We see that this cluster dominantly corresponds to "Sitting Spins." Image best viewed in color. See http://www.umiacs.umd.edu/~pturaga/VideoClustering.html for video results. Figure courtesy Turaga et al. [104].

Grassmann switching model would then represent a "summary" of the game, where the clusters of the model represent various elements of the game and the switching structure represents how the game progresses. This video consists of about 1700 frames. We extracted the motion-histogram features as proposed in Zhong et al. [8] for each frame of the video. The time-varying model parameters are estimated in sliding windows of size 10. The dimension of the state vector is chosen to be $d = 5$. To estimate the Grassmann switching model for the game of Blackjack, we manually set the number of clusters to 5. In Fig. 22, we show an embedding of the video obtained from the model parameters using Laplacian eigenmaps. Each point corresponds to a time-invariant model parameter (A, C) pair or equivalently a point on the Grassmann manifold. Each cluster was found to correspond dominantly to a

FIG. 18. Shown above are a few sequences from Cluster 2. Each row shows contiguous frames of a sequence. Notice that this cluster dominantly corresponds to "Standing Spins." Image best viewed in color. See http://www.umiacs.umd.edu/~pturaga/VideoClustering.html for video results. Figure courtesy Turaga et al. [104].

distinct element of the game as shown. The switching structure between the clusters is encoded in the transition matrix and is shown in Fig. 23. As can be seen the switching structure corresponds to a normal game of Blackjack. Since this is a data-driven procedure, it should be noted that the switching structure will not necessarily be the same for every individual Blackjack game. However, given two distinct Blackjack games we can now quantify the notion of how similarly the two games proceeded.

11. View and Rate Variations

The distance metrics defined in Section 8 will break down when there is a change in viewpoint or there is an affine transformation of the low-level features. Some features such as shape are invariant to affine transformations by definition. Features

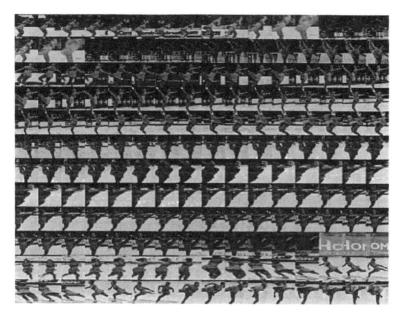

Fig. 19. Shown above are a few sequences from Cluster 3. Each row shows contiguous frames of a sequence. Notice that this cluster dominantly corresponds to "Spirals." Image best viewed in color. See http://www.umiacs.umd.edu/~pturaga/VideoClustering.html for video results. Figure courtesy Turaga et al. [104].

such as point trajectories can be easily made invariant to view and affine transforms. But, in general, it is not guaranteed that a given feature is invariant under these transformations (optical flow, background subtracted masks, motion history [23], and other "image-like" features). Reliance on the feature to provide invariance to these factors will tie the rest of the processing to that particular feature, which is not desirable as different features are appropriate for different domains and video characteristics. Thus, instead of relying on the feature, we propose a technique to build these invariances into the distance metrics defined above. This allows the algorithm flexibility in the choice of features.

11.1 Affine and View Invariance

In our model, under feature level affine transforms or view-point changes, the only change occurs in the measurement equation and not in the state equation. As described in Section 8, the columns of the measurement matrix (C) are the PCs of the observations of that segment. Thus, we need to discover the transformation between

FIG. 20. Shown above are a few sequences from Cluster 4. Each row shows contiguous frames of a sequence. This cluster dominantly corresponds to "Camel Spins." Image best viewed in color. See http://www.umiacs.umd.edu/~pturaga/VideoClustering.html for video results. Figure courtesy Turaga et al. [104].

the corresponding C matrices under an affine/view change. We begin by stating a theorem that relates low-level feature transforms to transformation of the PCs.

Theorem 1

Let $\{X(\bar{p})\}$ be a zero-mean random field where $\bar{p} \in D_1 \subseteq R^2$. Let $\{\lambda_n^X\}$ and $\{\phi_n^X\}$ be the eigenvalues and corresponding eigenfunctions in the K–L expansion of the covariance function of X. Let $T: D_2 \to D_1$, where $D_2 \subseteq R^2$ be a continuous, differentiable one-to-one mapping. Let $\{G(\bar{q})\}$, $\bar{q} \in D_2$ be a random field derived from X as $G(\bar{q}) = X(T(\bar{q}))$. If the Jacobian of T, denoted by $J_T(\bar{r})$, is such that $\det(J_T(\bar{r}))$ is independent of $\bar{r}$, then the eigenvalues and eigenfunctions of G are given by $\lambda_n^G = \lambda_n^X/|J_T|^{1/2}$ and $\phi_n^G(\bar{q}) = \phi_n^X(T(\bar{q}))/|J_T|^{1/2}$.

Proof

Refer to Turaga et al. [104].

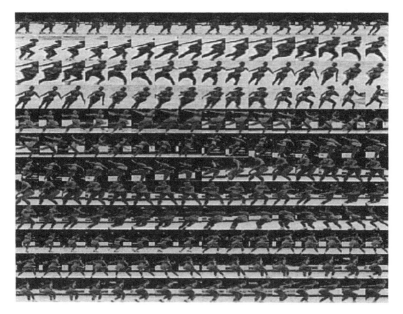

FIG. 21. Shown above are a few sequences from Cluster 5. Each row shows contiguous frames of a sequence. This cluster did not dominantly correspond to any "interesting" skating pose but seemed to capture the "usual" postures. Image best viewed in color. See http://www.umiacs.umd.edu/~pturaga/VideoClustering.html for video results. Figure courtesy Turaga et al. [104].

The utility of this theorem is that if the low-level features like flow/silhouettes undergo a spatial transformation which satisfies the conditions stated in the theorem, then the corresponding PCs also undergo the same transformation. It is important to note that we are not considering transformations of the pixel intensities, but we are interested in transformations of the "image-grid."

11.1.1 Modified Distance Metric

Proceeding from the above, to match two ARMA models of the same activity related by a spatial transformation, all we need to do is to transform the C matrices (the observation equation). Given two systems $S_1 = (A_1, C_1)$ and $S_2 = (A_2, C_2)$ we modify the distance metric as

$$d_{\text{compensated}}(S_1, S_2) = \min_T d(T(S_1), S_2) \tag{20}$$

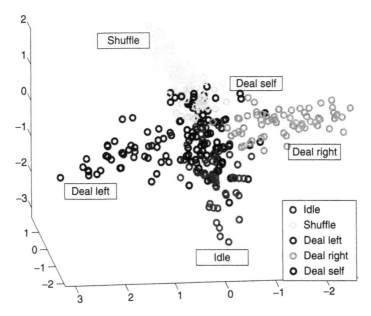

Fig. 22. An embedding of the entire Blackjack video sequence. Figure best viewed in color.
Figure courtesy Turaga et al. [110]. (See color insert at the back of the book.)

where $d(.,.)$ is any of the distance metrics given in Section 8, T is the transformation.
$T(S_1) = (A_1, T(C_1))$. Columns of $T(C_1)$ are the transformed columns of C_1. The
optimal transformation parameters are those that achieve the minimization in Equation (20). Depending on the complexity of the transformation model, one can use
featureless image registration techniques such as those in Refs. [107,117] to arrive at
a good initial estimate of T.

11.2   Invariance to Execution Rate of Activity

While building models for activities, one also needs to consider the effect of
different execution rates of the activity [118]. In the general case, one needs to
consider warping functions of the form $g(t) = f(w(t))$ such as in Veeraraghavan et al.
[119] where dynamic time warping is used to estimate $w(t)$. We consider linear
warping functions of the form $w(t) = qt$ for each action segment. Linear functions for
each segment give rise to a piece-wise linear warping function for the entire activity,
which accounts for variabilities in the execution rate well. It can be shown that,
under linear warps the stationary distribution of the Markov process in Equation (6)

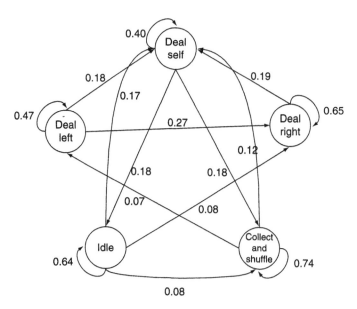

FIG. 23. Estimated structure of the game of Blackjack. For the sake of clarity arcs with low weights have not been shown. Figure courtesy Turaga et al. [110].

does not change. Hence, a linear warp will affect only the state equation and not the measurement equation, that is, the A matrices and not the C matrices. Consider the state equation of a segment: $X_1(k) = A_1 X_1(k-1) + v(k)$. Ignoring the noise term for now, we can write $X_1(k) = A_1^k X(0)$. Now, consider another sequence that is related to X_1 by $X_2(k) = X_1(w(k)) = X_1(qk)$. In the discrete case, for noninteger q this is to be interpreted as a fractional sampling rate conversion as encountered in several areas of DSP. Then, $X_2(k) = X_1(qk) = A_1^{qk} X(0)$, that is, the transition matrix for the second system is related to the first by $A_2 = A_1^q$.

11.2.1 Estimating q

Given two transition matrices of the same activity but with different execution rates, we need a technique to estimate the warp factor q. Consider the eigendecomposition of $A_1 = V_1 D_1 V_1^{-1}$, and $A_2 = V_2 D_2 V_2^{-1}$. Then, for rational q, $A_2 = A_1^q = V_1 D_1^q V_1^{-1}$. Thus, $D_2 = D_1^q$, that is, if λ is an eigenvalue of A_1, then λ^q is an eigenvalue of A_2 and so forth. Thus, we can get an estimate of q from the eigenvalues of A_1 and A_2 as

$$\hat{q} = \frac{\sum_i \log|\lambda_2^{(i)}|}{\sum_i \log|\lambda_1^{(i)}|} \tag{21}$$

where $\lambda_2^{(i)}$ and $\lambda_1^{(i)}$ are the complex eigenvalues of A_2 and A_1, respectively. Thus, we compensate for different execution rates by computing $\hat{q}$. In the presence of noise, the above estimate of q may not be accurate, and can be taken as an initial guess in an optimization framework similar to the one proposed in Section 11.1. Note that compensation for execution rate is done only for segments which have very similar $\hat{C}$ matrices.

12. Summary

Understanding human actions is part of the bigger goal of providing a machine the ability to see and understand as humans do. Synergistic research efforts in various scientific disciplines—computer vision, AI, neuroscience, linguistics, etc.—have contributed and enriched our understanding of this complex problem. Several technical and intellectual challenges need to be tackled before we get to the point of building an automatic system with these goals. The advances made so far need to be consolidated, in terms of their robustness to real-world conditions and real-time performance. This would then provide a firmer ground for further research. Methods that can leverage large unstructured databases such as those found on video-sharing websites form a fertile ground for further research. Contextual priming—for example, what activities can or cannot happen given that the scene is a snowy mountain—is another area that can significantly improve the performance of activity recognition algorithms.

ACKNOWLEDGMENTS

We would like to thank Prof. Anuj Srivastava (Florida State University) for helpful discussions. Research efforts summarized in this chapter were supported by the following grants and contracts: ONR MURI (N00014-08-1-0638), ARO MURI (W911NF0910408), NSF ITR (IIS-03-25715, CCF-03-25119), and a ONR grant (N00014-09-1-0664).

REFERENCES

[1] G. Johansson, Visual perception of biological motion and a model for its analysis, Percept. Psychophys. 14 (2) (1973) 201–211.
[2] J.K. Aggarwal, Q. Cai, Human motion analysis: A review, Comput. Vis. Image Underst. 73 (3) (1999) 428–440.

[3] C. Cedras, M. Shah, Motion-based recognition: A survey, Image Vis. Comput. 13 (2) (1995) 129–155.

[4] D.M. Gavrila, The visual analysis of human movement: A survey, Comput. Vis. Image Underst. 73 (1) (1999) 82–98.

[5] T.B. Moeslund, A. Hilton, V. Krüger, A survey of advances in vision-based human motion capture and analysis, Comput. Vis. Image Underst. 104 (2) (2006) 90–126.

[6] A. Yilmaz, O. Javed, M. Shah, Object tracking: A survey, ACM Comput. Surv. 38 (4) (2006) 13–57.

[7] S. Sarkar, P.J. Phillips, Z. Liu, I.R. Vega, P. Grother, K.W. Bowyer, The HumanID gait challenge problem: Data sets, performance, and analysis, IEEE Trans. Pattern. Anal. Mach. Intell. 27 (2) (2005) 162–177.

[8] H. Zhong, J. Shi, M. Visontai, Detecting unusual activity in video, in: Proceedings of IEEE Conference on Computer Vision and Pattern Recognition, 2004, pp. 819–826.

[9] N. Vaswani, A.K. Roy-Chowdhury, R. Chellappa, "Shape Activity": A continuous-state HMM for moving/deforming shapes with application to abnormal activity detection, IEEE Trans. Image. Process. 14 (10) (2005) 1603–1616.

[10] C. Stauffer, W.E.L. Grimson, Learning patterns of activity using real-time tracking, IEEE Trans. Pattern. Anal. Mach. Intell. 22 (8) (2000) 747–757.

[11] W. Hu, D. Xie, T. Tan, S. Maybank, Learning activity patterns using fuzzy self-organizing neural network, IEEE Trans. Syst. Man. Cybern. 34 (3) (2004) 1618–1626.

[12] A. Pentland, Smart rooms, smart clothes, in: Proceedings of International Conference on Pattern Recognition, vol. 2, 1998, pp. 949–953.

[13] D.A. Forsyth, O. Arikan, L. Ikemoto, J. O'Brien, D. Ramanan, Computational studies of human motion: Part 1, tracking and motion synthesis, Found. Trends Compu. Graph. Vis. 1 (2–3) (2005) 77–254.

[14] S.S. Beauchemin, J.L. Barron, The computation of optical flow, ACM Comput. Surv. 27 (3) (1995) 433–466.

[15] T. Huang, D. Koller, J. Malik, G.H. Ogasawara, B. Rao, S.J. Russell, J. Weber, Automatic symbolic traffic scene analysis using belief networks, in: Proceedings of National Conference on Artificial Intelligence, 1994, pp. 966–972.

[16] A.M. Elgammal, D. Harwood, L.S. Davis, Non-parametric model for background subtraction, in: Proceedings of IEEE European Conference on Computer Vision, 2000, pp. 751–767.

[17] M. Hu, Visual pattern recognition by moment invariants, IRE Trans. Inf. Theory 8 (1962) 179–187.

[18] H. Freeman, On the encoding of arbitrary geometric configurations, IRE Trans. Electron. Comput. 10 (2) (1961) 260–268.

[19] D.G. Kendall, Shape manifolds, procrustean metrics and complex projective spaces, Bull. Lond. Math. Soc. 16 (1984) 81–121.

[20] H. Blum, R.N. Nagel, Shape description using weighted symmetric axis features, Pattern Recogn. 10 (3) (1978) 167–180.

[21] A. Bissacco, P. Saisan, S. Soatto, Gait recognition using dynamic affine invariants, in: International Symposium on Mathematical Theory of Networks and Systems, 2004.

[22] J.W. Davis, A.F. Bobick, The representation and recognition of human movement using temporal templates, in: Proceedings of IEEE Conference on Computer Vision and Pattern Recognition, 1997, pp. 928–934.

[23] A.F. Bobick, J.W. Davis, The recognition of human movement using temporal templates, IEEE Trans. Pattern. Anal. Mach. Intell. 23 (3) (2001) 257–267.

[24] M. Blank, L. Gorelick, E. Shechtman, M. Irani, R. Basri, Actions as space-time shapes, in: Proceedings of IEEE International Conference on Computer Vision, 2005, pp. 1395–1402.

[25] L. Gorelick, M. Blank, E. Shechtman, M. Irani, R. Basri, Actions as space-time shapes, IEEE Trans. Pattern. Anal. Mach. Intell. 29 (12) (2007) 2247–2253.

[26] J. Malik, P. Perona, Preattentive texture discrimination with early vision mechanism, J. Opt. Soc. Am. A 7 (5) (1990) 923–932.

[27] O. Chomat, J.L. Crowley, Probabilistic recognition of activity using local appearance, in: Proceedings of IEEE Conference on Computer Vision and Pattern Recognition, vol. 2, 1999, pp. 104–109.

[28] L. Zelnik-Manor, M. Irani, Event-based analysis of video, in: Proceedings of IEEE Conference on Computer Vision and Pattern Recognition, vol. 2, 2001, pp. 123–130.

[29] R.A. Young, R.M. Lesperance, W.W. Meyer, The Gaussian derivative model for spatial-temporal vision: I. Cortical model, Spat. Vis. 14 (3–4) (2001) 261–319.

[30] H. Jhuang, T. Serre, L. Wolf, T. Poggio, A biologically inspired system for action recognition, in: Proceedings of IEEE International Conference on Computer Vision, 2007, pp. 1–8.

[31] I. Laptev, T. Lindeberg, Space-time interest points, in: Proceedings of IEEE International Conference on Computer Vision, 2003, pp. 432–439.

[32] I. Laptev, On space-time interest points, Int. J. Comput. Vis. 64 (2–3) (2005) 107–123.

[33] C. Harris, M. Stephens, A combined corner and edge detector, in: Proceedings of the 4th Alvey Vision Conference, 1988, pp. 147–151.

[34] P. Dollár, V. Rabaud, G. Cottrell, S. Belongie, Behavior recognition via sparse spatio-temporal features, in: Proceedings of IEEE International Workshop on Visual Surveillance and Performance Evaluation of Tracking and Surveillance (VS-PETS), 2005, pp. 65–72.

[35] J.C. Niebles, H. Wang, L. Fei Fei, Unsupervised learning of human action categories using spatial-temporal words, Proc. Br. Mach. Vis. Conf. 3 (2006) 1249–1258.

[36] C. Schuldt, I. Laptev, B. Caputo, Recognizing human actions: A local SVM approach, in: Proceedings of International Conference on Pattern Recognition, vol. 3, 2004, pp. 32–36.

[37] S. Savarese, A. Del Pozo, J.C. Niebles, L. Fei-Fei, Spatial-temporal correlations for unsupervised action classification, in: Proceedings of IEEE Workshop on Motion and Video Computing, 2008, pp. 1–8.

[38] S. Nowozin, G. Bakir, K. Tsuda, Discriminative subsequence mining for action classification, in: Proceedings of IEEE International Conference on Computer Vision, 2007, pp. 1–8.

[39] O. Boiman, M. Irani, Detecting irregularities in images and in video, Int. J. Comput. Vis. 74 (1) (2007) 17–31.

[40] S.F. Wong, T.K. Kim, R. Cipolla, Learning motion categories using both semantic and structural information, in: Proceedings of IEEE Conference on Computer Vision and Pattern Recognition, 2007, pp. 1–6.

[41] Y. Song, L. Goncalves, P. Perona, Unsupervised learning of human motion, IEEE Trans. Pattern. Anal. Mach. Intell. 25 (7) (2003) 814–827.

[42] J.C. Niebles, L. Fei-Fei, A hierarchical model of shape and appearance for human action classification, in: Proceedings of IEEE Conference on Computer Vision and Pattern Recognition, 2007, pp. 1–8.

[43] L.R. Rabiner, A tutorial on hidden Markov models and selected applications in speech recognition, Proc. IEEE 77 (2) (1989) 257–286.

[44] J. Yamato, J. Ohya, K. Ishii, Recognizing human action in time-sequential images using hidden Markov model, in: Proceedings of IEEE Conference on Computer Vision and Pattern Recognition, 1992, pp. 379–385.

[45] J. Schlenzig, E. Hunter, R. Jain, Recursive identification of gesture inputs using hidden Markov models, in: Proceedings of the Second IEEE Workshop on Applications of Computer Vision, 1994, pp. 187–194.

[46] T. Starner, J. Weaver, A. Pentland, Real-time American sign language recognition using desk and wearable computer based video, IEEE Trans. Pattern. Anal. Mach. Intell. 20 (12) (1998) 1371–1375.

[47] A. Kale, A. Sundaresan, A.N. Rajagopalan, N.P. Cuntoor, A.K. Roy-Chowdhury, V. Kruger, R. Chellappa, Identification of humans using gait, IEEE Trans. Image. Process. 13 (9) (2004) 1163–1173.

[48] Z. Liu, S. Sarkar, Improved gait recognition by gait dynamics normalization, IEEE Trans. Pattern. Anal. Mach. Intell. 28 (6) (2006) 863–876.

[49] M. Brand, N. Oliver, A. Pentland, Coupled hidden Markov models for complex action recognition, in: Proceedings of IEEE Conference on Computer Vision and Pattern Recognition, 1997, pp. 994–999.

[50] D.J. Moore, I.A. Essa, M.H. Hayes, Exploiting human actions and object context for recognition tasks, in: Proceedings of IEEE International Conference on Computer Vision, 1999, pp. 80–86.

[51] S. Hongeng, R. Nevatia, Large-scale event detection using semi-hidden Markov models, in: Proceedings of IEEE International Conference on Computer Vision, 2003, pp. 1455–1462.

[52] N.P. Cuntoor, R. Chellappa, Mixed-state models for nonstationary multiobject activities, EURASIP J. Appl. Signal Process. 2007 (1) (2007) 106–119.

[53] A. Bissacco, A. Chiuso, Y. Ma, S. Soatto, Recognition of human gaits, in: Proceedings of IEEE Conference on Computer Vision and Pattern Recognition, vol. 2, 2001, pp. 52–57.

[54] A. Veeraraghavan, A. Roy-Chowdhury, R. Chellappa, Matching shape sequences in video with an application to human movement analysis, IEEE Trans. Pattern. Anal. Mach. Intell. 27 (12) (2005) 1896–1909.

[55] M.C. Mazzaro, M. Sznaier, O. Camps, A model (in)validation approach to gait classification, IEEE Trans. Pattern. Anal. Mach. Intell. 27 (11) (2005) 1820–1825.

[56] N.P. Cuntoor, R. Chellappa, Epitomic representation of human activities, in: Proceedings of IEEE Conference on Computer Vision and Pattern Recognition, 2007, pp. 1–8.

[57] G. Doretto, A. Chiuso, Y.N. Wu, S. Soatto, Dynamic textures, Int. J. Comput. Vis. 51 (2) (2003) 91–109.

[58] A.B. Chan, N. Vasconcelos, Modeling, clustering, and segmenting video with mixtures of dynamic textures, IEEE Trans. Pattern. Anal. Mach. Intell. 30 (5) (2008) 909–926.

[59] R.H. Shumway, D.S. Stoffer, An approach to time series smoothing and forecasting using the EM algorithm, J. Time Ser. Anal. 3 (4) (1982) 253–264.

[60] P.V. Overschee, B.D. Moor, Subspace algorithms for the stochastic identification problem, Automatica 29 (3) (1993) 649–660.

[61] Z. Ghahramani, G.E. Hinton, Parameter estimation for linear dynamical systems, 1996. (Tech. Rep. CRG-TR-96-2, Department of Computer Science, University of Toronto, Technical Report).

[62] L. Ljung (Ed.), System Identification: Theory for the User, second ed., Prentice Hall PTR, Upper Saddle River, NJ, 1999.

[63] K.D. Cock, B.D. Moor, Subspace angles between ARMA models, Syst. Control Lett. 46 (2002) 265–270.

[64] P. Saisan, G. Doretto, Y.N. Wu, S. Soatto, Dynamic texture recognition, in: Proceedings of IEEE Conference on Computer Vision and Pattern Recognition, vol. 2, 2001, pp. 58–63.

[65] R.J. Martin, A metric for ARMA processes, IEEE Trans. Signal Process. 48 (4) (2000) 1164–1170.

[66] R. Vidal, P. Favaro, Dynamicboost: Boosting time series generated by dynamical systems, in: Proceedings of IEEE International Conference on Computer Vision, 2007, pp. 1–8.

[67] S.V.N. Vishwanathan, A.J. Smola, R. Vidal, Binet-Cauchy kernels on dynamical systems and its application to the analysis of dynamic scenes, Int. J. Comput. Vis. 73 (1) (2007) 95–119.

[68] A. Bissacco, S. Soatto, On the blind classification of time series, in: Proceedings of IEEE Conference on Computer Vision and Pattern Recognition, 2007, pp. 1–8.

[69] P. Turaga, A. Veeraraghavan, R. Chellappa, Statistical analysis on Stiefel and Grassmann manifolds with applications in computer vision, in: Proceedings of IEEE Conference on Computer Vision and Pattern Recognition, 2008, pp. 1–8.

[70] C. Bregler, Learning and recognizing human dynamics in video sequences, in: Proceedings of IEEE Conference on Computer Vision and Pattern Recognition, 1997, pp. 568–574.

[71] B. North, A. Blake, M. Isard, J. Rittscher, Learning and classification of complex dynamics, IEEE Trans. Pattern. Anal. Mach. Intell. 22 (9) (2000) 1016–1034.

[72] V. Pavlovic, J.M. Rehg, J. MacCormick, Learning switching linear models of human motion, Adv. Neural. Inf. Process. Syst. (2000) 981–987.

[73] V. Pavlovic, J.M. Rehg, Impact of dynamic model learning on classification of human motion, in: Proceedings of IEEE Conference on Computer Vision and Pattern Recognition, 2000, pp. 1788–1795.

[74] D. Del Vecchio, R.M. Murray, P. Perona, Decomposition of human motion into dynamics based primitives with application to drawing tasks, Automatica 39 (2003) 2085–2098.

[75] S.M. Oh, J.M. Rehg, T.R. Balch, F. Dellaert, Data-driven MCMC for learning and inference in switching linear dynamic systems, in: Proceedings of National Conference on Artificial Intelligence, 2005, pp. 944–949.

[76] R. Vidal, A. Chiuso, S. Soatto, Observability and identifiability of jump linear systems, in: Proceedings of IEEE Conference on Decision and Control, vol. 4, 2002, pp. 3614–3619.

[77] J. Pearl, Probabilistic Reasoning in Intelligent Systems: Networks of Plausible Inference, Morgan Kaufmann Publishers Inc., San Francisco, CA, 1988.

[78] H. Buxton, S. Gong, Visual surveillance in a dynamic and uncertain world, Artif. Intell. 78 (1–2) (1995) 431–459.

[79] S. Park, J.K. Aggarwal, Recognition of two-person interactions using a hierarchical Bayesian network, ACM J. Multimed. Syst. 10 (2) (2004) 164–179 (Special issue on video surveillance).

[80] C.A. Petri, Communication with automata, 1966. (Tech. rep., DTIC research report AD0630125.)

[81] C. Castel, L. Chaudron, C. Tessier, What is going on? A high-level interpretation of a sequence of images, in: ECCV Workshop on Conceptual Descriptions from Images, 1996, pp. 13–27.

[82] M. Albanese, R. Chellappa, V. Moscato, A. Picariello, V.S. Subrahmanian, P. Turaga, O. Udrea, A constrained probabilistic Petri net framework for human activity detection in video, IEEE Transactions on Multimedia 10 (8) (2008) 1429–1443.

[83] M. Brand, Understanding manipulation in video, in: Proceedings of the 2nd International Conference on Automatic Face and Gesture Recognition, 1996, pp. 94–99.

[84] Y.A. Ivanov, A.F. Bobick, Recognition of visual activities and interactions by stochastic parsing, IEEE Trans. Pattern. Anal. Mach. Intell. 22 (8) (2000) 852–872.

[85] D. Moore, I. Essa, Recognizing multitasked activities from video using stochastic context-free grammar, in: Eighteenth national conference on Artificial intelligence, 2002, pp. 770–776.

[86] J. Earley, An efficient context-free parsing algorithm, Commun. ACM 13 (2) (1970) 94–102.

[87] A.V. Aho, J.D. Ullman, The Theory of Parsing, Translation, and Compiling, Volume 1: Parsing, Prentice-Hall, Englewood Cliffs, NJ, 1972.

[88] S.W. Joo, R. Chellappa, Recognition of multi-object events using attribute grammars, in: Proceedings of International Conference on Image Processing, 2006, pp. 2897–2900.

[89] N. Rota, M. Thonnat, Activity recognition from video sequences using declarative models, in: Proceedings of the 14th European Conference on Artificial Intelligence, 2000, pp. 673–680.

[90] G. Medioni, I. Cohen, F. Brémond, S. Hongeng, R. Nevatia, Event detection and analysis from video streams, IEEE Trans. Pattern. Anal. Mach. Intell. 23 (8) (2001) 873–889.

[91] S. Hongeng, R. Nevatia, F. Bremond, Video-based event recognition: Activity representation and probabilistic recognition methods, Comput. Vis. Image Underst. 96 (2) (2004) 129–162.

[92] V.D. Shet, D. Harwood, L.S. Davis, VidMAP: Video monitoring of activity with prolog, in: Proceedings of IEEE Conference on Advanced Video and Signal Based Surveillance (AVSS), 2005, pp. 224–229.

[93] S. Tran, L.S. Davis, Visual event modeling and recognition using Markov logic networks, in: Proceedings of IEEE European Conference on Computer Vision, 2008.

[94] U. Akdemir, P.K. Turaga, R. Chellappa, An ontology based approach for activity recognition from video, in: ACM International Conference on Multimedia, 2008, pp. 709–712.

[95] P. Turaga, R. Chellappa, V.S. Subrahmanian, O. Udrea, Machine recognition of human activities: A survey, IEEE Trans. Circuits Syst. Video Technol. 18 (11) (2008) 1473–1488.

[96] D. Marr, W. H. Freeman, Vision, 1982.

[97] H.B. Barlow, The coding of sensory messages, in: W.H. Thorpe, O.L. Zangwill (Eds.), Current Problems in Animal Behaviour, 1960. Cambridge University Press, pp. 331–360 (Chapter 12).

[98] M.V. Srinivasan, S.B. Laughlin, A. Dubs, Predictive coding: A fresh view of inhibition in the retina, Proc. R. Soc. Lond. B Biol. Sci. 216 (1205) (1982) 427–459.

[99] M.R. Lemke, M. Schleidt, Temporal segmentation of human short-term behavior in everyday activities and interview sessions, Naturwissenschaften 86 (6) (1999) 289–292.

[100] V.S.N. Prasad, V. Kellokumpu, L.S. Davis, Ballistic hand movements, in: Proceedings of Conference on Articulated Motion and Deformable Objects (AMDO), 2006, pp. 153–164.

[101] Y. Chikuse, Statistics on Special Manifolds, Springer, New York, NY, 2003. (Lecture notes in statistics.)

[102] P. Turaga, A. Veeraraghavan, A. Srivastava, R. Chellappa, Statistical analysis on manifolds and its applications to video analysis, in: D. Schonfeld, C. Shan, D. Tao, L. Wang (Eds.), Video Search and Mining, Studies in Computational Intelligence, Springer, New York, NY, 2010, Chapter 5.

[103] D. Weinland, R. Ronfard, E. Boyer, Free viewpoint action recognition using motion history volumes, Comput. Vis. Image Underst. 104 (2) (2006) 249–257.

[104] P.K. Turaga, A. Veeraraghavan, R. Chellappa, Unsupervised view and rate invariant clustering of video sequences, Comput. Vis. Image Underst. 113 (3) (2009) 353–371.

[105] C. Rao, A. Yilmaz, M. Shah, View-invariant representation and recognition of actions, Int. J. Comput. Vis. 50 (2) (2002) 203–226.

[106] A. Yezzi, S. Soatto, Deformotion: Deforming motion, shape average and the joint registration and approximation of structure in images, Int. J. Comput. Vis. 53 (2) (2003) 153–167.

[107] B.S. Reddy, B.N. Chatterji, An FFT-based technique for translation, rotation, and scale-invariant image registration, IEEE Trans. Image. Process. 5 (8) (1996) 1266–1271.

[108] D. Weinland, R. Ronfard, E. Boyer, Automatic discovery of action taxonomies from multiple views, in: Proceedings of IEEE Conference on Computer Vision and Pattern Recognition, 2006, pp. 1639–1645.

[109] C. Vogler, D. Metaxas, ASL recognition based on a coupling between HMMs and 3D motion analysis, in: Proceedings of IEEE International Conference on Computer Vision, 1998, pp. 363–369.

[110] P.K. Turaga, R. Chellappa, Locally time-invariant models of human activities using trajectories on the Grassmannian, in: Proceedings of IEEE Conference on Computer Vision and Pattern Recognition, 2009, pp. 2435–2441.

[111] M. Hall, A.V. Oppenheim, A. Willsky, Time-varying parametric modeling of speech, in: Proceedings of IEEE Conference on Decision and Control, vol. 16, 1977, pp. 1085–1091.

[112] T.S. Rao, The fitting of nonstationary time-series models with time-dependent parameters, J. R. Stat. Soc. Series. B Stat. Methodol. 32 (2) (1970) 312–322.

[113] M. Tsatsanis, G. Giannakis, Subspace methods for blind estimation of time-varying FIR channels, IEEE Trans Signal Process. 45 (12) (1997) 3084–3093.

[114] L.H. Lee, Identification and Robust Control of Linear Parameter-Varying Systems, Ph.D. thesis at University of California, Berkeley, CA, 1997.

[115] V. Verdult, M. Verhaegen, Subspace identification of multivariable linear parameter-varying systems, Automatica 38 (5) (2002) 805–814.

[116] Y. Wang, H. Jiang, M.S. Drew, Z.N. Li, G. Mori, Unsupervised discovery of action classes, in: Proceedings of IEEE Conference on Computer Vision and Pattern Recognition, vol. 2, 2006, pp. 1654–1661.

[117] S. Mann, R.W. Picard, Video orbits of the projective group: A simple approach to featureless estimation of parameters, IEEE Trans. Image. Process. 6 (9) (1997) 1281–1295.

[118] Y. Sheikh, M. Sheikh, M. Shah, Exploring the space of a human action, in: Proceedings of IEEE International Conference on Computer Vision, 2005, pp. 144–149.

[119] A. Veeraraghavan, A. Srivastava, A.K. Roy Chowdhury, R. Chellappa, Rate-invariant recognition of humans and their activities, IEEE Trans. Image. Process. 18 (6) (2009) 1326–1339.

[120] A.K. Roy-Chowdhury, R. Chellappa, A factorization approach to activity recognition, in: CVPR Workshop on Event Mining, vol. 4, 2003, pp. 41–48.

Author Index

Subject Index

Contents of Volumes in This Series

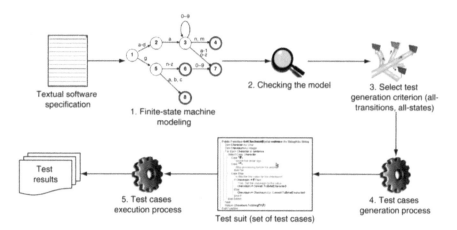

FIG. 2. A.C. DIAS-NETO AND G.H. TRAVASSOS (See Page 49 of this volume.)

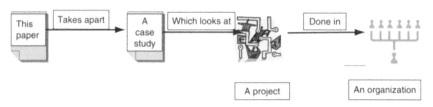

FIG. 2. RAVI I. SINGH AND JAMES MILLER (See Page 178 of this volume.)

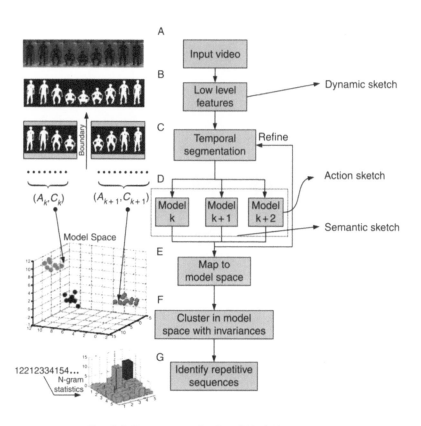

Fig. 9. P. Turaga *et al.* (See Page 264 of this volume.)

A

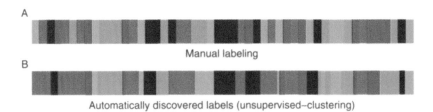

Manual labeling

B

Automatically discovered labels (unsupervised–clustering)

FIG. 11. P. TURAGA *ET AL.* (See Page 268 of this volume.)

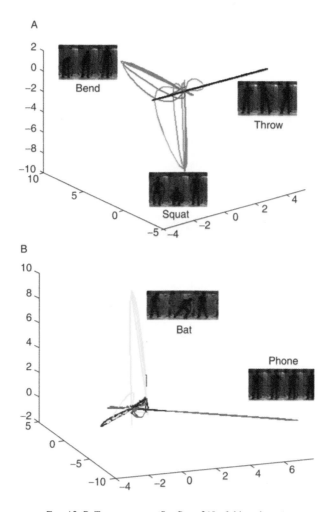

FIG. 12. P. TURAGA ET AL. (See Page 269 of this volume.)

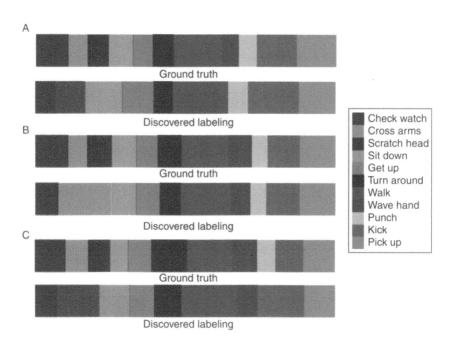

A

Ground truth

Discovered labeling

B

Ground truth

Discovered labeling

C

Ground truth

Discovered labeling

Check watch
Cross arms
Scratch head
Sit down
Get up
Turn around
Walk
Wave hand
Punch
Kick
Pick up

FIG. 13. P. TURAGA ET AL. (See Page 270 of this volume.)

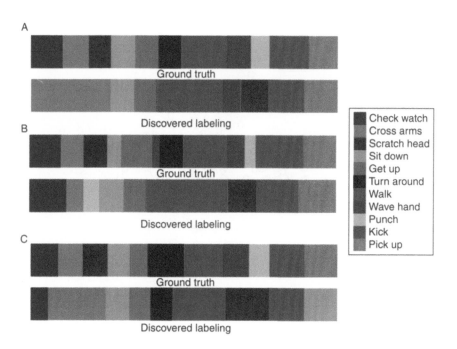

FIG. 14. P. TURAGA ET AL. (See Page 271 of this volume.)

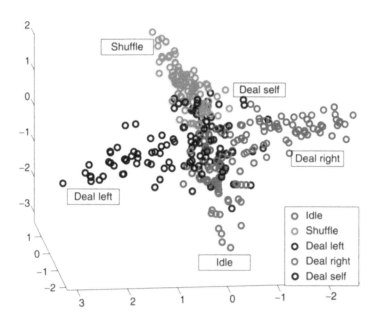

FIG. 22. P. TURAGA *ET AL*. (See Page 282 of this volume.)

Printed and bound by CPI Group (UK) Ltd, Croydon, CR0 4YY

03/10/2024

01040415-0005